STREETWISE
SPANISH

STREETWISE
SPANISH

Speak and Understand Everyday Spanish

Mary McVey Gill

Brenda Wegmann

with illustrations by Norma Vidal

PASSPORT BOOKS

NTC/Contemporary Publishing Group

Library of Congress Cataloging-in-Publication Data

Wegmann, Brenda, 1941–
    Streetwise Spanish : speak and understand everyday Spanish /
Brenda Wegmann and Mary McVey Gill.
        p. cm.
    ISBN 0-8442-7281-7
    1. Spanish language—Conversation and phrase books—English.
2. Spanish language—Slang.   I. Gill, Mary McVey.   II. Title.
PC4121.W38   1998
468.3'421—dc21   98-10556
                                                                          CIP

Published by Passport Books
A Division of The McGraw-Hill Companies

        6 7 8 9 0   LBM/LBM   1 0 9 8 7 6 5 4 3

ISBN 0-8442-7281-7

This book was set in Bembo
Printed and bound by Lake Book Manufacturing
Cover design by Nick Panos
Cover photograph copyright © David Barnes/Tony Stone Images
Interior design by Precision Graphics

McGraw-Hill books are available at special quantity discounts to use as premi-
ums and sales promotions, or for use in corporate training programs. For more
information, please write to the Director of Special Sales, Professional
Publishing, McGraw-Hill, Two Penn Plaza, New York, NY 10121-2298. Or contact
your local bookstore.

This book is printed on acid-free paper.

WE DEDICATE THIS BOOK TO ALL OUR MARVELOUS
LATIN AMERICAN AND SPANISH FRIENDS WHO
BRIGHTEN OUR LIVES WITH THEIR *CHISPA* AND CONTINUE
TO TEACH US THE MEANING OF *LA SIMPATÍA.*

Illustration Credits

All illustrations are by Norma Vidal, with the following exceptions:

page 5, advertisement courtesy of Mexican Tourist Board

page 10, cartoon by Hugo Díaz from his book *Díaz todos los días,* published by Editorial El Bongo, S.A., Costa Rica

pages 41, 42, 43, 75, 145, 216, and 217, cartoons by Manuel Héctor Falcón from his book *Cascajo,* published by Cal y Arena, Mexico

page 71, Honda advertisement courtesy of Automotores (SAVA)

page 107, cartoon by Antonio Mingote from his book *Los inevitables políticos*

page 113, cartoon by "Forges" from *Spanish à la Cartoon,* Passport Books

page 144, cartoon by "Tin-Glao" from *Spanish à la Cartoon,* Passport Books

page 184, cartoon by Oscar Sierra Quintero ("Oki") from *Spanish à la Cartoon,* Passport Books

page 247, TWA advertisement courtesy of Trans World Airlines

Acknowledgments

A big thank you goes to Jim Harmon and Christopher Brown of NTC/Contemporary Publishing Group for their inspiration, support, and excellent direction of this book, and to our artist, Norma Vidal, for her inventiveness and many fine suggestions concerning language and culture. We also want to express our heartfelt appreciation to the following people who so generously shared with us their extensive knowledge of idioms, slang, and culture during many hours of laughter and stimulating conversation: Frank Alomá, Ana Alomá Velilla, Adriana Alvarez, José Jaime Alvarez, Luz Adriana Alvarez, Ana Arcos, Cristina Cantú Díaz, Ingrid de la Barra de Muñoz, Sofía Domínguez de Malvárez, Juan Espinaco-Virseda, Dolores Fernández, Lucilda Flores, Nidia González Araya, Iván H. Jiménez Williams, Graciela Lam, Llanca Letelier, Naldo Lombardi, María López, Yolanda Magaña, Annie Ordónez, Susana Singer, and María Teresa Varese. Thanks also to our project editor at NTC/Contemporary, Sharon Sofinski, for her very competent handling of the production of the book.

Contents

CHAPTER 6: ¡QUÉ FLORES ME ESTÁ ECHANDO!   86

Giving and accepting compliments and praise • Gossiping

Vocabulary and Culture: *Names in Spain and Latin America* 98

CHAPTER 7: ¡QUÉ BÁRBARO!   104

Telling a story • Expressing surprise

CHAPTER 8: ¡JUNTOS PERO NO REVUELTOS!   120

Expressing love and affection • Using terms of endearment • Using the telephone

Vocabulary and Culture: *Talking about Sex*   132

CHAPTER 9: ¿QUIÉN ES ESE TIPO, EL PALANCÓN?   136

Describing people

CHAPTER 10: ¡QUÉ COCHINADAS HACEN!   152

Using expletives and swear words to express affection, surprise, or displeasure • Communicating in slang across two different dialects

Vocabulary and Culture: *The Varying Uses of Spanish Swear Words*   166

REPASO 2: REVIEW OF CHAPTERS 6–10   172

CHAPTER 11: ¡DÉJATE DE CUENTOS!   176

Expressing disagreement

CHAPTER 12: CUENTE USTED CONMIGO   190

Giving encouragement, advice, and emotional support • Expressing sympathy

Vocabulary and Culture: *Some Expressive Qualities of Spanish*   202

CHAPTER 13: ¡ESTOY HASTA LA MADRE!   208

Expressing anger

Introduction

—*¡Hola, compa! ¿Qué onda?* (—Hi, pal! What sound wave?)

(Uh, oh . . . What ever happened to *¿Cómo está Ud.?*)

Language is the key to culture. But a formal study of Spanish from text-books and classrooms touches on only a small part of the dynamic, color-ful, exuberant language spoken today on the street, at home, in the movies, on TV, over the Internet, between lovers, and in cafés and clubs all over the Hispanic world. Much of what people really say is slang, and as such it has been considered substandard and excluded from formal study.

Not any longer. *Streetwise Spanish* offers a simple and enjoyable teach-yourself method for learning to understand and use many of the practical, amusing slang expressions and idioms of the world's most user-friendly international language.

Different from other books, which present idioms and expressions alphabetically or mixed together, *Streetwise Spanish* uses a functional approach, with each chapter concentrating on a few related language functions, such as "Making, accepting, and declining invitations" or "Expressing love and affec-tion." Research has shown that we memorize and retain vocabulary better if we learn it in meaningful chunks related to specific needs. These functions are like hooks that hold together the words in our minds.

Like English, Spanish is a major medium for business, art, and science and is widely used around the globe. Many expressions are particular to certain regions, although with the expansion of travel, music, television, and the movie industry, a great convergence is occurring at present so that slang words that were once understood only in Mexico are now recognized and used in Chile or Spain, for example.

To help you to understand and master the Spanish that is really spo-ken and enjoyed by Latin Americans and Spaniards, *Streetwise Spanish* offers the following features:

Functional dialogues. Fifteen chapters, each one containing two functional dialogues that are situated in a particular part of the

Spanish-speaking world (including two placed in Spain). These include between 30 to 50 highlighted idioms and slang expressions.

English translations of the dialogues with literal meanings in parentheses.

Vocabulary notes in a section called **¡Ojo!** (Take note!, literally *¡Eye!*) at the end of each dialogue with detailed explanations of the idioms and slang from the dialogues, along with comparable or contrasting expressions used in other Spanish-speaking countries or regions.

Vocabulary list for easy reference immediately preceding the exercises.

A variety of exercises following the dialogues to test your recollection and aid your mastery.

Authentic jokes and cartoons from many corners of the Hispanic world.

Original drawings by Chilean illustrator Norma Vidal showing a humorous portrayal of a key idiom for each chapter.

Vocabulary and Culture, a short essay on a cultural theme, such as "Names in Spain and Latin America" or "The Varying Uses of Spanish Swear Words." These readings discuss how cultural attitudes are often reflected in the very words we use. They appear at the end of all even-numbered chapters and are followed by a short exercise.

Repasos (Review Sections) following every five chapters, each one with a crossword puzzle and several other exercises.

Answer Key at the end of the book, with answers for all exercises in the chapters and review sections.

A Spanish-English Glossary at the end of the book, containing the highlighted idioms and slang expressions from all fifteen chapters.

Finally, we wish you **¡Buena suerte!** (Good luck!) with your adventure into Spanish slang. **¡Que lo pase bomba!** (Have a heck of a time!)

STREETWISE
SPANISH

. CAPÍTULO 1 .

¡Hola, compa! ¿Qué onda?

GREETING PEOPLE
·
ASKING HOW THEY ARE
·
TELLING HOW YOU FEEL

CONVERSACIÓN 1

Rafael y Juan se ven en la calle Olvera de Los Ángeles, California.

RAFAEL   Hola, **compa**. **¿Cómo te va?**

JUAN   Bien. ¿Y tú? **¿Qué onda?**

RAFAEL   Pues, no me siento muy bien que digamos.

JUAN   **¿Y eso?**

RAFAEL   Es que anoche fui a un **reventón de primera** y **echamos mucho relajo**.

JUAN   Y además, **la cruda, ¿**no?

RAFAEL   No, hombre, no estoy **crudo**. Pero estoy **rendido, hecho pinole**. La fiesta fue **a toda madre**.

JUAN   ¿Había muchas **rucas** allí?

RAFAEL   ¡Cómo no! Vi a Silvia . . . Silvia Padilla.

JUAN   Oh, la amiga de Elena. **¡Qué padre!**

2

COMO COCODRILO EN FÁBRICA DE CARTERAS (SEE PAGE 6.)

Rafael and Juan see each other on Olvera Street in Los Angeles, California.

RAFAEL Hi, pal. How are things going for you?

JUAN Good. And you? What's new? (What sound wave?)

RAFAEL Well, let's just say I don't feel so good.

JUAN And why's that?

RAFAEL Last night I went to a first-class bash (blowout of first) and we had a blast (we threw off or made a rumpus).

JUAN And now you have a hangover (the rawness), eh?

RAFAEL No, man, I'm not hung over. But I'm wiped (pressed) out, ground down (made into a powder). The party was fantastic (at full mother).

JUAN Were there many girls there?

RAFAEL Yeah, I saw Silvia . . . Silvia Padilla.

JUAN Oh, Elena's friend. Fantastic! (What a father!)

RAFAEL Sí, es muy simpática. Y tú, **¿qué me cuentas?**

JUAN **Por aquí trabajando.** Nada de nuevo. Rafael, **te dejaron bien amolado,** ¿no? ¡Te ves horrible!

———————■———————

¡Ojo!*

- **Compa** is short for **compadre,** a close male friend.

- **¿Qué onda?** means *What wave?* (that is, sound wave, news). In some places, it is more common to say **¿Qué ondas?**

- **Un reventón** is literally *a "cracking up," bursting, or blowout (as a tire).*

- **La cruda** (rawness): There are many words for *hung over:* **estar de goma** (to be made of rubber, Central America); **tener resaca** (to have undertow, Argentina and Uruguay); **estar enguayabado(-a)** or **tener guayabo** (to have a guava tree, Colombia); **tener la mona** (to have the monkey, Chile), **tener un ratón** (to have a mouse, Venezuela), etc. **Estar crudo(-a)** or **tener una cruda** are common in Mexico and among Mexican-Americans.

- **Rendido(-a)** means *rendered;* for instance, like olives have been rendered after the oil has been pressed out or fruits or vegetables after processing. **Rendirse** means *to surrender.* People of Mexican origin often say **Estoy hecho pinole,** ground down like a powder (**pinole** is an aromatic powder that used to be used in making chocolate).

- **A toda madre** (**ATM**) means *good, fantastic.*

- **Una ruca** is a girl (often a pretty girl) or a woman; the expression is used in most of Latin America except the Southern Cone.

- **¡Qué padre!** or **¡Padrísimo!** are common Mexicanisms meaning *Great! Fantastic!* They are used in many situations, to describe things or people.

- **Por aquí** (**trabajando, estudiando,** etc.) is often used to indicate that things are the same, that nothing is new. In Mexico, you might also hear **Aquí nomás.**

———————

*Be aware. (Eye!)

RAFAEL   Yeah, she's really nice. And you, what have you been up to (what can you tell me)?

JUAN   I've just been working. Nothing new. Rafael, they wore you to a frazzle, didn't they? (They left you ruined/a wreck, didn't they?) You look horrible!

———————■———————

Mis vacaciones en México estuvieron padrísimas. Mi primo Javier me enseñó muchas cosas nuevas. Mis abuelitos nos llevaron a conocer Xochimilco. Dijo mi mamá que vamos a regresar muy pronto. Pero yo no veo por qué tengamos que regresar. Si fuera por mí, mejor nos quedamos.

¡Qué Padre Es México!

1 · 8 0 0 - 4 4   M E X I C O

MEXICO

ENCUÉNTRESE EN MÉXICO.

This ad for tourism in Mexico uses two very common Mexican expressions: **¡Qué padre!** and **padrísimo: Mis vacaciones en México estuvieron padrísimas.** (My vacation in Mexico was fantastic.)

CONVERSACIÓN 2

Silvia y Elena se encuentran en un café en la calle Olvera.

SILVIA   **¡Qui úbole!** ¿Cómo estás, **'manita?**

ELENA   **Estoy agüitada.** Tuve una pelea con Eduardo hoy por la mañana. Y tengo una entrevista de trabajo por la tarde.

SILVIA   ¿Es que buscas trabajo?

ELENA   Sí, en el centro de computación. Necesito **lana.** Pero la jefa allí es muy **fufurufa. Se cree la muy muy.** Así que me siento nerviosa . . .

SILVIA   **No te agüites,** chica, que vas a salir bien en la entrevista, estoy segura.

ELENA   Pues, ahora me siento **como cocodrilo en fábrica de carteras.** Bueno, pero tú, ¿cómo estás?

SILVIA   Bien.

ELENA   ¿Qué onda con **los chavos?**

SILVIA   **De película. ¿Qué crees?** Anoche vi a Rafael.

ELENA   Rafael, ¿eh? Y ¿qué hicieron? Cuéntame, cuéntame. ¡Te ves **feliz como una lombriz!**

SILVIA   **Encantada de la vida,** 'manita.

———— ■ ————

¡Ojo!

- **¡Qui úbole!**, from **Qué húbole,** uses **hubo,** the past form of **hay.** It's a common greeting, used something like **¡Hola!** Also heard is **¡Qu'ubo!**

- **'Manita** is from **hermanita,** *little sister.* **'Mano** is often used to mean *brother.*

Silvia and Elena meet at a café on Olvera Street.

SILVIA   What's up? How are you, **'manita?**

ELENA   I'm upset (down, stressed). I had a fight with Eduardo this morning. And I have a job interview this afternoon.

SILVIA   So you're looking for work?

ELENA   Yeah, in the computer center. I need money (wool). But the boss there is very stuck up. She thinks she's hot stuff (the very very). So I'm nervous . . .

SILVIA   Don't let yourself get down—you'll do well on the interview, I'm sure.

ELENA   Well, now I feel like a crocodile in a wallet factory. But anyway, how are you?

SILVIA   Fine.

ELENA   How's your love life? (What's happening with the guys?)

SILVIA   Like a movie. Guess what. (What do you think?) I saw Rafael last night.

ELENA   Rafael, eh? What did you do? Tell me, tell me. You look happy as a lark (as a worm)!

SILVIA   (I'm) On cloud nine (charmed or enchanted with life), **'manita.**

----■----

- **Agüitado(-a)** means *"down" (tired, low).* **No te agüites** means *Don't let yourself get down.*

- **Lana:** this expression survives from the day when there was great money to be made raising sheep in **Nueva España.**

- **Como cocodrilo en fábrica de carteras:** Another expression for *to be nervous* is **estar como perro en canoa,** *to be like a dog in a canoe.*

Chiste

Dos vascos se ven en un café.

IÑAKI   ¡Hola, Patxi! **¿Qué tal?** Meses de no verte. ¿Cómo estás?

PATXI   **Más o menos. Y tú, ¿cómo te ha ido?**

IÑAKI   Bien. Siéntate, Patxi . . . **Oye,** estaba pensando: ¿en el cielo habrá frontón? Tú, ¿qué crees?

PATXI   Pues yo creo que sí, Iñaki, porque si allí todo es perfecto, pues habrá frontón.

IÑAKI   Oye, pues el primero que se muera que se lo diga al otro, ¿no?

PATXI   De acuerdo.

Pasan los años, Patxi se muere y al día siguiente Iñaki oye una voz de ultratumba:

PATXI   Iñaaaaaki, Iñaaaaaki, Iñaaaaaki, soy Patxi.

IÑAKI   Patxi, ¡hola! Hombre, ¿qué tal? ¿Cómo estás?

PATXI   **En la gloria,** Iñaki. Mira, te tengo que dar dos noticias, una buena y otra mala.

IÑAKI   ¿La buena?

PATXI   Que yo tenía razón, que hay un frontón magnífico, de más de 60 metros de fondo.

IÑAKI   ¿Y la noticia mala?

PATXI   Que juegas mañana a las 11:00.

Two Basques (from northern Spain) see each other in a café.

IÑAKI   Hi, Patxi! How are things? I haven't seen you for months. How are you?

PATXI   Okay (More or less). How've you been?

IÑAKI   Fine. Sit down, Patxi . . . Listen, I've been thinking: is there a jai alai court (**frontón**) in heaven? What do you think?

PATXI   Well, I think so, Iñaki, because if everything is perfect there, there must be a **frontón.**

IÑAKI   Listen, then, the first one who dies will tell the other one, okay?

PATXI   Agreed.

The years go by, Patxi dies, and the next day Iñaki hears a voice from beyond the tomb:

PATXI   Iñaaaki, Iñaaaki, Iñaaaki. It's me, Patxi.

IÑAKI   Patxi, hi. How are things, man? How are you?

PATXI   In seventh heaven (in my glory), Iñaki. Look, I have to give you two pieces of news, one good and one bad.

IÑAKI   What's the good news?

PATXI   That I was right, there's a magnificent **frontón,** more than 60 meters long.

IÑAKI   And the bad news?

PATXI   That you're playing tomorrow at 11:00.

———■———

¡Ojo!

- **Jai alai** is often called **la pelota vasca** *(Basque ball)* because it originated in the Basque region in northern Spain. It's a fast-moving game played on a court (the **frontón**) with walls on three sides and a fourth side with wire netting that spectators watch through. The players catch and throw the ball in curved wicker baskets strapped to their arms; sometimes the ball travels up to eighty miles an hour. Betting is common in jai alai.

- **¿Qué tal?** means *How are things?* It can be used with nouns: **¿Qué tal la fiesta?** *How is/was the party?* **¿Qué tal las niñas?** *How are the girls?* In Spain, one also hears **¿Qué tal andas?**

- **¿Cómo te ha ido?** is like **¿Cómo te va?** but in a different tense: *How have things gone for you?* instead of *How are things going for you?*

- **Estar en la gloria** means *to be in seventh heaven, very happy or comfortable.*

VOCABULARIO DEL CAPÍTULO

a toda madre	great, fantastic (Mexico, Central America)
agüitado(-a)	"down," tired, low (Mexico, Central America)
aquí nomás	(I'm) Just here—i.e., nothing is new. (Mexico, Central America)
el chavo, la chava	guy, girl
como cocodrilo en fábrica de carteras	(like a crocodile in a wallet factory) nervous
como perro en canoa	(like a dog in a canoe) nervous
¿Cómo te ha ido?	(How has it gone for you?) How have you (**tú**) been?

In Latin America, **telenovelas**, miniseries or soap operas, are very popular. Here Marcela asks how her friend Brígida has been. How does Brígida measure time? Not in weeks or months, but in **telenovelas**! (Hugo Díaz is a popular Costa Rican cartoonist.) © Hugo Díaz.

¿Cómo te va?	(How's it going for you?) How are you (**tú**)?
el compa	close male friend (from **compadre**)
la cruda	(rawness) hangover (Mexico, Central America)
de película	like a movie, great
echar relajo	(to throw off or make a rumpus) to have a blast (Mexico)
encantado(-a) de la vida	charmed or enchanted with life, very happy
estar crudo(-a)	(to be raw) to be hung over (Mexico, Central America)
estar de goma	(to be made of gum, rubber) to be hung over (Central America)
estar en la gloria	(to be in one's glory) to be in seventh heaven, on cloud nine
feliz como una lombriz	happy as a lark (worm)
hecho(-a) pinole	ground down, exhausted (Mexico)
fufurufo(-a)	stuck up
la lana	(wool) money
'mana ('manita)	forms of **hermana**, sister (used to address a female friend)
'mano ('manito)	forms of **hermano**, brother (used to address a male friend)
Más o menos.	(More or less.) Okay.
No te agüites.	Don't let yourself (**tú** form) get down, upset. (Mexico, Central America)
Oye (tú).	Listen. Hey.
padrísimo(-a)	fantastic, super (Mexico)
Por aquí (trabajando, estudiando).	Just here working, studying—i.e., nothing is new.
¿Qué crees?	(What do you [**tú**] think?) Guess what?
¿Qué me cuentas?	(What do you [**tú**] tell me?) What's happening?
¿Qué onda?	(What sound wave?) What's happening?

¡Qué padre!	(What a father!) Great! How fantastic! (Mexico)
¿Qué tal?	How are things?
¡Qui úbole!	a greeting, like **¡Hola!**
rendido(-a)	(rendered) exhausted
un reventón de primera	(a blowout of first) a first-class bash (Mexico, Central America)
la ruca	girl, woman (most of Latin America except the Southern Cone)
Se cree el (la) muy muy.	He (She) thinks he's (she's) hot stuff (the very very).
Te dejaron bien amolado(-a).	(They left you [**tú**] ruined, a wreck.) They wore you to a frazzle.
tener guayabo	(to have a guava tree) to be hung over (Colombia); also, **estar enguayabado**
tener la mona	(to have the monkey) to be hung over (Chile)
tener resaca	(to have undertow) to be hung over (Argentina, Uruguay, Spain)
tener un ratón	(to have a mouse) to be hung over (Venezuela)
¿Y eso?	(And that?) What does that mean?

¡A USTED LE TOCA!*

A. Responda, por favor.   Circle the appropriate response.

Modelo: ¿Qué onda con los chavos?
a. Estoy rendido.
(b.) De película.
c. ¡Qué cruda!

1. ¿Qui úbole? ¿Cómo estás?
   a. No huele nada.
   b. Aquí nomás.
   c. ¿Tienes lana?

2. Me siento como cocodrilo en fábrica de carteras.
   a. Cálmate, pues.
   b. No seas tan agresivo.
   c. ¿Por qué estás de goma?

3. Estoy en la gloria.
   a. Sí, te dejaron bien amolada.
   b. Así que tienes la mona, ¿eh?
   c. ¿Por qué estás tan contenta?

4. Hombre, ¡qué padre!
   a. Sí, es muy fufurufo.
   b. De veras, es estupendo.
   c. Tampoco me gusta.

5. ¿Cómo te ha ido?
   a. Bien, estoy hecho pinole.
   b. De película, todo fantástico.
   c. A un reventón de primera.

_____

*It's your turn!

6. Se cree la muy muy.

       a. Sí, está agüitada.

       b. ¿Qué crees?

       c. Sí, se cree muy importante.

B. Sinónimos. Match the synonyms.

_h_	1. a toda madre	a. tener resaca
__	2. lana	b. chicos
__	3. chavos	c. encantado de la vida
__	4. reventón	d. dinero
__	5. feliz como una lombriz	e. chica, mujer
__	6. estar crudo	f. amigo
__	7. compa	g. fiesta
__	8. ruca	h. excelente

C. Y tú, ¿qué tal? Someone asks how you are. Give an appropriate response for each situation, choosing from expressions in this chapter.

1. You're very happy; everything is going well.

    _____

2. You're feeling great.

    _____

3. You're okay.

    _____

4. Nothing is happening; you've just been working.

    _____

5. You're hung over.

    _____

6. You're exhausted.

    _____

7. You're "down" (nervous, tired).

    _____

D. ¿Cómo se dice . . . ? Write three ways to ask someone how things are going.

_____

_____

_____

. CAPÍTULO 2 .

No te hagas mala sangre

COMPLAINING ABOUT THE WEATHER AND
UNFAIR TREATMENT
·
GIVING SOMEONE A PIECE OF YOUR MIND

CONVERSACIÓN 1

*Jury Williams y su mujer Paz **hacen cola** en una oficina de gobierno en Santiago, Chile. Quieren hacer una queja por el exceso de impuestos que les cobraron.*

JURY **Por la flauta** que **hace calor**. **¡Se caen los patos asados!**

PAZ **La pura verdad** y esta **cola** no avanza. ¡Qué **despelote**! Hay tres **fulanos** y uno solo atiende a la gente. Están allí **copuchando** y **no nos dan bola**. ¡Qué idiotas! ¡Vamos a perder toda la tarde!

JURY **No te hagai mala sangre.** Estos **trámites redemoran**.

PAZ Mejor que no hablemos con el **gallo** de la barba. **Es muy mala leche.**

16

SE CAEN LOS PATOS ASADOS.

Jury Williams and his wife Paz are waiting in line (making a tail) at a government office in Santiago, Chile. They want to file a complaint for the extra taxes they were overcharged.

JURY   Gee whiz (By the flute), it's hot. You could fry an egg on the sidewalk (Roasted ducks are falling from the sky)!

PAZ   Right you are (the pure truth), and this line (tail) is not moving. What a mess (unravelling pile of balls)! Three so and so's **(fulanos)** are there and only one is helping people. There they are gossiping (cupping it up) and they don't pay any attention (give a ball) to us. What idiots! We are going to waste (lose) the whole afternoon!

JURY   Don't get upset (make bad blood for yourself)! These office procedures **(trámites)** take a really long time.

PAZ   It would be better not to talk with the guy (rooster) with the beard. He's a real pill (very bad milk)!

JURY   ¿Cuál? ¿Ese flaco como **palo de escoba?**

PAZ   Sí, lo recuerdo de la última vez. **Tuvo un ataque de caspa** y **se mandó un discurso** porque nos faltaba una estampilla en un documento. Es un **siútico tal por cual.**

JURY   Bueno, cambiémonos a la otra cola **por si las moscas . . .**

———————■———————

¡Ojo!

- **No te hagas mala sangre** is a plea to calm down and not get too angry (not to make your blood bad by getting stirred up) since the situation isn't worth it. Here, the common Chilean usage of the **vos** form (as a substitute for the **tú** form) changes the verb from **hagas** to **hagai.** (See page 124 for more about **vos** forms.)

- **Cola** (line or queue) means literally *tail* and probably originates because lines of people often wind around like an animal's tail. *To wait or get in line* or *to queue up* is **hacer cola.**

- **Se caen los patos asados** (Roasted ducks are falling out of the sky) is a common expression in Chile to complain that the weather's too hot.

- **¡Qué despelote!** means *What a mess!* in Chile, Uruguay, Venezuela, and Argentina. In Argentina, **¡Qué burdel!** or **¡Qué quilombo!** (What a bordello!) are also common. In Peru, it's **¡Qué laberinto!** (What a maze!), in Costa Rica, **¡Qué zambrote!** (What a Moorish party!) and in Spain, **¡Qué follón!** (What a ruckus!) The latter comes from the verb **follar,** which means to have sex, but the expression is not vulgar. However, the standard expression understood everywhere is **¡Qué lío!** (What a bundle!)

- **Fulano** or **fulana** refers a bit pejoratively to someone you don't know. In English we might say *That "so and so."* **Fulano** or **fulana de tal** means *John* or *Jane Doe.* To extend the reference to other unknowns, add **mengano** or **zutano.**

- **Copuchar** is the common verb for *to gossip* in Chile and may derive from the word **copa,** which means *wine glass* (and by extension, any alcoholic drink), since it is often over a **copa** or two that gossiping takes place.

JURY   Which one? That thin one who looks like a broomstick?

PAZ   Yes, I remember him from last time. He threw a fit (had a dandruff attack) and delivered a lecture because a stamp was missing on our document. He's an out-and-out (such for which) pretentious snob (**siútico**).

JURY   OK, let's change to the other line just in case (just in case the flies). . .

———————————————

- **Trámites** refers to the filling out of forms, standing in lines, or general procedures that must be done with papers in a bank, office, or business. There is no exact translation in English for this useful word.

- **Redemorar. Demorar** means *to take a long time* and **re-** is an intensifying prefix, so **redemoran** means (they) are taking a *really* long time. (See page 202 for more on intensifiers.)

- **Gallo.** Animal names are common slang many countries. For example, in Chile any man can be referred to as a **gallo** (rooster). A common word for young people is **cabros.** Introverts lacking social skills are **pavos(-as)** (turkeys) or **gansos(-as)** (geese). Many other countries have similar uses.

- **Mala leche** (bad milk) turns sour and a person described in this way is the kind who causes problems and conflicts for everyone.

CONVERSACIÓN 2

La misma oficina, dos horas más tarde. Las colas casi no han avanzado.
La gente empieza a perder la paciencia, y un funcionario llega para calmarlos.

PAZ	¡Mira a esa **patuda** con minifalda! Llegó recién y ya está en la ventanilla.
JURY	Y **el palo de escoba le muestra los dientes, está todo derretido** con ella.
SR. X	¡Qué ridículo! El jefe está mirando y **hace la vista gorda.**
JURY	Y nosotros tenemos que **comernos el buey.**
SRA. X	Sí, claro. Estamos aquí **sudando la gota gorda** y llega ella, moviendo el **poto,** y se coloca al frente **como si nada**.
SRA. Y	**Eso no es justo.** Voy a hablar con ella. *(Se dirige a la señorita con la minifalda.)* Ya pues, señorita, ¡**un poco de respeto**, por favor! Tiene que ponerse al final de la cola y esperar su turno como todos.
SRTA. CON MINI	¿Y quién es Ud. para **meter la cuchara?**
SRA. X	**¡Qué descaro! Tenemos que reclamar.**
FUNCIONARIO	Un momento, por favor. ¿Su nombre, señorita?

In many places you also can say someone **tiene mala leche,** which means he or she is in a grouchy mood.

- A **siútico(-a)** is an affected snob who tries to pretend he or she is upper-class but is not. This word seems to exist only in Chile.

- **Por si las moscas** is a common humorous rephrasing of **por si acaso** (just in case).

The same office, two hours later. The lines have hardly advanced. People are beginning to lose patience and a government worker (functionary) comes over to calm them down.

PAZ	Look at that pushy chick (ugly bigfoot) with the miniskirt! She just arrived and already she's up at the counter (little window).
JURY	And the broomstick is smiling all over at her (showing her his teeth). He's completely in her power (melted by her).
MR. X	How ridiculous! The director is looking and pretending that he sees nothing (making the fat look).
JURY	And we have to put up with it!
MRS. X	Yeah, right. Here we are sweating it out (sweating the fat drop) and she comes along, moving her buns (rear) and is put at the front just like that (as if nothing).
MRS. Y	That's not fair. I'm going to talk with her. (*She goes over to the girl with the miniskirt.*) Enough, now, miss, a little respect, please! You have to go to the end of the line and wait your turn like everyone else.
GIRL IN MINI	And who are you to butt in (put in your soup spoon)?
MRS. X	What nerve! We have to make a complaint.
FUNCTIONARY	One moment please. Your name, miss?

SRTA. CON MINI	Teresa Wilson.
FUNCIONARIO	Buenas tardes, señorita Wilson. **Tenga la bondad de pasar por aquí.**
SRA. Y	Probablemente la señorita es su **polola.**
SR. X	¡Seguro que tiene **santos en la corte!**
FUNCIONARIO	Calma, señores. La señorita Wilson tiene una cita previa.
PAZ	**Claro, y los chanchos vuelan. ¡Cuñas!** En este país todo se arregla con cuñas.

———■———

¡Ojo!

- **Patudo(-a)** (big-footed person) in Chile refers to someone who breaks the norms of respect or good manners; for example, the friend who enters your house and opens up your refrigerator without asking. The word derives from **pata** (which refers to the foot of an animal but is used comically for human feet) with the negative ending -**udo,** since **patudos** stick their feet in places where they don't belong. (See page 203 for a discussion of negative and positive word endings.) In Venezuela, a person like this is a **rajado(-a),** literally, one who rips or tears.

- **Hacer la vista gorda** (to make the fat view) is to ignore someone or something, looking straight past him or it, or in the other direction.

- **Comernos el buey** (to eat up the ox) means to tolerate or put up with a situation.

- **Poto** is the Chilean term for what you usually land on when you fall down, equivalent to *buttocks, butt,* or *buns* in the U.S., or *bum* in Canada or the U.K. It is not as strong or vulgar as **culo,**

GIRL IN MINI	Teresa Wilson.
FUNCTIONARY	Good afternoon, Miss Wilson. Please be so kind as to step this way.
MRS. Y	She's probably his sweetie (bumblebee).
MR. X	For sure she has connections (saints at court)!
FUNCTIONARY	Calm down, ladies and gentlemen. Miss Wilson has a previously scheduled appointment.
PAZ	Sure, that's likely (and pigs fly). Connections (construction supports)! In this country everything is arranged with connections.

———■———

ass, and is used in many contexts to indicate *bottom* such as when talking about the **poto de la silla** *the bottom of the chair.* In Mexico the word for this part of the anatomy is usually **pompis,** possibly from **pompas,** *bubbles,* as in **pompas de jabón;** in Argentina **traste,** and in many other places, **trasero,** both words from **atrás,** *behind* or *in back.*

- **Pololo(-a)** (bumblebee) is a very Chilean word for boyfriend or girlfriend, called **novio(-a)** in most other places, and implies a steady romantic relationship. In Chile, to go with someone in this way is **pololear** (to buzz like bumblebees).

- **Cuñas** (literally *small wooden props*) means *connections,* the kind that get you in the door somewhere because you know the right people. It is a synonym in Chile for the term **santos en la corte** (saints at court), an obvious remnant from colonial times, which is used and understood in many countries. In Venezuela, to make the right connection for someone is **hacerle la esquina** (to make the corner for him or her).

Vocabulario del capítulo

el ataque de caspa	(dandruff attack) fit, tantrum
los cabros, las cabras	(goats) kids (Chile, Peru)
Claro, y los chanchos vuelan.	Right, and that's likely (pigs fly). [sarcastic]
la cola	(tail of an animal) line or queue of people waiting
comerse el buey	(to eat up the ox) to put up with something you don't like
como si nada	(like if nothing) just like that, as if there were no problem
copuchar	to gossip (Chile)
el culo	ass [vulgar]
las cuñas	(props, wedges) connections (social, political, etc.) (Chile)
dar bola a alguien	(to give the ball) to pay attention to someone
Eso no es justo.	That is not fair (just).
estar todo(-a) derretido(-a)	to be completely under the spell (melted)
el fulano, la fulana	so and so (to refer to someone you don't know)
el fulano or **la fulana de tal**	John or Jane Doe
el gallo	(rooster) guy (Chile, Peru, some parts of Central America)
hacer cola	(to make a tail) to wait in line
hacerle la esquina	to get you (him, her) the right connections (Venezuela)
hacer la vista gorda	(to do the fat look) to ignore
mala leche	(bad milk) conflictive or difficult person
mandarse un discurso	to deliver a sermon (speech)
meter la cuchara	(to put in [your] soup spoon) to butt into someone else's business
mostrar (ue) los dientes	(to show teeth) to smile

No te hagas mala sangre.	Don't get upset (make bad blood for yourself).
el palo de escoba	(broomstick) person who is too skinny
patudo(-a)	(ugly bigfoot) pushy or nervy person (Argentina, Chile, Uruguay)
pololo(-a)	(bumblebee) sweetheart, steady boyfriend or girlfriend (Chile)
los pompis	buttocks, *buns* in the sense of rear end (Mexico)
por si las moscas	(for if the flies) just in case (Chile, Peru)
por la flauta	(by the flute) gee whiz, good heavens
el poto	rear end, butt, bottom (Chile)
la pura verdad	(pure truth) right you are
¡Qué burdel!, ¡Qué quilombo!	(What a bordello!) What a mess! (Argentina, Uruguay)
¡Qué descaro!	What nerve (brazenness)!
¡Qué despelote!	(What an unravelling ball!) What a mess! (Chile, Uruguay, Argentina)
¡Qué laberinto!	(What a labyrinth!) What a mess! (Peru)
¡Qué lío!	(What a bundle!) What a mess! (used everywhere)
¡Qué zambrote!	(What a Moorish party!) What a mess! (Costa Rica)
rajado(-a)	(ripper) pushy or nervy person (Venezuela)
redemorar	to take a really long time
los santos en la corte	connections (saints at court)
Se caen los patos asados.	(Roasted ducks are falling.) It's too hot. (Chile)
siútico(-a)	affected and pretentious snob (Chile)
sudar la gota gorda	(to sweat the fat drop) to sweat bullets, sweat it out
tal por cual	(such for which) out-and-out, dyed-in-the-wool

Tenemos que reclamar.	We have to demand our rights.
tener mala leche	(to have bad milk) to be in a grouchy mood
Tenga la bondad de . . .	(Have the goodness of) Be so good as to . . .
los trámites	bureaucratic procedures
el trasero	rear end, bottom (*bum* in Canada and England)
el traste	pot, dish, or pan (Mexico); rear end, backside (in many other countries)
un poco de respeto	a little respect

¡A USTED LE TOCA!

A. ¿Qué dicen realmente? Sometimes the literal meaning of an idiom is far away from the real meaning. Choose the response that best gives the *real* meaning.

1. Ese hombre es **mala leche.**
   - a. criminal
   - b. una persona conflictiva
   - c. un individuo triste

2. El empleado **le muestra los dientes** a la muchacha.
   - a. Está enojado *(angry)*.
   - b. Está sonriendo *(smiling)*.
   - c. Está asustado *(scared)*.

3. **¡Caen los patos asados!**
   - a. Hace mucho calor.
   - b. Es muy tarde.
   - c. No nos gustan.

4. A veces tenemos que **comernos el buey.**
   - a. trabajar mucho
   - b. gozar de la vida
   - c. aguantar la situación

5. **Seguro, y los chanchos vuelan.**
    a. Lo que dice Ud. es muy probable.
    b. Lo que dice Ud. es posible.
    c. Lo que dice Ud. es una mentira.

B. Chilenismos. Choose the Chilean slang from the list for each of the standard words in italics.

cola	cuñas	escobas	pololear	reclamar
copuchar	despelote	gallos	el poto	siútico

1. La oficina está mal organizada. ¡Qué *lío* _____!
2. El hermano de Clara es *un esnob pretencioso* _____.
3. El jefe quiere *andar de novio* _____ con su joven secretaria.
4. Esos *hombres* _____ no piensan en las consecuencias.
5. Miren la botella de vino. *La base* _____ está rota (roto).
6. Quiero charlar acerca de nuestros amigos. ¡Vamos a *chismear* _____!
7. Tratan bien a Tomás en la compañía. Tiene *santos en la corte* _____.

C. Palabras revueltas. Unscramble the letters to get each message.

1. She's really thin. She's a
   lopa ed seboca. _____

2. They are ignoring what's going
   on: **chena al sativ radog.** _____

3. That isn't fair! **¡On se tosuj!** _____

4. Instead of minding his own
   business, he wants to **reemt al
   churaca.** _____

5. She was so upset. **¡Es oid
   nu qaueta ed pacas!** _____

6. Juan is infatuated with Ana:
   táse doot idorreted noc alle _____

D. ¿Qué falta? Complete the expressions on the left. Then match them to their English equivalents on the right.

1. **como si** _____   a. just in case *(for if the flies)*

2. **un siútico tal por** _____   b. to pay no attention to us *(to not pass us the ball)*

3. **no darnos** _____   c. to work very hard *(sweat the fat drop)*

4. **por la** _____   d. just like that *(as if nothing)*

5. **por si las** _____   e. an out-and-out *(such for which)* pretentious snob

6. **sudar la gota** _____   f. gee whiz *(by the flute)*

E. Responda, por favor. React to the following, using different expressions from this chapter.

1. You're waiting in line at an office and all of the employees are socializing with each other and ignoring you completely. Then a friend of yours arrives and you want to describe to him what's happening.

_____

_____

_____

2. Another friend is very angry about the situation and looks ready to have a heart attack. You want to calm her down and tell her that things are just like that and we have to accept them.

_____

_____

_____

3. A man barges into the line in front of you when the employees aren't looking and you decide to give him a piece of your mind.

_____

_____

_____

Vocabulary and Culture

"Chilenismos" and Other Expressions of Spanish Diversity

Do you know where you are if you order "regular" (pronounced *"regulah"*) coffee and it comes with cream? Or if a lady asks where the "bubbler" is because she wants a drink of water? Coffee with cream in Boston and water fountains in Milwaukee are special words that are examples of the language of place, language that differs throughout the many regions of the English-speaking world.

Signature Words   Spanish also has special words, *signature words,* that distinguish particular regions in the twenty-one countries where it is spoken as a main language. Sometimes these expressions give clues to national obsessions, as is the case with the English word *workaholic* and other expressions relating to hard work. Chilean Spanish, on the other hand, has numerous special adjectives describing fine nuances in social class that reflect the national obsession for delineating social status. A **roto** is a low-class bum with bad manners; a **roto con plata,** a low-class bum with money, or *nouveau riche* (General Pinochet, the dictator from 1973–88, is considered by many as a prime example of this type); a **pituco** is an affected snob tending toward tacky; a **pepepato,** a vain rich person with no brains; a **cuico,** an ostentatious snob flaunting high status; and a **siútico,** an overly fastidious person pretending to be high class when he isn't, to name only a few! In the English translation of the novel *Paula* by the Chilean author Isabel Allende, there is not even an attempt to translate several of these words, but instead they are included in italics in Spanish.

Indigenous Influences   In many regions a strong linguistic influence is the local native culture. Mexico, for example, has common words derived from the ancient Aztec language, Náhuatl, such as **güero(-a)** which means *blond(e)* and is often used instead of the more universal **rubio(-a),** and **esquintle(-a),** which means *street dog* after the tiny hairless dogs the Aztecs once raised for food, but which is often used today as an insult meaning *twerp* or *insignificant youngster.* The Peruvian word **mita** (forced labor) from Quechua, the Venezuelan **arepa** (corn bread) from Arawak, and **chicle** (universally used for "chewing gum") from the Maya language are other examples of native influences.

Every region possesses local variants, even when the universal terms are understood. Mexicans, for example, understand the word **autobús** (bus) but generally use **camión** (truck) for bus as well as for truck (specifying **camión de carga** for the latter if they wish to make the meaning clear). They frequently say **¿Mande?** (literally, "Your command?") when they haven't heard or don't understand something, instead of **¿Cómo?,** which is the usual word employed to translate *What?* or *Huh?*

The Tango Connection   In Argentina and Uruguay, conversations are peppered with words derived from *lunfardo,* the special dialect used in tango songs. *Lunfardo* evolved from sailors who worked around the wharves at the turn of the century and so many of its words have spicy connotations contrasting with the normally conservative speech habits of the region. The plaintive tangos with their distinctive beat, often accompanied by dancers, speak of the ungrateful **mina** from the **conventillo** who has betrayed her man: **¡Qué quilombo!** (What a disaster—literally, bordello!) Translated literally, the woman is referred to as a "mine" because her boyfriend in those long-ago times was a **cafiche** (a pimp) who used her as a source of money to live on, and this all took place in a run-down tenement, which may have been a "little convent" at one time. But the literal meaning does not matter, for it is the intense emotion of the tango that is dear to the hearts of Uruguayans and Argentines. Modern tangos are invented each year (nowadays by women as well as men) and sung along with traditional ones, but the old dialect persists and is part of everyday speech. Another strong influence is the tradition of the **gaucho,** or Argentine cowboy, which gives rise to expressions such as **una gauchada,** meaning *a really big favor.* The **huaso** in Chile, the **charro** in Mexico, and the **llanero** in Venezuela and Colombia have similar cowboy traditions which spill over into everyday ways of speaking.

Toward a Language and a Culture "Sin fronteras" ("Without Borders") And so it is in every part of the Spanish-speaking world. If you were to wake from a dream and hear someone say, **¿Qué te apetece?** (What do you feel like having?), you could be pretty sure you were in Spain, but if instead you heard, **¿Te provoca un tinto?** (Are you in the mood for some coffee?), you'd know instantly that you were in Colombia. Colloquial and slang expressions vary from place to place, particularly insults, swear words, or off-color expressions, generally called **groserías** or **palabrotas.** Nevertheless, much slang (including insults) is understood almost everywhere and this universalizing trend is gaining force.

With the expansion of travel, music, and the movie industry, Spanish, like English, is moving toward a higher degree of universalization. Slang words that were once understood only in Mexico are now sung by Chilean adolescents, as they listen to Mexican music on their Walkmans®. Soap operas, magazines, movies, the Internet—all are vehicles for spreading words and expressions. At the same time, these media are stimulating minority cultures and dialects which in the past had little access to communication. In fact, some cultures and dialects once in danger of extinction have now gained new life. So, paradoxically, regionalization is also flourishing. Spanish is on the move, evolving by becoming more universal and by including and expanding its many regional variants, two counter-tendencies occurring in parallel to enrich and diversify this amazing international language across and beyond all borders.

Selecciones. Choose the correct option to finish each statement.

1. Spanish is the official language of __ countries.
    a. 6
    b. 21
    c. 80

2. In Chile, **pololo** means
    a. lower class
    b. snob
    c. boyfriend

3. The Mexican word **esquintle** derives from the
    a. Mayas
    b. Incas
    c. Aztecs

4. In Mexico a **camión** is a
    a. truck
    b. bus
    c. truck or bus

5. Some Uruguayan and Argentine signature words, like **mina**, are derived from the tango dialect called
    a. gaucho
    b. lunfardo
    c. huaso

6. If someone asks you, **¿Qué te apetece?**, you are probably in
    a. Madrid
    b. Bogotá
    c. Los Angeles

7. Two counter-tendencies occurring in Spanish today are
    a. movies and Internet
    b. rapidity and borders
    c. universalization and regionalization

UN MALENTENDIDO REGIONAL:
UN CHILENO BIEN VALIENTE

Un chileno que tenía la reputación de ser malgeniudo hizo un viaje de negocios a México. De regreso a Chile, se puso a charlar con su hermana sobre el viaje. Le contó que en México se había asombrado de ver que todo el mundo lo alababa constantemente por su valentía.

    —Mira, hermana querida—le dijo—. Me siento orgulloso porque los mexicanos me tienen por muy valiente, pero la verdad es que no comprendo por qué.

La hermana, que había vivido en México varios años, le preguntó:

    —Pero, dime, ¿qué te decían exactamente?

    —Me decían—respondió—, que yo siempre tenía coraje.

    —Pues, se aclara el misterio, hermano mío—explicó su hermana, riéndose—, porque en México ¡**"tener coraje"** quiere decir **estar enojado**!

A Chilean who had the reputation of being very bad-tempered made a business trip to Mexico. After returning to Chile, he began to chat with his sister about the trip. He told her that in Mexico he had been amazed to find that everyone constantly praised him for his courage. "Look, sister dear," he said. "I feel proud because the Mexicans consider me courageous, but the truth is that I don't understand why." The sister, who had lived in Mexico for several years, asked him, "But tell me, what exactly did they say to you?" "They said to me," he replied, "that I always had **coraje.**"

1. b 2. c 3. c 4. a 5. b 6. a 7. c

"Well, the mystery is solved, dear brother," she explained, laughing, "because in Mexico, to have **coraje** means 'to be angry'!"

Personas y personajes *(People and Characters)* Certain names are used in Chilean proverbs and sayings as examples of particular personality types. While these may be especially Chilean, they have equivalents in many cultures.

1. Eso es como **el padre Gatica:** predica pero no practica.
2. Eso es como **el capitán Araya:** embarca a su gente y él se queda en la playa.
3. Eso es como **el maestro Ciruela:** no escribe ni lee pero tiene escuela.
4. **Juan Seguro** vivió muchos años.
5. Más perdido que **el teniente Bello.**★

1. That's like Father Gatica: he doesn't practice what he preaches.
2. That's like Captain Araya: he sends out his people on the sea and he stays behind on the beach.
3. That's like the teacher Ciruela: he can't read or write but he has a school.
4. John Safety lived many years.
5. More lost than Lieutenant Bello.

Los dichos de una abuelita chilena *(Sayings of a Chilean Grannie)*
A Chilean lady who emigrated to Canada remembers her grannie's sayings that were earthy and **"salpicados de chilenismos"** (peppered with Chilean expressions). In English she heard close friends, for example, described as two peas in a pod, but her grandmother used to say they were like **la uña y la carne** (the nail and the flesh under it), or like **dos potos en un calzón** (two rear ends in one pair of pants).

★Lieutenant Bello was a famous Chilean aviator who disappeared one day on a routine flight to Santiago and was never seen again.

. Capítulo 3 .

¡*Vamos a vacilar!*

Making, accepting, and declining invitations

En un centro comercial de Miami, Florida.

FELIPE   ¡Qui ubo, Marta! ¿Cómo estás?

MARTA   Bien, bien. Y tú, ¿qué onda?

FELIPE   **Por aquí, vagando.** Oye, pensaba ir a escuchar a Gloria Estefan el sábado . . . **¿Qué te parece?** ¿Me quieres acompañar?

MARTA   ¿Gloria Estefan? Sí, **hombre, ¡chévere!** Me encantaría.

FELIPE   Entonces, **¡vamos a vacilar!** A ver . . . Comamos antes, ¿no?

MARTA   **¡Simón,** con mucho gusto! ¿A qué horas?

FELIPE   Nos vemos a las seis, ¿de acuerdo?

MARTA   ¿Dónde?

FELIPE   Pasaré por tu casa.

MARTA   **Asómate** a las seis, pues. Y **no me dejes plantada.**

NO ME DEJES PLANTADA.

In a shopping center in Miami, Florida.

FELIPE   Hi, Marta! How are you?

MARTA   Good, good. And you, what's up?

FELIPE   Same as usual (I'm just here), goofing (wandering) around. Listen, I was thinking of going to see Gloria Estefan on Saturday . . . What do you think? Do you want to go with me?

MARTA   Gloria Estefan? Yes, fantastic! I'd love it.

FELIPE   Then let's party! Let's see. Let's eat first, okay?

MARTA   Yeah, good (with great pleasure). What time?

FELIPE   Let's meet (see each other) at six, okay?

MARTA   Where?

FELIPE   I'll go by your house.

MARTA   Show up at six, then. And don't stand me up (leave me planted).

FELIPE   No, no. A las seis en tu casa, **así quedamos**.

MARTA   **No veo la hora de salir, chico**. Gloria Estefan . . . ¡**es lo máximo!**

———————◾———————

¡Ojo!

- **Hombre:** While it may seem strange, **¡Hombre!** is a term of address used for a woman as well as a man. The exception is the southern part of Latin America, where it may seem a bit rude when used for a woman. It is also common in most regions to say **¡mujer!** to a woman in the same way.

- **Chévere** means *great, wonderful, super,* etc., and is very commonly used in Latin America except in the southern areas. It supposedly originated in a Cuban song lyric and spread throughout the Caribbean and then southward.

- **Vacilar** is *to have a good time,* or it can mean *to joke around, kid.*

- **Simón** is a variant of **sí.**

- **Asomarse** means *to go near, appear,* but in this case *to show up.*

CONVERSACIÓN 2

En una calle de Miami.

JAIME   Hola, chula. **Dichosos los ojos que te están viendo. Estás como nunca.**

MARISOL   Hola.

JAIME   ¿Qué tal, corazón?

MARISOL   Bien.

JAIME   Bien bonita. Oye, este viernes hay una **pachanga** en casa de un amigo mío. ¿Vamos juntos?

FELIPE   No, no. At six at your house, that's how we'll leave it (remain).

MARTA   I can't wait (see the hour) to go out. Gloria Estefan—she's the best (the maximum)!

———■———

- **Dejar plantado(-a)** means literally *to leave someone planted in the ground,* that is to stand him or her up; this expression is used in most of the Spanish-speaking world. In Spain, one hears **No me dés plantón.** In the Caribbean, **tirar bomba** is used also, and Mexican-Americans say **dar calabazas,** *to give pumpkins.* A similar expression is **No me dejes con los churquitos (colochos) hechos,** *Don't leave me with my curls done,* that is, all spruced up and ready to go. (In Chile, you might hear **No me dejes con los ruleros puestos,** *Don't leave me with my rollers in.*)

- **No veo la hora** means literally, *I can't see the hour*—that is, I am looking forward to it.

- **Chico(-a)** is used as a form of address by Cubans and others to mean *friend, pal.*

On a street in Miami.

JAIME   Hello, beautiful. Great to see you (lucky the eyes that are looking at you). You look better than ever.

MARISOL   Hello.

JAIME   How are things, my love (heart)?

MARISOL   Good **(Bien).**

JAIME   Very **(Bien)** pretty. Listen, this Friday there's a party at the house of a friend of mine. Shall we go together?

MARISOL ¿Cómo . . .? ¿Tú y yo?

JAIME Sí, **mamacita**. ¿Qué dices? **Vamos a pasarla bien.**

MARISOL No puedo. **Este** . . . Tengo mucho que hacer. Gracias, de todos modos.

JAIME **Nos watchamos** otro día, pues.

MARISOL (a sí misma) **¡Caray! ¡Qué mujeriego! Un cero a la izquierda.**

JAIME (a sí mismo) ¡Uuf! **¡Qué fresa! No está en na'a.**

———————■———————

¡Ojo!

- **Dichosos los ojos** is also heard, or **Dichosos los ojos que te ven.** Similar is **¡Qué habré hecho yo para merecerme tal preciosura!** *What could I have done to deserve such beauty (such preciousness)!*

- **Pachanga:** There are many words for *party* or *dance*: **pachanga** or **pachangón, danzón, rumbón** (like **rumba**). Other expressions: **bachata** (Dominican Republic), **farra** (Colombia), **guachafita** (Venezuela), **fanfarria** (Puerto Rico), **jarana** (Mexico, Spain, Peru), **bailorio** (Ecuador), **bayú** or **bembé** (the Caribbean).

- **Mamacita** is a term of affection deriving from **mamá.** In many Latin American countries, even young girls are called **mamacita, mamita,** or **mami** with affection. Also used is **mamasota,** for a gorgeous or appealing woman, a "cheesecake"; this expression is, of course, rather sexist.

- **Pasarla bien** (also, **parsarlo bien**): In Spain, people say **pasarlo en grande,** *to have a great time.*

- **Este** is a hesitation word, used to buy time, sort of like "uh, well . . ." in English. **Bueno** or the very common **pues** often

MARISOL   What . . .? You and me?

JAIME   Yes, **mamacita** (little mama). What do you say? We'll have a
            great time.

MARISOL   I can't. Uh . . . I have a lot to do. Thanks, anyway.

JAIME   We'll see each other another day, then.

MARISOL   (to herself) Jeeze! What a womanizer! Worthless (a zero to the
            left).

JAIME   (to himself) Uuf! What a **fresa** (strawberry). She's nowhere.
            (She's not in anything.)

———■———

function in the same way, to fill in when one is thinking of
what to say. Spanish speakers don't usually say *uh* or *um*.

- **Nos watchamos** comes, obviously, from the English expression
  to watch. **Nos lukeamos,** from the English *to look,* is also used.
  Both mean basically *See you.*

- **¡Qué mujeriego!** A man who chases women is a **mujeriego** or
  mujerero. Other expressions similar in meaning include: **¡Qué
  gorila!, ¡Qué cocodrilo!** and **¡Qué buitre!** (literally, *What a
  gorilla! What a crocodile! What a vulture!*), meaning something like
  What a wolf! Also heard is **¡Qué don Juan!,** from the story of
  Don Juan Tenorio, a famous womanizer created by Spanish play-
  wright Tirso de Molina, but the meaning in Spanish is not as
  negative as in English. The term **¡Qué descarado!** is also heard,
  meaning *What a scoundrel!*

- **Una fresa,** literally, *a strawberry,* refers to a young woman who
  is innocent but also a bit disdainful or spoiled, usually living with
  her parents.

CHISTE

En Ecuador, una señorita va a la iglesia a confesarse.—Perdóneme, padre, porque he pecado—dice ella.

—Bueno, hija, cuéntame tus pecados—le responde el cura.

—El otro día estaba caminando por la calle cuando me encontré con un viejo amigo. Me invitó a tomar un café, empezamos a charlar, de allí me invitó a su departamento e hicimos el amor. Y como yo soy tan frúgil. . . .

—Frágil, hija, frágil—dice el padre.

—Bueno—dice la señorita—, al día siguiente estaba sentada en la plaza cuando de repente se asoma otro amigo. Iba para la casa de un **pana** suyo porque allá **se iba a formar un vacilón.** Me invitó a acompañarlo. Como estaba libre y no quería ser **aguafiestas,** fui con él. Después terminamos en mi departamento e hicimos el amor. Y como yo soy tan frúgil. . . .

—Frágil, hija, frágil—dice otra vez el cura.

—Ayer me llamó mi novio—empieza **de nuevo** la señorita—. "¿Quieres ir a un **danzón?**", me dijo. Bueno, **fuimos de juerga** y después fuimos a su departamento y como yo soy tan, ay, ¿cuál es esa palabra, padre?

—Puta, hija, puta.

———— ■ ————

In Ecuador, a young lady goes to church to make her confession. "Forgive me, father, for I have sinned," she says. "Well, my child (daughter), tell me your sins," the priest replies. "The other day I was walking down the street when I met an old friend. He invited me to have coffee, we began to chat, from there he invited me to his apartment and we made love. And since I am so frugile . . . ." "Fragile, my child, fragile," says the priest. "Well," says the young lady, "the next day I was sitting in the plaza when suddenly another friend showed up. He was going to the house of a friend of his because a party was going to get going there. He invited me to go with him. Since I was

Nota cultural: Manuel Héctor Falcón is a popular Mexican cartoonist. He tends to spoof character types like **el capitán nerd**, who is always trying to invite women out or getting in the way of someone else who is, and Güilson (Wilson) **el dios de la güeva**, a boring, lazy fellow. The cartoons on this page, page 42, and page 43 are from his book *Cascajo*.

ligarse *to connect with, pick up*

free and I didn't want to be a party-pooper, I went with him. Afterwards we ended up in my apartment and we made love. And since I'm so frugile . . . ." "Fragile, my child, fragile," says the priest again. "Yesterday my boyfriend called me," the young lady begins again. "'Do you want to go to a dance?' he asked. Well, we went out on the town and then we went to his apartment and since I'm so . . . uh, what was that word, father?" "Slut ('prostitute'), my child, slut."

EL capitán NERD, a la OFENSiva, iNteNta atrapar CHavas coN su extraordiNaRio álbum de FiLatelia asiática...

intenta *tries;* filatelia *stamp collecting*

¡Ojo!

- **Pana** comes from **panal,** *honeycomb,* and means *a good friend.* It is used mainly in Venezuela, Ecuador, and Colombia.

- **Allá se iba a formar un vacilón** means that a party was taking shape or beginning. A **vacilón** can also be a comic, the life of the party, someone who is entertaining: **José es un vacilón, siempre contando chistes.**

- **Aguafiestas:** this word, *party-pooper,* conjures up a vision of someone pouring water over a party, to ruin it.

- **Ir de juerga** or **ir de parranda** both mean *to party, go out on the town.*

velada *evening get-together;* captó *got;* lárgate *get lost*

VOCABULARIO DEL CAPÍTULO

Así quedamos.	(That's how we'll remain.) That's how we'll leave it, agreed.
asomarse	to show up
¡Caray!	Jeeze! (from **¡Carajo!**, vulgar)
un cero a la izquierda	(a zero to the left) worthless, no good
chévere	great, fantastic (most of Latin America except the Southern Cone; most common in Caribbean areas, Venezuela, Colombia)
chulo(-a)	cute, good-looking
el danzón	dance
de nuevo, nuevamente	again
dejar plantado(-a)	(to leave someone planted) to stand (someone) up
Dichosos los ojos que te están viendo.	(Fortunate the eyes that are looking at you.) Great to see you. Also **Dichosos los ojos.**

el don Juan	Don Juan, womanizer
¡Es lo máximo!	It's (He's, She's) fantastic (the maximum)!
Estás como nunca.	(You [**tú**] are like never.) You look better than ever.
Este . . ., Bueno . . ., Pues . . .	Uh . . ., Well . . . (hesitation words)
una fresa	(a strawberry) a young woman who is innocent but also a bit disdainful or spoiled, usually living with her parents
Gracias, pero tengo mucho que hacer.	Thanks, but I have a lot to do.
¡Hombre!	(Man!) term of address for either a man or a woman
ir de juerga	to go out on the town, party
ir de parranda	to go out on the town, party
la jarana	party (Mexico, Spain, Peru)
mamacita	(little mama) term of address derived from **mamá,** used with affection to a girl or woman; also, **mamita**
mamasota	(big mama) term of address a bit vulgar, meaning *cheesecake,* good-looking woman
el mujeriego (mujerero)	womanizer
No está en na'a (nada).	He or she is out of it (not in anything).
No me dejes con los churquitos (colochos) hechos.	Don't leave me waiting (with my curls done). (Carribean, Central America)
No veo la hora de salir.	I can't wait (see the hour) to go out.
Nos lukeamos./Nos watchamos.	See you. We'll see each other. (from the English *to look, to watch,* used where there is English influence)
la pachanga, el pachangón	party
el, la pana	(male or female) friend (from **panal,** honeycomb)
pasarla (o pasarlo) bien	to have a good time

pasarlo en grande	(to pass or spend it big) to have a great time (Spain)
un plantón	(a planting) a standing up (of someone) or someone who stands someone else up
Por aquí, vagando.	Same as usual. (I'm just here, goofing [wandering] around.)
¡Qué gorila (buitre, cocodrilo)!	(What a gorilla [vulture, crocodile]!) What a wolf!
¿Qué te parece (si . . .)?	(How does it seem to you [**tú**] [if . . .]?) How about (if . . .)?
ser aguafiestas	(to be a water-party) to be a party-pooper
simón	yeah (variant of **sí**)
tirar bomba	(to throw a bomb) to stand (someone) up (Caribbean)
vacilar	to party, have a good time; to kid or joke
¡Vamos a vacilar!	Let's party!
un vacilón	comic (amusing person); good time
Allá se formaba un vacilón.	A party was taking shape (getting going) there.

¡A USTED LE TOCA!

A. Sinónimos. Match the synonyms.

___1. ir de juerga   a. tirar bomba

___2. chévere   b. un mujeriego

___3. de nuevo   c. aparecer

___4. dejar plantado   d. lo máximo

___5. pana   e. nuevamente

___6. un don Juan   f. nos watchamos

___7. asomarse   g. pachanga

___8. nos lukeamos   h. compañero(-a), amigo(-a)

___9. jarana   i. ir de parranda

B. **¿Qué es?** Give a word or phrase that best fits each description. Choose from the following: **aguafiestas, cero a la izquierda, chulo, fresa, gorila, pana, vacilón.**

Modelo:

Andrés es muy guapo y atractivo. Es muy _____ **chulo**_____.

1. Beto es muy chistoso. Le gusta pasarla bien. Es un _____.
2. Carlos es un buen amigo. Es un buen _____.
3. Daniel es inútil; no tiene muchas cualidades buenas. Es un

   _____.
4. Eva es una señorita que vive con sus papás y está mimada *(pampered);* trata a los admiradores con desdén. Es una _____.
5. Paco no sabe divertirse y no le gusta que otra gente se divierta tampoco. Es un _____.
6. Gerardo es muy mujeriego, agresivo con las mujeres. Es un

   _____.

C. **¿Qué falta?** Complete the expressions on the left, then match them to the English equivalents on the right.

___1. No me dejes con los colochos _____.

a. Hi, friend. Great to see you.

___2. Juan no _____ en na'a.

b. Don't stand me up.

___3. Hola, pana. _____ los ojos.

c. You look better than ever.

___4. Por aquí, _____.

d. That's how we'll leave it, at eight o'clock.

___5. Estás como _____.

e. Jeeze! Jaime and Alicia are together again.

___6. Así _____, a las ocho.

f. Juan is out of it (nowhere).

___7. ¡Caray! Jaime y Alicia están juntos _____ nuevo.

g. I'm just here, goofing (wandering) around.

D. ¿Qué dice usted . . .?

1. cuando necesita tiempo para pensar (tres expresiones)

   _____

2. cuando alguien le invita a una fiesta y de verás quiere ir

   _____

3. cuando alguien le invita a una fiesta y NO quiere ir

   _____

E. Invitaciones.

1. Invite a friend to a get-together or party in two different ways:

   _____

   _____

2. Tell him or her to show up at 8:00.

   _____

3. Tell him or her not to stand you up.

   _____

4. Tell him or her you can't wait to go out.

   _____

Oiga, señora, ¿dónde está el excusado?

GETTING SOMEONE'S ATTENTION
·
ASKING POLITELY FOR INFORMATION
·
UNDERSTANDING DIRECTIONS
·
INTRODUCING YOURSELF

CONVERSACIÓN 1

*Una calle en Santander, España. Amalia Benavides, una joven turista, detiene a una vieja señora, doña Mariela, para **preguntarle cómo llegar a la plaza.***

AMALIA **¡Oiga, señora! ¿Podría Ud. decirme** cómo llegar a la Plaza de las Américas?

DOÑA M. **Desde luego,** hija. Espera un minuto, que **estoy hecha polvo** después de subir esta calle . . . Bien. **Camina derecho** cuatro **manzanas** . . .

AMALIA **¿Cómo?** ¿Manzanas? ¿Manzanas para comer?

DOÑA M. No eres de aquí, ¿verdad? Manzanas, **hija,** son calles, . . . **Baja** por esta calle cuatro manzanas y llegarás a la Calle Cortes. **Tuerce** pa' la izquierda y **ve subiendo** hasta ver una farmacia grande en la esquina a la derecha, Farmacia Estrella. Sigue **calle arriba** dos manzanas más y allí está la plaza. ¿Qué buscas en la plaza? ¿El museo?

48

¿DÓNDE ESTÁ EL EXCUSADO?
- CAMINA DERECHO CUATRO MANZANAS. . .

A street in Santander, Spain. Amalia Benavides, a young female tourist, stops an older lady, Doña Mariela, to ask her how to get to the square.

AMALIA   Excuse me, ma'am. Could you please (would you be able to) tell me how to get to the Plaza de las Américas?

DOÑA M.   Of course, my dear. Wait a minute since I'm all worn out (turned to dust) after going up this street . . . All right. Walk straight for four blocks (apples) . . .

AMALIA   Pardon me? (How?) Apples? Apples for eating?

DOÑA M.   You're not from around here, are you? "Apples," my dear (daughter), are streets, blocks. Go down this street for four blocks (apples) and you'll get to Cortes Street. Turn to the left and keep on going up until you see a big pharmacy on the corner on the right, Estrella Pharmacy. Go up the street two more blocks, there you'll see (is) the plaza. What are you looking for in the plaza—the museum?

Amalia	No, señora. Quiero saber **dónde está el excusado.** Me dijeron que en la plaza hay **servicios públicos.**
Doña M.	Mira, te voy a dar un consejo. **Por acá** hay **baños** mucho más **cerquita.** Ese café, por ejemplo. Entras y vas derecho hacia los teléfonos. Al lado de los teléfonos siempre hay baños. **No seas tímida.** Entras como si nada. Yo te espero aquí.
Amalia	**Ud. me saca de un apuro.** Gracias, señora. *(Se dirige al café.)*
Doña M.	¿Para qué, niña? ¿Para qué?

———■———

¡Ojo!

- **¡Oiga!** literally means *Hear!*, but the real meaning is closer to something like *"Excuse me, please. May I talk with you?"* This is the magic word to get attention on the street in Spain and many parts of Latin America. Although it is a command, it's in the formal **(Ud.)** form and so is courteous. In Venezuela, the word **¡Epa!** is used in a similar fashion, but is less formal.

- The **excusado** (excused place) is a euphemism for **el cuarto de baño** (the bathroom). Nowadays certain other expressions are more common: **los servicios, el water** (short for *water closet* or *W.C.* and pronounced **"vater"**), **el cuarto para señoras y el cuarto para caballeros,** and (in Latin America) **los baños.**

- **Doña** is a title of respect used with the first name for older women or women with authority. The equivalent for men is **Don.** There is no English equivalent.

- **Preguntar cómo llegar a** means *to ask the way to* or *to ask directions for.* The Spanish word **dirección** is a false cognate meaning *address,* e.g., **¿Cuál es su (tu) dirección?** (What is your address?)

AMALIA No, ma'am. I want to know where the restroom (excused place) is. I was told (they told me) that there are public washrooms (services) in the plaza.

DOÑA M. Look, I'm going to give you some advice. Right around here there are bathrooms (baths) much closer by. That café, for example. You go inside and walk straight toward the telephones. Next to the telephones there are always bathrooms. Don't be shy (timid). Go in as if it were natural (as if nothing). I'll wait for you here.

AMALIA You are really helping me out (taking me out of a pressing difficulty). Thank you, ma'am. *(She heads off toward the café.)*

DOÑA M. No problem at all. (For what, miss? For what?)

- **¿Podría Ud. . . .?** This is a good formula to remember when asking for help or a favor. The verb **poder** is in the conditional mood, which makes the phrase more polite. Any one of a number of infinitives may follow with the pronoun **me** attached: **¿Podría Ud.** (Could you?) **. . . decirme** (tell me), **ayudarme** (help me), **mostrarme** (show me), etc.

- **Estar hecho(-a) polvo** (to be made into dust) is used to describe extreme fatigue and is roughly the equivalent of *to be worn out.*

- **Camine Ud. derecho** means *Walk straight* and is not to be confused with **a la derecha** (on the right), which is the opposite of **a la izquierda** (on the left). The similarity in form between **derecho** and **derecha** can cause misunderstandings for English speakers, so it's important to listen for the word ending. The word **derecho** also means *law,* when referring to the legal profession (e.g., la facultad de derecho, *law school*).

- **Manzanas** means *apples,* but in Spain it also means *blocks.* In many countries, **cuadras** is used for *blocks,* but in Spain it means *stables,* not *blocks.*

- **¿Cómo?** literally means *How?* It is used when you have not understood what was just said, as *What?, Huh?, Excuse me?* or *Pardon me?* are used in English.

- **Hija** (daughter) and **hijo** (son) are friendly and affectionate terms, often used by an older person to a younger one or among friends and colleagues; they are similar to **querido(-a)** *dear,* except that they are never used in a romantic way. In Mexico, **m'hijo** and **m'hija** (meaning *my daughter, my son*) are commonly used even by friends or relatives of the same age.

- **Baja por esta calle** means *Go down this street* and may refer either to a street that goes downhill or to one with numbers that are going down in sequence. **Subir** (to go up), **calle arriba** (up the street) and **calle abajo** (down the street) are used similarly in giving directions. **Torcer (ue)** (to turn) is common in Spain; **doblar** and **dar la vuelta** are used in Latin America.

- **Por acá** means *around here.* **Acá** and **allá** may be used instead of **aquí** or **allí** when the reference is vague and non-specific.

- **Cerquita** is the diminutive of **cerca** and means *very near.*

- **No seas tímido(-a)** or **No te intimides** (Don't be intimidated) are ways of reassuring someone who may feel shy or uneasy about doing something. In Mexico the common expression for this is **No tengas pena** (literally, Don't have sorrow).

CONVERSACIÓN 2

Mariela espera a Amalia cuando llega su primo, Julián.

JULIÁN   Buenos días, Mariela. **¿Cómo te sientes** hoy?

MARIELA   La verdad es que no estoy muy bien. **Me duelen hasta los huesos** porque ayer limpié toda la casa. Trabajé **a brazo partido.** Pero, ¿por qué tanto interés en mi salud? ¿No será que has visto a la joven turista y **tienes ganas** de conocerla?

Mariela is waiting for Amalia when her cousin Julián comes up to her.

JULIÁN   Good morning, Mariela. How are you feeling today?

MARIELA   The truth is that I'm not feeling well. I ache all over (even my bones are hurting me) because I cleaned the whole house yesterday. I worked hard (to a broken arm). But why so much interest in my health? Could it be that you saw the young lady tourist and want (have desires) to meet her?

JULIÁN   Ah, pero **¡las tías sois la pera! Os mosqueáis por todo.**
¿O es que te levantaste **de mal talante,** Mariela?

MARIELA   **No me cabrées,** Julián. Y no te hagas ilusiones. Esta chica
parece **una niña bien** y decente. No es como esas **guarras**
con que sueles andar tú.

JULIÁN   **Te estás cachondeando de mí,** prima. **Tengo intenciones
honradas.** Sólo quisiera una pequeña presentación . . .

(En este momento, Amalia vuelve y saluda a los dos.)

AMALIA   Hola. Buenos días. Soy Amalia Benavides. *(Les da la mano a los
dos.)*

MARIELA   **Encantada,** hija. Soy Mariela Sánchez.

JULIÁN   **Mucho gusto.** Me llamo Julián Romeralo Velázquez y **estoy
a sus órdenes.**

¡Ojo!

- **A brazo partido** is one way of telling how hard you work, literally *until your arm breaks apart.*

- **¡Las tías sois la pera!** The familiar plural **vosotras** form is
used here because Julián is including Mariela in the group of "all
women" whom he is addressing familiarly and all together
because he suggests they are all alike. The words **tíos** (uncles)
and **tías** (aunts) are common in Spain to refer casually to men
and women, more or less like *guys, fellows* and *dames, broads.* (In
Latin America, the equivalent is **tipo(-a)** or **viejo(-a).**) **La pera**
is *pear,* but in this context it means *the limit.*

JULIÁN   Ah, you women (aunts) are the limit! You smell a rat in every-thing. Or is it that you awoke in a bad mood (disposition), Mariela?

MARIELA   Don't make me mad (Don't act like a goat), Julián. And don't go getting any illusions. This girl seems like a proper young lady (a well girl) and decent. She's not like those hussies (pig women) that you usually go around with.

JULIÁN   You are making fun of (batting horns with) me, cousin. I have honorable intentions. I only wish for a little introduction . . .

(At this moment, Amalia returns and greets both of them.)

AMALIA   Hello. Good day. I'm Amalia Benavides. *(She offers both of them her hand.)*

MARIELA   Delighted (to meet you), dear. I am Mariela Sánchez.

JULIÁN   Pleased to meet you. My name is Julián Romeralo Velázquez and I am at your service (at your orders).

- **Os mosqueáis por todo,** you smell a rat in (get suspicious about) everything. This expression comes from the word **mosca** (fly) as though the doubts and suspicions were like flies buzzing around. A secondary use in Spain and Latin America is **No me mosquées,** which can be translated as *Don't bug me.*

- **De mal talante** (with a bad disposition) is another way of say-ing **de mal humor** (in a bad mood).

- **No me cabrées** means *Don't make me mad (with your crazy actions or talk)* and comes from the word **cabra** (goat), an animal that tends to jump around in an uncontrolled way.

- **La niña bien** and **el niño bien** refer to young people from the privileged upper class who are assumed to have good manners and moral conduct.

- **Guarras** is a very strong and vulgar insult, coming from a word associated with pigs and suggesting slovenly women with low morals.

- **Cachondearse de alguien** (to make fun of or tease someone) is used in Spain and many other places but only among close friends and colleagues because it is a bit vulgar. It comes from **cachón,** meaning a large horn on an animal, and has a somewhat sexual connotation since animals in heat may be called **cachondos.** A similar expression common everywhere is **tomarle el pelo a alguien** (*to tease,* literally, *to pull someone's hair*).

- **Encantado(-a)** (Charmed, Enchanted [to meet you]) and **Mucho gusto** (Much pleasure) are the standard ways of saying *Pleased to meet you.* **A sus órdenes** is considered rather excessively polite in some circles and charming in others, but it is generally said by a man to a woman or to someone considered higher in importance or authority.

VOCABULARIO DEL CAPÍTULO

a brazo partido	(to a broken arm) to the limit (describing how hard you're working)
a la derecha	to the right
a la izquierda	to the left
bajar	to go down, get off
los baños	bathrooms
calle abajo	down the street
calle arriba	up the street
cerquita	very near (diminutive of **cerca**)
como si nada	(as if nothing) like you don't have a care in the world

¿Cómo te sientes hoy?	How are you feeling today?
¿Cómo?	(How?) Pardon me? What?
las cuadras	blocks of a street (Latin America)
el cuarto de baño	bathroom
el cuarto para caballeros	men's room
el cuarto para señoras, el cuarto para damas	ladies' room
de mal talante	in a bad mood
derecho	straight ahead
la dirección	address
encantado(-a)	(enchanted) pleased to meet you
la esquina	corner of two streets (corner of two walls is **rincón**)
Estoy a sus órdenes.	I am at your service.
Estoy hecho(-a) polvo.	(I'm made into dust.) I'm exhausted.
el excusado	(the excused place) bathroom (euphemism)
la facultad de derecho	law school
las guarras	hussies, sluts, loose women
hija(-o)	(daughter, son) my dear
ir subiendo	(to go ascending) to keep on going up
¡Las tías sois la pera!	You women are the limit (the pear)! (Spain)
las manzanas	(apples) blocks of a street (Spain)
Me duelen hasta los huesos.	(Even my bones ache.) I'm aching all over.
mosquearse	(to have flies) to smell a rat (be suspicious) (Spain)
Mucho gusto.	Pleased to meet you.
niño(-a) bien	well brought up (upper-class) boy (girl)
No me cabrées.	(Don't be a goat, **tú** form.) Don't make me mad. (Spain)

No me mosquées.	(Don't put flies on me, **tú** form.) Don't bug me. (Spain)
No seas tímido(-a).	(**tú** form) Don't be shy.
No te intimides.	(Don't be intimidated, **tú** form.) Don't be shy.
No tengas pena.	(Don't have pain, **tú** form.) Don't be shy. (Latin America)
¡Oiga!	(Listen! **Ud.** form) Excuse me, may I speak with you? (used to get attention of passer-by, waiter, etc.)
¿Para qué?	(For what?) You're welcome.
¿Podría Ud. decirme . . . ?	Could you please tell me . . . ?
por acá	around here
por allá, por ahí	around there
preguntar cómo llegar a . . .	(to ask how to arrive at) ask for directions to . . .
los servicios públicos	public washrooms
Te estás cachondeando de mí.	You are making fun of (batting horns with) me. (Spain)
tener ganas de . . .	to feel like . . .
las tías	(aunts) girls, women (Spain)
los tíos	(uncles) guys, fellows (Spain)
torcer (ue)	to turn (Spain)
Ud. me saca de un apuro.	You get me out of a difficulty.
el water	(from *water closet,* pronounced "vater") bathroom

¡A USTED LE TOCA!

A. Sinónimos. Match the words or phrases with similar meanings.

___1. bloques   a. mucho gusto
___2. excusado   b. querida
___3. encantado   c. tener ganas

___4. muy cansado

___5. desear

___6. hija

d. calles, cuadras (*manzanas* en España)

e. servicios, cuarto de baño, water

f. hecho polvo

B. Antónimos. Match the words or phrases with opposite meanings.

___1. suba

___2. a la derecha

___3. de mal talante

___4. guarras

___5. arriba

___6. acá

a. de buen humor

b. niñas bien

c. allá

d. baje

e. a la izquierda

f. abajo

C. ¿Qué falta? Complete the expressions to fit the situations.

1. You want to ask someone how to get to the drugstore.
   ¿P_____ _____ _____ **cómo llegar a la farmacia?**

2. You want to tell someone to walk straight. **Camine Ud.**
   _____.

3. You accuse a friend of making fun of you. **Te estás** _____ **de mí.**

4. You are describing how hard you worked yesterday. **Trabajé a**
   _____.

5. After working out, you feel like complaining about your aching body, so you say: **¡Me duelen hasta** _____!

6. Someone has just solved a big problem for you and to thank her you say: **Gracias, Ud. me saca de** _____.

D. La palabra exacta. Choose the most correct word to finish each statement.

1. En España la palabra común para indicar **calles** o **bloques** en una ciudad es
   a. cuadras
   b. manzanas
   c. peras

2. En España, para decir **doblar** o **dar la vuelta,** a veces se dice
   a. torcer
   b. marchar
   c. ir

3. Un español que habla con sus tres hermanas les dice
   a. ustedes
   b. vosotros
   c. vosotras

4. Para llamar la atención de alguien en la calle, se dice
   a. atención
   b. oiga
   c. perdón

5. Los abogados *(lawyers)* estudian las complicaciones del sistema legal en la facultad de
   a. ordenes
   b. izquierdo
   c. derecho

6. Otra manera de decir **turbarse** o **enojarse** es
   a. cabrearse
   b. estar hecho polvo
   c. intimidarse

E. ¿Qué dice Ud.? Tell what you could say in each situation, using some expressions from this chapter.

1. Stop a man on the street and ask him how to get to the **Hotel Colonial.**

_____

_____

2. He introduces himself to you. You acknowledge this and tell him your name.

_____

_____

3. Tell a friend how to get to the **Café La Perla,** where you will meet him later. He has to walk straight for five blocks and then turn left on **Calle Flores** and he will see it on the right.

_____

_____

4. You're at a restaurant and you ask the waiter where the bathroom is.

_____

_____

Vocabulary and Culture

IT HAD TO BE (SINGULAR, PLURAL, FORMAL, INTIMATE, SEXUAL) YOU!

What word do we use to address other people? In English the answer is simple. We say *you* to everyone from the president or prime minister to the panhandler on the street. In standard Latin American Spanish, there's a choice of three options: **tú, Ud.,** or **Uds.** and in the Spanish of Spain, there are five options: **tú, Ud., Uds., vosotros,** or **vosotras.** In addition, in Central America, some regions of Colombia and Venezuela, Argentina, Chile, and Uruguay, **vos** forms are used informally among close friends. (See page 124 for more about **vos.**) This is one reason Spanish is considered a more personal language than English, since every time Spaniards or Latin Americans speak to someone else, they must classify that person according to several parameters, and then choose *not only pronouns but all verb forms* accordingly. (See drawing on page 53.)

Three Parameters for Choice   The first parameter for choosing a pronoun is number (singular or plural). Everyone knows that hurtful consequences result at times from stating in a group what would better be reserved for private conversation. It's been suggested that such errors occur less in Spanish since its grammar forces speakers to remember whether they are speaking publicly or intimately. This may partly explain why Spanish speakers in international circles are not generally perceived as too blunt the way English speakers are. In Latin America, you use **tú, Ud.** (or **vos**) for singular and **Uds.** for any group of more than one, but in Spain, you have also the possibility of **vosotros** or **vosotras** for groups.

The second parameter is the social and affective relationship between speaker and audience, but it also depends to some degree on age and respect. In general, use **Ud.**, the formal, for anyone older or in a position of authority, but you can also take your cue from how the other person addresses you. The ease with which the familiar form is used varies from country to country and in different time periods. At present, Spain, Cuba, the Dominican Republic, and Venezuela are countries where people easily use the **tú** form, and Costa Rica is just the opposite. **Ticos** (as Costa Ricans often call themselves) use **usted** almost exclusively, except for a few intimate friends whom they address as **vos**. As a general rule, stick to the formal **Ud.** if you are not sure, especially in Central America.

The third parameter is gender (male or female), and it applies only to usage in Spain with a group of good friends, when you use **vosotros** for males or for a group of both males and females and **vosotras** for females only.

The Power of tú   In general, the intimate forms give the Spanish language a special affective power, often exploited in poetry and song. For example, the oft-quoted *Rimas** of Spain's most famous romantic poet, Gustavo Adolfo Bécquer, would be inconceivable without the **tú** form:

¿Qué es poesía? dices mientras	What is poetry? You ask while
clavas tu pupila en mi pupila azul.	you nail your eye in my eye of blue.
¿Qué es poesía? ¿y tú me lo preguntas?	What is poetry? And you ask me this?
¡Poesía eres tú!	Poetry is you!

There is sometimes a magic moment when one friend decides to **tutear** (**tratar de tú**) the other and the relationship can change to a more per-

---

*The book called *Rimas* by G.A. Bécquer is available in most libraries or Spanish bookstores. It is a poem cycle that describes the many aspects of a love relationship with a short verse for each aspect. These verses, or *rimas,* are well-known and sometimes recited by lovers.

sonal level. On the other hand, the listener may ignore the change and continue on in the formal mode, thus refusing the offer of intimacy.

Here, There, This or That in Three Dimensions   Another distinctive aspect of Spanish is the three dimensionality of certain pronouns and adverbs. Instead of dividing the world into *this* and *that, here* and *there* according to what is near or far from the speaker, Spanish takes into account the person being spoken to and what is near or far from him or her. For example, **estas casas** are *these houses* (near to me), **esas casas** *those houses* (near to you) and **aquellas casas,** *those houses* (far from both of us). **Aquí** (here), **ahí** (*there,* near to you), and **allí** (*there,* away from both of us) are parallel. This third dimension is another example of how Spanish is a personal language, since it obliges a speaker to be more conscious of the situation of the person being addressed.

Selecciones.   Choose the best way of completing each statement.

1. Spaniards have _____ ways of saying *you* as compared with Latin Americans.
   - a. the same number of
   - b. more
   - c. fewer

2. In Latin America, when speaking with a group of women, you use
   - a. Uds.
   - b. vosotros
   - c. vosotras

3. In Spain, when speaking with a group of your close women friends, you use
   - a. Uds.
   - b. vosotros
   - c. vosotras

4. Costa Ricans (**Ticos**) commonly use this form of address with almost everyone:
   - a. Ud.
   - b. tú
   - c. vos

5. Gustavo Adolfo Bécquer is famous in Spanish culture for his
    a. dictionary of expressions
    b. scientific discoveries
    c. love poetry

6. If a native Spanish speaker refers to **esa casa,** he is speaking about a house that is
    a. near to him
    b. near to you
    c. far away from both of you

7. If a native Spanish speaker says something is **allí,** he means a place that is
    a. near to him
    b. near to you
    c. far away from both of you

Un Malentendido Regional: **Una pregunta equivocada**

A Regional Misunderstanding: **The Wrong Question**

It just so happens that one of the most common words in Spain, **coger** (to catch, take, grab) is a very vulgar expression in Argentina and Uruguay, where it means the equivalent of the English "f" word. (Recently this usage has also spread to other parts of Latin America.) In Argentina, for example, avoidance of this verb takes such forms as saying "I *received* the fish" or "I *accepted* the ball." So you can imagine the difficulties a Spaniard had when he moved to Buenos Aires, Argentina, and would often use **coger** in the normal way it is used in Spain. One fine day he was walking down the street looking for the bus stop and asked a passerby, **"Oiga, señor, ¿sabe Ud. por dónde se coge el autobús?"** The Argentine looked at him as if he were examining an insect and replied, **"Por atrás, ¡cochino!"**

. CAPÍTULO 5 .

Porfa . . .

ASKING FOR A FAVOR
·
CONVINCING OR PERSUADING SOMEONE TO
DO SOMETHING
·
UNDERSTANDING SHORT FORMS OF WORDS
AND EXPRESSIONS

CONVERSACIÓN 1

Miguel habla con su primita, que está de visita en San Salvador, El Salvador.

CRISTINA   Oye, Miguel, ¿me **haces un paro**?

MIGUEL   ¿De qué?

CRISTINA   Acompañarme al lago mañana. **Va'cer** mucho calor.

MIGUEL   No puedo. Tengo que **chambear**.

CRISTINA   Vamos, Miguel, no seas tan **pesado. Llévame de paseo.**
Porfa . . .

MIGUEL   **Que no,** Cristina, que no. Mira, me van a regañar si no llego
al trabajo.

CRISTINA   Es que no quiero ir sola **pa'l** lago. El jueves tengo que regresar
a la capital.

MIGUEL   ¿No te puede llevar **la** Mercedes?

SE CREE LA DIVINA GARZA.

Miguel is talking to his little cousin, who is visiting in San Salvador, El Salvador.

CRISTINA Hey, Miguel, will you do me a favor (a stop)?

MIGUEL What?

CRISTINA Go with me to the lake tomorrow. It's going to be very hot.

MIGUEL I can't. I have to work.

CRISTINA Let's go, Miguel, don't be such a drag (so heavy). Take me on an outing. Please . . .

MIGUEL No, Cristina, no. Look, they're going to give it to me (scold me) if I don't go to work.

CRISTINA It's just that I don't want to go to the lake alone. Thursday I have to go back to the capital.

MIGUEL Can't Mercedes take you?

CRISTINA   No la pude convencer. Pero tú ya sabes como es . . . **se cree la divina garza.** Pídele permiso a tu jefe y nos vamos.

MIGUEL   ¡Ay, ay, ay! ¡Qué necia eres! **Que hostigas.** Pero **okey, sale y vale.**

———————■———————

¡Ojo!

- **Hacer un paro** is used in some areas, such as Central America and Mexico, to mean *to do a favor.* In Colombia, people say **hacer un catorce.**

- **Va'cer calor: Va a hacer calor.** Sometimes words are "linked" in Spanish by omitting the second of two repeating vowel sounds so some letters are not pronounced. Linking often occurs because of a silent *h*. Other examples: **m'hijo (m'hija) = mi hijo (mi hija), s'iciera = si hiciera, l'ay = la hay.** Occasionally, in informal Spanish, these forms are written as pronounced.

- **Chambear** (also **chambiar**), *to work,* has a related noun: **chamba,** *work, job.* Also common are **camellar,** *to work,* and **camello,** *work, job* (literally, *camel*).

| CONVERSACIÓN 2

Cerca de la Universidad de San Carlos de Guatemala, Ciudad de Guatemala.

YOLANDA   Hola, 'manita, ¿qué tal?

ELENA   Tengo una **depre** que no me deja pensar en **na'a.**

YOLANDA   ¿Cuál es el problema?

ELENA   **Me tronaron** en el último examen de la clase de **mate.** El **profe** es fatal. Si no apruebo la clase, **estoy frita.**

CRISTINA   I couldn't convince her. But you know how she is . . . she thinks she's hot stuff (the divine heron). Ask your boss for permission and let's go.

MIGUEL   Ay, ay, ay! How stubborn (foolish) you are! How you bug (a person). But okay, it's a deal (It goes/turns out, it's worth it.).

—————■—————

- **Pesado(-a)** means *heavy;* by extension it is something weighty, cumbersome, boring, a drag.

- **Pa'l lago.** Because of linking, **para el** becomes **pa'l** in spoken Spanish. Other examples: **pa'cá = para acá, hasta'hora = hasta ahora, aunqu'está = aunque está, desdel día = desde el día, d'él = de él,** etc.

- **La Mercedes:** Sometimes **el** or **la** is used before a first name in informal Spanish: **el Felipe, la Yolanda.** This usage varies with region; in Spain, it is considered a bit "uneducated," but it is often used by educated people to suggest that a person is a bit of a character.

Near the University of San Carlos de Guatemala, Ciudad de Guatemala.

YOLANDA   Hi, **'manita,** how are you?

ELENA   I'm so depressed I can't think. (I have a depression that won't let me think about anything.)

YOLANDA   What's the problem?

ELENA   I failed (They blasted me in) the last exam in math class. The prof is the pits (fatal). If I don't pass the class, I'm sunk (fried).

YOLANDA ¿De qué clase hablas?

ELENA De geometría . . . con el profe Sánchez.

YOLANDA Ah, sí, seguí ese curso el trimestre pasado. Fue **requete difícil.** ¿Quieres estudiar conmigo?

ELENA Sí, **primero Dios** eso me ayude.

YOLANDA Ahora iba para la **U,** a la biblioteca. ¿Vamos juntas?

ELENA **Chasgracias,** Yolanda. Ya me siento mejor.

YOLANDA Sólo que vamos a pasar por el Café Sol, que allí me espera un amigo. Es un gran **cuate, muy buena onda.**

¡Ojo!

- **Depre = depresión**

- **Me tronaron** means literally, *They blasted (thundered at) me.* In Spain, students say **Me catearon** (They searched me); in Colombia, **Me tiré** (I threw myself); and in Venezuela, **Me rasparon** (They grated me).

- **Fatal** is used in most parts of the Spanish-speaking world, meaning *awful, terrible, the pits.* In Puerto Rico, a very strict (hard) professor is **limero(-a).**

- **Estar frito:** *to be fried.* In many areas, people might say **estar en la olla,** *to be in the pot,* that is, in hot water.

- **Requete** is an intensifier that can be used with most adjectives or adverbs: **requete bueno, requete bien.**

- **Primero Dios,** like **si Dios quiere,** is often heard in Central America, especially when some kind of action is proposed or some statement of optimism is made. It has behind it a cautionary stance, a humble position of "let's not be too cocky; this is wishful thinking, after all." Perhaps it stems from living in an area where there have been so many natural and political disasters.

YOLANDA What class are you talking about?

ELENA Geometry . . . with Professor Sánchez.

YOLANDA Oh, yeah, I took that class last quarter. It was really hard. Do you want to study with me?

ELENA Yes; God willing (first God), that will help me.

YOLANDA I was just going to the university, to the library. Shall we go together?

ELENA Thanks, Yolanda. I feel better already.

YOLANDA But let's go by the Café Sol, where a friend is waiting for me. He's a great pal, a good egg (very good wave).

- **Chasgracias = Muchas gracias.** Similarly, one hears **Chogusto (Mucho gusto).**

- **El cuate (la cuata)** comes from the Náhuatl (Aztec) word **cóatl,** meaning *snake* or *serpent* but also *twin,* and specifically from Quetzalcóatl, the "plumed serpent," the god who was the alter ego of Xólotl. The word is used commonly in Mexico and Central America. Another word for *friend,* used in many areas of South America, is **el (la) cole,** short for **colega,** *colleague.*

- **Buena onda** can be used for things as well as people, meaning *a good deal or thing.*

CHISTES

LA CARTA

Un 22 de diciembre, Pepito saca un **boli** y una hoja de papel para escribir-
le al Niño Jesús: "Estimado Niño Jesús*: Me he portado muy bien este
año; favor regálame una bicicleta y un Nintendo. Atentamente, Pepito."
Lleva la carta a la sala a ponerla debajo del árbol de Navidad. Junto al
árbol, en la **tele,** hay una pequeña estatua de la Virgen María. Pepito mira
la estatua, **se arrepiente,** se da la vuelta y regresa a su cuarto. Allí escribe
una nueva carta: "Estimado Niño Jesús: Es cierto que no me he portado
tan bien este año, pero creo que por las acciones buenas me merezco un
Nintendo y una **bici.** Atentamente, Pepito." Cuando llega a la sala, **vuelve
a ver** la estatua de la Virgen y otra vez se arrepiente. Va a su cuarto y
escribe una tercera versión de la carta: "Estimado Niño Jesús: Es verdad,
me he portado mal este año, pero yo sé que si me regalas un Nintendo y
una bici, será suficiente incentivo para portarme bien el próximo año.
Atentamente, Pepito." Va a la sala y otra vez ve la estatua. **Echando chispas,** destroza la carta y **no sabe qué hacer del mal genio.** Hasta que **de
pronto** toma la estatua de la Virgen, la trae de regreso a su cuarto, le
cubre los ojos y la boca con cinta pegante, la mete en un baúl, se sienta
encima del baúl y escribe una carta: "Estimado Niño Jesús: Si quieres
volver a ver a tu madre, dame un Nintendo y una bici. Pepito."

THE LETTER

One December 22, Pepito gets out a pen and a piece of paper to write to
the Christ child. "Dear Christ child: I've behaved very well this year; please
give me a bicycle and a Nintendo game. Sincerely, Pepito." He takes the letter to the living room to put under the Christmas tree. Next to the tree, on
the TV, there's a small statue of the Virgin Mary. Pepito looks at the statue,
has second thoughts, turns around, and goes back to his room. There he
writes a new letter: "Dear Christ child: It's true that I haven't behaved so
well this year, but I think that for my good deeds I deserve a Nintendo and
a bike. Sincerely, Pepito." When he gets to the living room, he sees the statue of the Virgin and again has second thoughts. He goes to his room and

---

*In some areas of Latin America, such as Ecuador and Peru, children expect gifts not from
Santa Claus but the Christ child. In still others, gifts are expected from the Three Kings or
Wise Men.

writes a third version of the letter: "Dear Christ child: It's true, I behaved badly this year, but I know that if you give me a Nintendo game and a bike, it will be enough incentive for me to behave well next year. Sincerely, Pepito." He goes to the living room and again sees the statue. Fuming (Throwing off sparks), he destroys the letter and is in such a bad mood he doesn't know what to do. Suddenly, he takes the statue of the Virgin, brings it back to his room, covers its eyes and mouth with adhesive tape, puts it in a trunk, sits on top of the trunk, and writes a letter: "Dear Christ child: If you want to see your mother again, give me a Nintendo and a bike. Pepito."

¡Ojo!

- **Arrepentirse (ie) de** means *to regret, to be sorry or have second thoughts.* **Me arrepentí de haber comprado ese auto.** I regretted buying (having bought) that car. **¿Te arrepentiste?** Were you sorry?

- **Volver a** + infinitive means *to do something again.* **Volví a leer la novela.** I read the novel again.

- **De pronto** means quickly, suddenly. **Pronto** means *soon, quick*; it is used in other idioms, such as **por lo pronto,** *for now, for the moment.*

———■———

LOS PERROS

Un tipo y **una mina** pasean por la calle con sus perros: un doberman y un chihuahua. El dueño del doberman le dice a su **ñera:**

—Mira, tengo hambre . . . vamos a comer algo en aquel restaurante.

La dueña del chihuahua responde:

—Pero no podemos. **O sea,** tenemos los perros, y no se dejan entrar en el restaurante.

—No hay problema. Mira y aprende.

Cuando el tipo entra en el restaurante, el maitre le dice:

—Lo siento, señor, pero usted no puede entrar en el restaurante con un perro.

—Por favor, amigo . . . es que soy ciego, y éste es mi perro-guía.

—¿Un doberman?

—Sí, hoy en día los han empezado a usar.

—Bueno, pase usted entonces.

La dueña del chihuahua piensa: "Nada se pierde con tratar."
Y entra en el restaurante.

—Lo siento, señorita, pero usted no puede entrar en el restaurante
con un perro—dice el maitre.

—Pero, señor, déjeme explicar. Es que soy ciega, y éste es mi
perro-guía, **se lo juro.**

—¿Un chihuahua?

—¿Me dieron un chihuahua?

The Dogs

A guy and a girl are walking down the street with their dogs: a
Doberman and a Chihuahua. The owner of the Doberman says
to his friend:

"Look, I'm hungry. Let's eat in that restaurant."

The owner of the Chihuahua answers:

"But we can't. That is, we have the dogs, and they won't let us in
the restaurant."

"No problem. Look and learn."

When the guy goes into the restaurant, the *maitre d'* (host) says to
him:

"I'm sorry, sir, but you can't come into the restaurant with a dog."

"Please, friend, (it's that) I'm blind and this is my guide dog."

"A Doberman?"

"Yes, these days they've started using them."

"Well, come in then."

The owner of the Chihuahua thinks, "You don't lose anything by trying." And she goes into the restaurant.

"I'm sorry, miss, but you can't come into the restaurant with a dog," says the *maitre d'*.

"But sir, let me explain. (It's that) I'm blind, and this is my guide dog, I swear to you."

"A Chihuahua?"

"They gave me a Chihuahua?"

¡Ojo!

- **Una mina** is used for *girl* in many South American countries.

- **Ñera** is short for **compañera; ñero,** for **compañero.** The derivation of **compañero(-a)** is **con + pan** (bread), *someone to break bread with.*

Nota cultural: Esta mujer habla con su psicólogo. Parece que tiene dinero, que es de la alta sociedad. ¿Cuál es su problema? ¿Qué revista lee? ¿Conoce usted esa revista?

- **O sea . . .** This hesitation phrase is used a lot to buy time or clarify something, meaning something like *That is . . . , That's to say . . .*

Vocabulario del capítulo

arrepentirse (ie)	to regret, have second thoughts
la bici	(short for **bicicleta**) bicycle
el boli	(short for **bolígrafo**) pen
camellar, el camello	(to camel, the camel) to work, work or job
chambear, la chamba	to work, work or job
chasgracias	(short for **muchas gracias**)
chogusto	(short for **mucho gusto**)
el, la cole	(short for **colega**) colleague, friend, pal
creerse la divina garza	to think you're (one is) hot stuff (the divine heron)
el cuate, la cuata	pal, good friend (Central America, Mexico)
la depre	(short for **depresión**) depression
echar chispas	(to throw off sparks) to fume, be angry
estar frito(-a)	(to be fried) to be sunk, in trouble
estar en la olla	(to be in the pot) to be in hot water, in trouble
fatal	(fatal) terrible, the pits
hacer un paro	(to make a stop) to do (someone) a favor (Central America, Mexico)
hostigar	to annoy, badger, bug
Que hostigas.	How you bug a person.
Llévame (tú) de paseo.	Take me on an outing.
m'hijo (m'hija)	short for **mi hijo (mi hija)** my son (my daughter)

las mate	(short for **matemáticas**) math
Me tronaron.	(They blasted me.) I failed. (Central America, Mexico)
la mina	girl (South America)
na'a (nada)	nothing
el ñero (la ñera)	companion, friend (short for **compañero** or **compañera**)
no saber qué hacerse del mal genio	to be in such a bad mood one doesn't know what to do
Okey.	OK (from the English).
onda: ser buena onda	to be a good thing, a good deal, a good person
pesado(-a)	heavy, boring, a drag
porfa' (short for **por favor**)	please
el, la profe	(short for **profesor** or **profesora**) professor
pronto: de pronto	suddenly
por lo pronto	for now
Que no.	No.
requete	intensifier used with adjectives or adverbs, meaning *very* + adjective or adverb
Sale y vale.	(It goes/turns out and it's worth it.) It's a deal.
Se (te) lo juro.	I swear to you.
sea: o sea. . .	that is . . .
la tele (short for **televisión**)	television
la u (short for **universidad**)	university
volver (ue) a + inf.	(to return to + inf.) to do (something) again

¡A USTED LE TOCA!

A. La palabra completa. Match the shortened forms of the words on the left with their endings on the right.

__1. bolí (boli)	a. sión
__2. cole	b. cleta
__3. profe	c. grafo
__4. mate	d. ga
__5. depre	e. máticas
__6. tele	f. visión
__7. bici	g. sor

B. En otras palabras. Choose the slang term from the following list that best corresponds to the underlined word or phrase.

buena onda	de pronto	fatal	mina
camellar	la divina garza	frita	paro
cuate	estoy de mal genio	me tronaron	requete

1. Enrique, ¿me haces un <u>favor</u>?
2. <u>De repente</u> tuvo una idea.
3. <u>Echo chispas</u> por la mañana.
4. <u>Fracasé</u> *(I failed)* en el examen de francés; ¡me siento horrible!
5. ¿Quién es esa <u>chica</u>?
6. Fuimos al cine ayer, pero la película fue <u>muy mala</u>.
7. Si no llego a casa antes de las once estaré <u>en la olla</u>.
8. ¿No sabes hacer arroz con pollo? Pero es <u>muy</u> fácil.
9. Miguel es un buen <u>amigo</u>.
10. ¿Tienes que <u>trabajar</u> mañana?
11. Se cree <u>muy importante</u>.
12. Esa bicicleta es <u>una cosa muy buena</u>.

C. ¿Qué falta? Write the long forms of the underlined expressions.

1. ¿Qué quieres, <u>m'hija</u>? _____
2. Ese chavo no está en <u>na'a</u>. _____
3. Voy para la <u>U</u> . . . ¿Me acompañas? _____

4. Volveré a llamarte. —<u>Chasgracias</u>. _____

5. Me arrepiento de haber venido; <u>e'toy</u> muy cansado. _____

6. <u>Na'ma'</u> mira allí y vas a ver. _____

7. Hoy <u>v'acer</u> frío. _____

D. Una conversación por teléfono. For each underlined word or expression, give a synonymous word or expression, choosing from the following:

ojalá	**por lo pronto**	**okey**
volveré a llamar	**de paseo**	**una nueva chamba**

MANUEL   Hola, Dolores. ¿Qué estás haciendo?

DOLORES   <u>En este momento</u> (1), nada.

MANUEL   Entonces, vamos al centro <u>a pasear</u> (2), ¿no?

DOLORES   <u>Está bien</u> (3), sólo que necesito esperar el correo. <u>Primero Dios</u> (4) me hayan mandado un cheque de la compañía donde trabajaba antes. Sabías que tengo <u>un nuevo trabajo</u> (5), ¿no?

MANUEL   Sí, felicitaciones, Dolores.

DOLORES   Mira, ¿podríamos hablar a mediodía?

MANUEL   Entonces <u>llamaré otra vez</u> (6) a eso de las doce.

DOLORES   Perfecto. Hasta luego, pues.

E. Favores.

1. Ask a friend if he/she will do you a favor, using a slang expression from this chapter.

_____

2. Tell him or her, "Don't be a drag."

_____

3. When your friend asks you for a favor, tell him or her, "I can't because I have to work."

_____

4. Your friend suggests you help him (her) another time. Tell him or her, "OK, it's a deal."

_____

Review of Chapters 1–5
(50 points)

A. **Crucigrama.** Solve the following crossword puzzle. (1–14)

Horizontal:
  2. inútil; un . . . a la izquierda
  3. trabajar mucho; sudar la gota . . .
  4. comediante, persona muy chistosa
  5. terrible, muy mal
  9. *party-pooper* en inglés
  11. cuadra
  12. trabajo

Vertical:
  1. una chica inocente pero muy mimada *(spoiled)*
  2. Cuando está enojada, echa . . .
  6. Hace mucho calor; se caen los patos . . .
  7. trabajar mucho, a . . . partido
  8. Se cree muy importante; se cree la . . . garza.
  9. situación difícil; sacarle a alguien de un . . .
  10. dinero; quiere decir *wool* en inglés

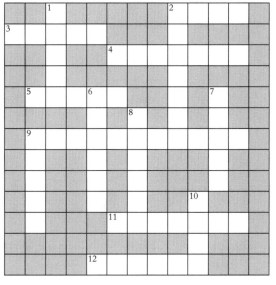

B. ¿Qué podemos decir de los hermanos Sánchez? What can we say about the Sánchez brothers? Many things. Match each Spanish description to the correct English meaning. (Two English meanings will not be used.)

15. __Hacen cola.
16. __Les da un ataque de caspa.
17. __Muestran los dientes.
18. __No nos dan bola.
19. __No saben qué hacerse del mal genio.
20. __No se hacen mala sangre.
21. __Redemoran.
22. __Se comen el buey.
23. __Se están cachondeando de nosotros.
24. __Van de parranda.

a. They aren't paying attention to us.
b. They take a long time.
c. They put up with the situation.
d. They are making fun of us.
e. They are going out on the town.
f. They do the right thing.
g. They are smiling.
h. They aren't getting upset.
i. They aren't having any fun.
j. They have a fit.
k. They are in such a bad mood they don't know what to do.
l. They are waiting in line.

C. La terminación perfecta. Find the right word from the list to end each sentence. (Two words will not be used.)

escoba	leche	madre	pataleta	corte
amolado	cuchara	moscas	relajo	canoa
churquitos	huesos	paro	trámites	

25. Hoy mi hermano está nervioso. Está como perro en _____.
26. He trabajado mucho y ahora me duelen hasta los _____.
27. Eduardo recibe sus papeles pronto porque tiene santos en la _____.
28. ¡Qué bien lo pasamos! Esta fiesta está a toda _____.
29. Es tan flaco el profesor. Es un palo de _____.

30. Ese señor causa problemas porque siempre quiere meter la

    _____.
31. Mis primos no estudian en verano; sólo echan _____.
32. Oye, mi pana, ¿no puedes hacerme un _____?
33. No quiero hablar con Gertrudis. Es mala _____.
34. Nuestros amigos nos dejaron con los _____ hechos.
35. Vamos a cerrar la puerta con llave por si las _____.
36. Pareces muy cansado. ¡Te dejaron bien _____!

D. Palabras revueltas. Unscramble the words and write the Spanish expressions from the list that are hidden in the mixed-up letters. Two expressions from the list will not be used.

es lo máximo	**está muy bolo**	**me provoca un tinto**
está en la gloria	**está toda derretida**	**me tronaron**
está en la olla	**feliz como una**	
	lombriz	

37. Norma has a high opinion of her new boss. She thinks that
    (he) . . . **[se ol oxámmi]** ¡ _____!
38. Daniel has a bad feeling about his exams. He says, "I'm afraid
    that . . .**[em nratoonr]** _____.
39. Iván just got a good job. (He) . . . **[tasé ne al rilago]**
    ¡ _____!
40. Esmeralda won a free ticket to Panama. She is . . . **[zefil mooc anu
    bozlirm]** _____.
41. Margarita just hit a baseball right through the neighbor's window.
    Now (she) **[sáte ne al allo]** _____.
42. Linda is madly in love. (She) **[tesá odat tirredade]** _____
    with her boyfriend.

E. Pero, ¿qué querrán decirme? Choose the correct meaning for the following Spanish words or expressions.

43. You get to a meeting and your Costa Rican friend says, **"¡Qué zambrote!"**
    a. How marvelous!
    b. What great organization!
    c. What a mess!

44. You make a comment to your friend from Spain, and he says, **"¡No me cabrées!"**
    a. Don't go away!
    b. Don't make me mad!
    c. Don't be ridiculous!

45. Someone asks you for your **dirección.** What do they want to know?
    a. how to get to your house
    b. your address
    c. your place of work

46. In Chile, a girl introduces you to her **pololo.** Who is he?
    a. her boyfriend
    b. her brother
    c. her best buddy

47. Your Mexican friend tells you there is a restaurant that is **padrísimo.** That means that it is
    a. great
    b. horrible
    c. old-fashioned

48. Your Uruguayan friend calls and says, **"Tengo resaca."** That means he or she is
    a. depressed
    b. hung over
    c. confused

49. On a crowded street in Barcelona, someone approaches you and shouts, **"¡Oiga!"** What does it mean?

    a. Watch out!

    b. Get out of the way!

    c. I want to talk to you!

50. A friend says to you, **"No veo la hora de salir."** She's telling you that

    a. she doesn't know what time it is

    b. she can't wait to go out

    c. she doesn't know where the exit is

· CAPÍTULO 6 ·

¡Qué flores me está echando!

GIVING AND ACCEPTING COMPLIMENTS AND PRAISE
·
GOSSIPING

CONVERSACIÓN 1

*Lima, Perú, a las 10:30 de la noche. Es la **sobremesa** en casa de la familia Flores. Marta Flores, su hijo y su sobrina están con un invitado, el doctor Jesús Silva.*

MARTA   ¿Un **poquitín** más de **pisco,** doctor?

DR. S.   **Sólo un pelito,** gracias, Marta. **¡Qué delicia!** En esta casa se **manya** bien. **Papear** con los **amigos del alma**—esto le hace la felicidad a cualquier **zapallo.** ¡Felicitaciones, Marta! La cena fue sabrosísima.

MARTA   **¿Cómo cree? Yo no tengo el mérito de esto.** Déle las gracias a la **sirvienta,** que ella preparó el **papeo.**

DR. S.   Pero Ud. planeó la lista de platos tan exquisitos y arregló la casa con un ambiente tan alegre.

MARTA   Ay, don **Jesús, ¡qué flores me está echando!**

¡QUÉ FLORES ME ESTÁ ECHANDO!

---

*Lima, Peru, 10:30 P.M. It's after-dinner discussion (**sobremesa**) time at the Flores home. Marta Flores, her son, and her niece are with a guest, Dr. Jesús Silva.*

MARTA   A teeny little bit more pisco brandy, doctor?

DR. S.   Only a tiny bit (a little hair), thanks, Marta. How delicious! In this house we eat well. Chowing down (potatoing) with good old buddies (friends of the soul)—that is what brings happiness to any person from Lima (zucchini squash person)! Congratulations, Marta! Supper was very tasty.

MARTA   Not at all! (How can you think that?) I can't take credit for this. Thank the maid since she prepared the supper (potato dish).

DR. S.   But you planned the menu of exquisite dishes and arranged the house with such a cheery atmosphere.

MARTA   Oh, Jesús (the doctor's first name), what compliments (flowers) you are giving (throwing at) me!

LAURA   Es verdad, tía. En tu casa, la cena más sencilla se convierte en una jarana.

DR. S.   Además, ¡qué **buena moza está** Ud. esta noche! ¡Muy **guapa!** Ese color violeta le sienta muy bien. **Está como una reina.**

MARTA   **¡Qué ocurrencia!** Ud. es muy amable, doctor. Creo más bien que ando **chapada a la antigua.**

FLAVIO   No es cierto, mamá. Estás tan guapa como para que te dén **piropos** en la calle.

MARTA   **Basta ya. Ahorita** vamos a tomar el postre y el café.

————————■————————

¡Ojo!

- **¡Qué flores me está echando!** (What compliments you are giving me!) Literally, **echar flores a alguien** means *to throw flowers at someone.*

- **Sobremesa** (On top of the table) is the Hispanic custom of sitting around the table after dinner and talking for an hour or two.

- **Pisco** is a strong brandy made from grapes or potatoes in Peru, Bolivia, and Chile. When lime juice, egg white, sugar, and ice are added, it becomes a pisco sour.

- **Manyar** and **papear** are the usual ways of saying *to eat* in Lima. **Chupar** means *to drink* but it is considered vulgar by some. **Papear** and **papeo** (meal) come from **papa,** the word for *potato* in Latin America (in contrast with **patata,** which is used in Spain). These words remind us that potatoes were discovered in pre-Columbian times in the highlands of Peru and Bolivia, developed further by the Incan Empire, and later spread throughout the world after the Spanish conquest.

LAURA   It's true, Auntie. In your house the simplest supper becomes a fiesta.

DR. S.   Besides, how lovely you are tonight! Very attractive. That purple color really suits you (sits very well on you). You look like a queen.

MARTA   Not at all! (What a strange idea!) You are very kind, doctor. I rather think that I look a bit old-fashioned (turned out in the antique style).

FLAVIO   That's not true, Mom. You are so attractive that you could get street compliments (**piropos**).

MARTA   That's enough. Right now let's have coffee and dessert.

———■———

- **Zapallos** (zucchini squashes) is the word **limeños** (people from Lima) often use when speaking about themselves, just as people from Buenos Aires call themselves **porteños,** Guatemalans call themselves **chapines,** Costa Ricans call themselves **ticos,** Nicaraguans call themselves **nicas,** and Salvadorans call themselves **guanacos.**

- **¿Cómo cree?** (How can you think that?) This is a phrase that can be said after someone gives you a compliment. In Spanish it is not the custom to say thank you for compliments as people frequently do in English. However, humble disclaimers like this one are used when one feels the compliment is excessive or simply wants to appear modest. Other phrases that can be used in a similar way: **¡Qué ocurrencia!** (What a strange idea!), **No debe decir eso.** (You shouldn't say that), **Ud. es muy amable** (You are very kind), or the somewhat old-fashioned **Favor que Ud. me hace** (How nice of you to say so).

- **Sirvienta** is a standard way to say maid or servant. **Servilleta** means *napkin* (*servillette* in Canada), but in Peru it is also a common word for *maid, female servant,* although it is considered slightly pejorative by some people. Particular regional words to indicate this useful person, the housemaid, abound: **mucama** (Argentina), **empleada** (Chile), **muchacha** (Mexico), **criada** (Spain).

- **Jesús** and the feminine form **Jesusa** are traditional names that are commonly used in Spain and many parts of Latin America, though they are not as popular as they used to be. Nicknames are **Jesusito, Jesusita,** or **Chuchi, Chucha.** (The word **Chucha** has a vulgar connotation in Chile, however, and should not be used as a nickname there.)

- To compliment a woman (man) on how well she (he) looks, the words **buena moza** (**buen mozo** for the man) or **guapa** (**guapo** for the man) are always appropriate for all ages and sexes. In Argentina and Uruguay, a common compliment is to tell a woman she looks very **paquete** (literally "package").

- **Piropos** (street compliments given by men to passing women) are still common in Lima and in many other parts of Spain and Latin America. They range from the artistic, poetic, and sincere to the rude or cliché, depending on circumstances and local inclination. (See examples on page 101.)

| CONVERSACIÓN 2

Más tarde, los dos jóvenes charlan a solas en el living.

LAURA   Y ese doctor Silva, ¿quién es? Parece el **trome** del barrio.

FLAVIO   **Nada de eso.** Tiene la costumbre de **caerse por acá** de vez en cuando y comer **a la suerte de la olla.**

- **Ahorita** means *right now* in Peru, Mexico, and many parts of Central America, and **ahora** means *now* in the sense of *pretty soon,* or *in a little while.* (Among Cubans and Venezuelans, it is just the reverse: **ahora** means *right now* and **ahorita,** *in a little while.*) **Ahorita** is not used at all in the Southern Cone. In Chile, the expression for *right now* is **al tiro** (at the gun shot).

Later, the two young people chat by themselves in the living room.

LAURA   And that Dr. Silva, who is he? He seems like the neighborhood expert.

FLAVIO   Not at all (nothing of that). He has the habit of dropping in (falling down around here) from time to time and eating potluck (to the luck of the pot).

LAURA	No me digas. ¿Es **paracaidista**?
FLAVIO	Más o menos, pero también es un **gallo** simpático. No **lo pasa piola** pero tampoco es de los **"Silvas que silban." Pobre pero caballero.**
LAURA	**Elogia** mucho a tu mamá, pero creo que es sincero. **Me cae bien**.
FLAVIO	La que es insoportable es su mujer. Es tu **tocaya,** la doña Laura. No me gusta **tirar arroz** a nadie, pero esa vieja es muy creída.
LAURA	¿Laura Walton es su mujer? La conocí en la **despedida de soltera** de Manuela Salazar. **Se cree la divina pomada.** Entró con la nariz parada, hablando con grandes **ínfulas** de su casa del campo.
FLAVIO	He visto esa casa. Es una **chacra** destartalada en un **pueblucho.**
LAURA	¿Por qué no vino esta noche?
FLAVIO	Obvio. Hoy es **martes 13.** Doña Laura es una supersticiosa **de remate.** A lo mejor no le gusta salir los días de mala suerte.
LAURA	¡Qué cosa! ¡Pero precisamente es cuando debe salir, como es tan **bruja**!

———— ■ ————

¡Ojo!

- **Trome** means *expert* or *wizard* in Peruvian slang. In El Salvador they speak of the **cacique del barrio** in this sense.

- The **paracaidista** *(parachutist)* is one of the traditional character types in Lima. This is the person who drops down "out of the sky" at dinner time in other people's houses.

- **Gallo** *(rooster)* is one of the many animal words used in common slang, and it means *fellow, guy.* See page 20 (Chapter 2).

LAURA   No kidding! (Don't tell me.) He's a freeloader (parachutist)?

FLAVIO   More or less, but he's also a good egg. He's not in the gutter (passing it **piola**) but neither is he one of the "rich Silvas" (the Silvas that whistle). Poor but honorable (a gentleman).

LAURA   He praises your mother a lot, but I think he's sincere. He seems nice enough to me (he falls well on me).

FLAVIO   The one who is unbearable is his wife. She's got the same name as you (she's your **tocaya**), doña Laura. I don't like to criticize (throw rice at) anyone, but that old gal is very conceited (believed).

LAURA   Laura Walton is his wife? I met her at the wedding shower for Manuela Salazar. She thinks she's God's gift (divine hand cream)! She came in with her nose up in the air (standing up), talking with great airs about her house in the country.

FLAVIO   I've seen that house. It's a tumble-down shack in a one-horse (ugly old) town.

LAURA   Why didn't she come tonight?

FLAVIO   Obvious. Today is Tuesday the 13th. Doña Laura is hopelessly (terminally) superstitious. She probably doesn't like to go out on bad luck days.

LAURA   Isn't that something? But that's just when she should go out since she's such a witch!

———■———

- The **"Silvas que silban"** is a pun because the letters *b* and *v* are pronounced exactly the same way in Spanish.

- **Tocayo(-a)** refers to a person with the same first name as yours, so Laura is the **tocaya** of Laura Walton.

- **Tirar arroz** (to throw rice) at someone is to criticize or talk badly about that person.

- The **despedida de soltera,** *the sending away of the single girl,* is a good-bye party for the bride before her wedding and is really more in the spirit of a female stag party than a wedding shower.

- **Chacra** is a small country house. Almost every region has its particular term for a home in the country. However, strong class distinctions exist. For instance, in Peru and Chile, a **chacra** is for the lower or middle class and a **fundo** is a large estate for wealthier people (equivalent to **hacienda** in many regions or **estancia** in Argentina).

- The ending **-ucho(-a)** is negative, indicating that something is large, ugly, or bad in some way, such as **pueblucho** implying a town (**pueblo**) that is probably small and run down. (See page 203 for more on negative endings.)

- The unlucky days in Hispanic culture are not Friday the 13th, but Tuesday or Thursday the 13th or, in the case of Lima, also Sunday the 7th.

Vocabulario del capítulo

a la suerte de la olla	(to the luck of the pot) potluck
ahorita	(diminutive of **ahora**) right now, sooner than now (not used in Spain or Southern Cone); in Cuba and Venezuela it means the opposite: in a little while, not now but later.
al tiro	(at the throw) right away (Chile)
los amigos del alma	(friends of the soul) buddies, pals
la bruja	witch
caerse por acá	to drop in here
la chacra	country cottage (Peru)
chapado(-a) a la antigua	old-fashioned
los chapines	slang term for Guatemalans
chupar	to drink alcohol (considered vulgar in some regions)

¿Cómo cree?	How can you think that? (disclaimer after a compliment)
la criada	maid (Spain)
de remate	(terminally) hopelessly, completely
la despedida de soltera	send-off party for the bride before her wedding
echar flores	(to throw flowers) to compliment
la empleada	maid, employee (Chile)
Está (Ud.) como una reina.	You look like (as beautiful as) a queen.
la estancia	large country estate (Argentina and Uruguay)
Favor que Ud. me hace.	(Favor that you do me.) How nice of you to say so.
guapo(-a)	good-looking, attractive
los guanacos	slang term for Salvadorans
la hacienda	large country estate (used in many regions)
las ínfulas	airs, pretentious attitude
los limeños	people from Lima, Peru
manyar	to eat (Peru)
martes 13, jueves 13	Tuesday the 13th, Thursday the 13th (considered unlucky days in Spanish-speaking countries)
Me cae bien.	He (She, It) pleases (suits) me.
la mucama	maid (Argentina)
la muchacha	maid, girl (Mexico)
Nada de eso.	Not at all. None of that.
los nicas	slang term for Nicaraguans
No debe decir eso.	You shouldn't say that.
papear	(to potato) to eat (Peru)
el papeo	dinner

paquete	(package) chic, well-turned out (referring to a woman) (Argentina)
el paracaidista	(parachutist) freeloader
pasarlo piola	to be in a bad way economically (Peru)
los piropos	street compliments
el pisco	grape brandy (Chile, Peru)
Pobre pero caballero.	(common saying) Poor but dignified (a gentleman).
los porteños	people from Buenos Aires
el pueblucho	one-horse town
¡Qué delicia!	(What a delight!) How delicious!
¡Qué ocurrencia!	The very idea!
Se cree la divina pomada.	She thinks she's hot stuff (the divine cream).
la servilleta	the maid (Peru), napkin
la sobremesa	after-dinner conversation at the table
sólo un pelito	just a tiny bit (little hair)
los ticos	slang for Costa Ricans
tirar arroz	(to throw rice) to criticize
el trome	expert, wizard (Perú)
tu tocayo(-a)	a person with the same first name as yours
Usted es muy amable.	You are very kind.
los zapallos	people from Lima

¡A usted le toca!

A. ¡Misterio, misterio! Identify the following people or objects.

1. ¡Qué casualidad! *(What a coincidence!)* Muchas veces yo llego a la casa de mis amigos a la hora de comer y resulta que me invitan a la mesa. ¿Qué soy yo? Un(a) **p**_____.

2. Soy una bebida alcohólica muy fuerte, hecha a base de uva *(grape)* que se sirve en Perú y Chile. ¿Cómo me llamo? **El** _____.

3. Soy hombre y tengo el mismo nombre que mi amigo. ¿Qué somos mi amigo y yo? Somos **t**_____.

B. Sinónimos. Match the synonyms.

__1. echar flores
__2. manyar
__3. papeo

__4. servilleta
__5. tirar arroz
__6. trome
__7. zapallo

a. comida
b. experto
c. criada (empleada, muchacha, mucama)
d. limeño (hombre de Lima)
e. elogiar
f. comer
g. criticar

C. Completar la frase.

1. Es la hora de comer y te invitamos **a la suerte de la**

_____.

2. Ese hombre es buena persona. **Es pobre pero** _____.

3. Mi tía lleva ropa que no está de moda. Es **chapada a la**

_____.

4. Mirella Flores es mi mejor amiga. Somos **amigas del** _____.

5. Ese hombre es simpático. **Me cae muy** _____.

6. Mis primos no tienen dinero. **Lo pasan** _____.

D. Situaciones. Follow the instructions, using expressions from this chapter.

1. Tell your hostess how lovely she looks and how nicely she has arranged the house. Then say something complimentary to your host.

_____

_____

2. Someone has just told you at a dinner party that you are brilliant and that a project you did is superb. Say some disclaimers so that you don't appear too vain or lacking in modesty.

_____

_____

3. It's the day after a party and you want to describe someone you met there and liked.

_____

_____

4. It's the day after a party and you want to describe someone you met there and did not like.

_____

_____

VOCABULARY AND CULTURE

NAMES IN SPAIN AND LATIN AMERICA: HOW IMPORTANT IS A NAME?

In Spain and Latin America, names are important, diverse, and evolving, in many ways similar to and in others different from English names. They are often linked to social responsibility. In the seventeenth-century play **El burlador de Sevilla** (*The Joking Playboy of Seville,* which was written by a priest as a moral allegory), the main character tries to escape his role in society and so, when he arrives in the dark to deflower a young maid and is asked to identify himself, he replies, **"Un hombre sin nombre"** (a man without a name). Ironically, the many versions of this story have been so popular over the years that the name of this character, Don Juan, has become well known in many languages as an eponym for a heartless seducer, and his last name, **Tenorio,** is also used in Spanish to denote a man of this inclination.

Not surprisingly, Hispanic last names (**apellidos**) often tell people the nationality or origin of a person's ancestors, since Spain and Latin America have received many generations of immigrants. Bernardo O'Higgins, for example, is the national hero of Chile, and Carlos Menem and Alberto Fujimori are recent political figures. Even with Spanish surnames, many people can tell which part of Spain a person's family came from. For instance, most long complicated names with few vowels and many consonants are Basque and so from the north. However, because people in Spain and Latin America have traditionally been less socially and economically mobile than North Americans, it is common in many places for people there to be able to tell socioeconomic status from a surname. This is what young Flavio means when he tells his cousin that Dr. Silva is **"de los Silvas que no silban"** (from the Silvas who don't whistle, i.e., don't have money).

Last names (**apellidos**) sometimes reflect professions from the past as they do in English, like **Herrero** for (black)smith or **Guerrero** for warrior, or they refer to the father or grandfather with the ending **-ez**, as in **Martínez** (son of Martín) or **González** (son of **Gonzalo**). Hispanic people often have more last names than English speakers, since they frequently keep both father's and mother's surnames, in that order (with **y** for *and* in between). A woman retains her maiden name (**apellido de soltera**) after marriage as her legal name. On some occasions, however, she may add **de** and her husband's last names too which means her full name can become quite long. For example, Helena Domínguez y González marries Daniel Álvarez y Prieto and then becomes Helena Domínguez y González de Álvarez y Prieto. (See the jokes at the end of this chapter for some humorous examples of this.)

First names, usually called **nombres cristianos** (Christian names), have a special importance because it is common to celebrate not only your birthday but also **el día de tu santo,** your *saint's day,* the date assigned to your name saint on the traditional religious calendar. For example, March 19 is the feast of **San José** (St. Joseph), so all the **Josés** or **Josefinas** will get presents and parties on that day. **Tocayos** (people with the same first name) often celebrate together. Many Spanish names have close English equivalents, like Mary (**María**), Joseph (**José**), George (**Jorge**), or Margaret (**Margarita**). Other first names sound strange to English ears for various reasons. Many come from the Christian tradition. **Concepción** (*Conception*), **Refugio** *(Refuge),* and **Amparo** *(Shelter)* are all common names for girls because they signify attributes of the Virgin Mary. Similarly, boys are often called **Jesús, Rafael** or **Ángel,** or they may be named for classical figures, such as **Héctor, Aristóteles, Aquiles,** or **Platón.**

The picture becomes even more complex because of the very popular habit of using nicknames of all sorts: **Pancho** for **Pedro, Paco** for **Francisco, Pepe** for **José, Chuchi** or **Chus** for **Jesús,** and many more. Frequently, friends or families will invent their own particular **apodos** (nicknames), often referring to some physical attribute. A Mexican boy with curly hair may be called **Chino** (Mexican for *curly*), and a girl with a pug nose, **Chata.** This custom is not considered offensive in any way. Indeed, terms like **gordo(-a)** (fat, chubby), **flaco(-a)** (thin), or **negro(-a)** are affectionate terms of endearment. (See page 122.)

Selecciones. Choose the best way to finish each statement.

1. In Spain or Latin America, a **tenorio** is a man who
   a. has lots of money
   b. runs after women
   c. writes poetry

2. An example of cultural diversity is the national hero of Chile, whose name is
   a. Alberto Fujimori
   b. Carlos Menem
   c. Bernardo O'Higgins

3. The literal meaning of the last name **Enríquez** is
   a. very rich
   b. warrior
   c. son of Enrique

4. Marta Muñoz Vaca gets married to Paco Vidal Blanco; then her legal name is
   a. Marta Muñoz Vaca
   b. Marta Muñoz de Blanco
   c. Marta Vidal

5. Besides their **cumpleaños** (birthday), every year Hispanics also celebrate their
   a. **apellido de soltera**
   b. **día de santo**
   c. **derecho al apodo**

6. The names **Refugio** and **Amparo** are
    a. men's names of classical origin
    b. women's names of religious origin
    c. surnames of Basque origin

7. One difference in the use of nicknames between English and Latino cultures is that Latinos
    a. don't like nicknames that refer to physical attributes
    b. use **gordo** (chubby) as an affectionate term instead of an insult
    c. don't like to use nicknames at all

EL ARTE DEL PIROPO Y DEL CONTRAPIROPO

The custom or art of the street compliment is alive and well in many parts of Spain and Latin America. Here are a few traditional ones.

> (México) "¡Cómo me gustaría tener pulgas como ésa en mi petate!"
>
> *"How I'd like to have fleas like that in my sleeping mat!"*

> (Perú) "Oh, mi vecina, ¡cómo me gusta! ¡Es bien robusta y cómo se ajusta!"
>
> *"Oh, my neighbor lady, how I like you! You are so healthy and how you hold yourself together!"*

> "¡Qué buen lomo! ¡Tu cuerpo es un monumento y quiero estudiar arquitectura!"
>
> *"What a good back! Your body is a monument and I want to study architecture!"*

There is also a tradition of clever comebacks on the women's part that are sometimes in the form of rhyming putdowns. For example:

> Gil de la calle: "¡Ay, chula linda, eres mi delirio!"
>
> *Guy on the street: "Oh, gorgeous babe, you are my delirium!"*

Respuesta de mujer: "Más bien para mí ¡serías un martirio!"
Answer from the woman: "Rather for me you would be 'inferium'
(martyrdom)!"

————■————

CHISTES SOBRE NOMBRES

Los chistes sobre nombres abundan en español. Aquí hay algunos ejemplos:

1. Una chica que se llama Linda Botella se casó con Juan Leche. Ahora su marido la presenta como su "Linda Botella de Leche."

2. ¡Pobre Zoila Concha! Se casó con Carlos Fierro y ahora se llama "Zoila Concha de Fierro" (Soy la concha de fierro).

3. Dolores Fuertes se casó con Sergio Barriga y ahora se llama "Dolores Fuertes de Barriga."

4. Elsa Pito tomó como marido a Eduardo Madera y ahora se llama "Elsa Pito de Madera" (El sapito de madera).

5. Lucilda Casas y Marco Mesa tuvieron un bebé y lo llamaron Armando. Debe estudiar carpintería porque se llama "Armando Mesa y Casas."

JOKES ABOUT NAMES

There are many jokes about names in Spanish. Here are a few examples:

1. A girl named Linda Botella marries Juan Leche. Now her husband presents her as his Linda Botella de Leche (lovely milk bottle). (Linda is a common first name which also means *lovely,* and **Botella** and **Leche** are common surnames that also mean *bottle* and *milk.*)

2. Poor Zoila Concha! She married Carlos Fierro and now her name is Zoila Concha de Fierro, "I am the iron seashell." (**Concha** means *seashell* but in Chile and some other places it is also a vulgar term for the woman's organ.)

3. Dolores Fuertes got married to Sergio Barriga and now she's called Dolores Fuertes de Barriga, "Strong Pains of the Belly." (**Dolores** is a common first name but also means *pains,* **fuertes** means *strong,* and **barriga** means *belly.*)

4. Elsa Pito took Eduardo Madera as her husband and now she's called Elsa Pito de Madera, "the little wooden toad." (**Sapito** means *little toad* and **madera** means *wood*.)

5. Lucilda Casas and Marco Mesa had a baby boy and they named him Armando. He should study carpentry because his name is Armando Mesa y Casas, "Setting up a table and houses." (**Armar** means *to set up or construct*, **mesa** *table*, and **casas** *houses*.

CHAPAS, MOTES Y APODOS DE LOS LIMEÑOS

En los barrios de Lima es costumbre inventar *chapas* a la gente y muchas veces éstas son picantes. Aquí están algunos comentarios al respecto:

> ¿Qué le ponen a esa chica tan bien dotada con el cuerpo que asesina?
>
> La llaman *La extremista* porque cuando camina "agita las masas".
>
> ¿Qué apodo le dan a ese borracho sinvergüenza que siempre pelea con todo el mundo?
>
> Lo llaman *Parroquia abandonada* porque "no tiene cura."

NICKNAMES IN THE STYLE OF LIMA, PERU

In the neighborhoods of Lima it's customary to make up nicknames for the residents and often these are quite "spicy." Here are a few commentaries about them:

> What are they calling that girl who is so well endowed with the killer body?
>
> They call her "The Extremist" because when she walks she "agitates the masses."
>
> What nickname are they giving that good-for-nothing drunk who always fights with everyone?
>
> They call him "abandoned parish" because he doesn't have any cure. (In Spanish this is a pun because **cura** means both *cure* in the sense of *remedy* and *priest*.)

· CAPÍTULO 7 ·

¡Qué bárbaro!

TELLING A STORY
·
EXPRESSING SURPRISE

CONVERSACIÓN 1

Dos amigas, muy chismosas y **metiches,** *se encuentran en la calle en San Juan, Puerto Rico. Empiezan a* **montar un cotorreo en plena calle.**

MATILDE   ¿Qué **notas** me cuentas, Amalia? ¿Cómo están Fernando y Ana?

AMALIA   Pues, la verdad . . . Bueno, ¿cómo diré?

MATILDE   **Destápate, comay** . . . ¿Qué pasa?

AMALIA   Parece que **rompieron.**

MATILDE   **¡Diantre!**

AMALIA   Es que, pues . . .

MATILDE   **Saca los trapos al sol,** que yo no diré nada a nadie.

AMALIA   Si prometes no decir nada, es que Ana **salió embarazada** y . . .

MATILDE   **¡Ay, bendito! Así que se comió el sanduche antes del recreo,** ¿eh?

SE HA ESFUMADO. ES EL AS DE LA BARAJA.

Two very gossipy and nosy friends run into (meet) each other on a street in San Juan, Puerto Rico. They start a long chat (gab session) in the middle of the street.

MATILDE   What news is there (What notes will you tell me), Amalia? How are Fernando and Ana?

AMALIA   Well, the truth is . . . Uh, what shall I say?

MATILDE   Spit it out (uncap yourself), **comay**. What's happening?

AMALIA   It seems they've broken up.

MATILDE   Holy smoke (Devil)!

AMALIA   It's just that, well . . .

MATILDE   Give me the low-down (take the rags/clothes out into the sun), I won't tell anyone.

AMALIA   If you promise not to say anything, Ana got pregnant and . . .

MATILDE   Bless my soul! (Blessed one!) So they ate the sandwich before recess, huh?

AMALIA   Y Fernando se ha esfumado. Es el as de la baraja.

MATILDE   **¡Híjole! ¡Qué bárbaro!**

AMALIA   Sí. Y tú, ¿qué me cuentas? ¿Hay algo nuevo sobre el divorcio de Jaime y María?

MATILDE   **Oh, está que arde.** Pero, **ya tú sabe'** que no me gusta repetir **chismorreos.**

AMALIA   **Claro.**

MATILDE   Entonces escucha atentamente la primera vez . . .

¡Ojo!

- **Pleno(-a)** means *whole, complete.* It can also mean *in the middle of,* as **en pleno desierto** *in the middle of the desert,* **en pleno invierno** *in the middle of winter.*

- **Notas,** like **noticias,** can be **buenas** or **malas.** In some countries, **una mala nota** refers to a thing or a person that is disagreeable.

- **Comay** is short for **comadre,** a close friend who is sometimes also the godmother of one's child (the original meaning of **comadre**). In times past, the **comadre** was the person designated to care for a child in case of illness or death of the mother, something like modern-day insurance.

- **¡Diantre!** (also **¡Dianche!**) means *devil* and is used to express surprise or dismay, something like **¡demonios!** It sometimes ends in an /s/ sound (**¡diantres!**). In some areas, such as Mexico and Puerto Rico, people say **¡Chanfle!** with this meaning. Another expression for this purpose, now a bit old-fashioned, is **¡Rayos!** (lightning rays), still used in expressions like **¿Qué rayos pasa?** *What the dickens is happening?*

- **¡Ay, bendito!** (blessed one) expresses sympathy and is very common in Puerto Rico.

AMALIA   And Fernando has disappeared into thin air. He's made himself scarce (the ace of the deck).

MATILDE   Wow! Good grief! (How barbaric!)

AMALIA   Yes. And you, what news do you have? Is there anything new about Jaime and María's divorce?

MATILDE   Oh, it's at a fever pitch (it's burning). But you know I don't like to repeat gossip.

AMALIA   Of course not.

MATILDE   So listen carefully the first time . . .

———■———

- **Se comió el sanduche antes del recreo** (Puerto Rico) or **Se comió la torta antes de la fiesta** (they ate the cake before the party) mean that something was enjoyed before it should have been.

- **¡Qué bárbaro!** means literally, *How barbaric!* It roughly equals *Good grief!* or *How shocking!* **¡Qué barbaridad!** is similar in meaning. (The word *barbaric* comes from the Greek word for *foreigner, stranger.*)

- **Ya tú sabe':** The letters *s* and *d* frequently go unpronounced, especially in Caribbean Spanish, and these forms are sometimes written as they sound in dialogue. So **na'ma' = nada más, uste' = usted, e'toy = estoy, una' diez = unas diez,** etc. **Ya tú sabes** may be reduced even further in speech in the Caribbean, sometimes sounding almost like **Ya tú sa'.**

- **Claro** is very common, meaning *Sure, yes, of course (not), clearly.*

LA MADUREZ DEL HOMBRE

© Antonio Mingote

CONVERSACIÓN 2

En una plaza en San Juan, Puerto Rico.

JOSÉ   Hola, compa. ¡Otra vez nos encontramos! **Eres como arroz blanco: te veo hasta en la sopa. ¿Cómo está la movida?**

FERNANDO   **Nítida,** bien chévere. **Chócala.** *(Se dan la mano.)*

JOSÉ   **Y de la vida, ¿qué más?**

FERNANDO   **To'el tiempo pa'lante. Éjele,** ¿has oido el cuento del monje?

JOSÉ   No, pues no sé. *(Se sientan en un banco a **platicar**.)*

FERNANDO   Un monje va a comprar un loro, **¿viste?,** y le dice al dueño del loro:

—Quiero que esté **bien educado, ¿**eh? Nada de **palabrotas,** que es para el monasterio.

—**Huy,** no se preocupe, tengo el loro que usted necesita—le dice el dueño—. **Fíjese,** fíjese qué bonito es, y si le tira de la pata derecha le reza el Padre nuestro.—Y al tirarle de la patita derecha, el loro **se pone a** recitar el Padre nuestro.

—**¡Cielo verde!** Eso está muy bien, con tal que no diga **groserías**—dice el monje.

—No se preocupe; es un loro muy religioso. **Imagínese,** si le tira de la patita izquierda se pone a cantar misa en latín.—Y al tirarle de la patita izquierda el loro se pone a cantar misa en latín.

—¡Qué maravilla, qué maravilla! Bueno, pues si no dice palabrotas me lo llevo.

—**Total que** el monje se lleva el loro al monasterio. Reúne al resto de los hermanos para decirles:

In a plaza in San Juan, Puerto Rico.

JOSÉ   Hi, pal. So we see each other again! You're like white rice; I see you even in the soup (i.e, everywhere). How's the action?

FERNANDO   Great, very good. Put it here. (Hit it, referring to a hand.) *(They shake hands.)*

JOSÉ   And what else is happening in your life? (And of life, what more?)

FERNANDO   Onward and upward. (All the time forward.) Hey, have you heard the story about the monk?

JOSÉ   No. Well, I don't know. *(They sit down on a bench to chat.)*

FERNANDO   A monk goes to buy a parrot, see, and he says to the parrot's owner: "I want it to be well brought up, eh? No swear words because it's for the monastery." "Oh, don't worry, I have just the parrot that you need," says the owner. "Look, just look at how pretty he is, and if you pull his right foot he says the Lord's Prayer." And when he pulls his right foot, the parrot begins to recite the Lord's Prayer. "Good grief! (Green sky!) That's very good, provided that he won't say anything gross," says the monk. "Don't worry; he's a very religious parrot. Just imagine, if you pull his left foot he begins to sing the mass in Latin." And when he pulls his left foot, the parrot begins to sing the mass in Latin. "What a marvel! What a marvel! Well, if he doesn't say swear words I'll take him." And so the monk takes the parrot to the monastery. He gets the rest of the brothers together to tell them: "Look, I've bought this parrot to keep us company. He's a marvel; he doesn't say swear words, and if we pull his right foot he says the Lord's Prayer. But that's nothing, because if we pull his left foot he sings the mass in Latin."

—Miren, he comprado este loro para que nos haga compañía. Es una maravilla; no dice palabrotas y si le tiramos de la patita derecha reza el Padre nuestro. Pero eso no es nada, porque si le tiramos de la patita izquierda canta misa en latín.

—Y si le tiramos de las dos patitas, ¿qué pasa?—pregunta uno de los hermanos—. Y contesta el loro:

—¡Me caigo de la **puta** percha y estrello contra el **jodido** suelo, idiota!

¡Ojo!

- **Eres como arroz blanco:** In the Caribbean and in many other Hispanic areas, rice is a common staple. **Sales hasta en la sopa** is a similar expression to indicate that someone is seen everywhere.

- **La movida** is movement, action; to be **en la movida** is like being **en la onda,** "with it."

- **Nítido(-a)** can mean *excellent, perfect, correct, very acceptable.*

- **Chócala** means literally, *hit it,* referring to one's hand; this is the **tú** form.

- **¿Viste?** (past form of **¿ves?**) is used commonly to make sure a listener is following. **¿Cachas?** *(Get it?)* has the same use but is even more colloquial; it comes from the English *to catch,* as in *Catch the drift? ¿Cachaste?* (the past form) is also heard. These are **tú** forms.

- **¡Huy!** expresses surprise or admiration, something like *Wow!* It is sometimes used to express pain, meaning *Ouch!*

- **Ponerse a,** followed by an infinitive, is *to begin to,* literally *to set or put oneself to* doing something.

- **Total que** is used to sum up, meaning *So . . .*

"And if we pull both feet, what happens?" asks one of the brothers. And the parrot answers: "I fall off the damn perch and see stars on the friggin' floor, idiot!"

———■———

- **Puto** is used in many places to mean *pimp* or *homosexual.* **Puto(-a)** can be used as an adjective; **no hicieron ni puto caso, ¿dónde está el puto problema (la puta máquina)?,** etc. The expression is of course vulgar.

- **Jodido(-a)** comes from the verb **joder,** which can mean *to screw, bother, trick, or just plain "bug" someone.* It normally just means *to bother* but is much stronger than **molestar** and can be vulgar. It can also mean *to break,* as in **Ese niño jodió el televisor.**

CHISTE

Un joven reportero decide hacer una entrevista al hombre con la mejor memoria del mundo. Llega a un pequeño pueblo en las montañas, donde vive el anciano.

—Disculpe —le dice al viejo— he oído decir que es usted el hombre con la mejor memoria del mundo. ¿Es cierto?

—Sí, sí, joven. Eso dicen.

—Sólo por curiosidad, por ejemplo . . . ¿me podría decir qué comió, tal día como hoy, hace cuarenta y tres años?

—Huevos . . .

—¡Dios mío! ¡Increíble!

El reportero **todo emocionado** le hace la entrevista de su vida y **realiza** un espléndido reportaje que **tiene éxito** mundial. El hombre gana el Pulitzer y **se hace famoso.** Pasan los años y nuestro joven reportero, ya

cincuentón, reflexiona: "Todo lo debo a aquel reportaje que le hice al **vejete.** Voy a visitar su tumba; creo que debería darle las gracias."

Al llegar al pueblo del anciano, va al cementerio pero no encuentra la tumba del vejete. **Extrañado,** pregunta si lo enterraron en otra parte.

—¡No, si no ha muerto! —le contesta una señora.

—¿No ha muerto? **No puede ser.** ¡Si ya era un viejo hace treinta años!

Y sale hacia la casa del viejo. Allí lo encuentra, de nuevo, sentado en la misma silla, leyendo un libro.

—Pero, ¿cómo? . . .

—Fritos.

———————■———————

A young reporter decides to interview the man with the best memory in the world. He arrives at a small town in the mountains, where the old man lives. "Excuse me," he says to the old man, "I've heard that you are the man with the best memory in the world. Is it true?"

"Yes, yes, young man. That's what they say."

"Just out of curiosity, for example . . . could you tell me what you ate, on just such a day like today, forty-three years ago?"

"Eggs . . ."

"My goodness! (My God!) Incredible!"

The reporter, all excited, interviews him about his life and creates (brings into effect) a splendid report which has worldwide success. The man wins the Pulitzer and becomes famous. The years go by and our young reporter, now fiftyish, reflects: "I owe everything to that report that I did of the old man. I'm going to visit his tomb; I think I should pay him my thanks." Upon arriving at the old man's town, he goes to the cemetery, but he can't find the old fellow's tomb. Surprised, he asks if they buried him in another place.

"No, since he hasn't died!" a woman answers him.

Forges (Spain)

Oculista sordo angustiando a un paciente

—La B.
—No señor.
—¡Dios mío, estoy ciego!

sordo *deaf;* angustiando *causing anguish;* ciego
blind

"He hasn't died? It can't be! He was already an old man thirty
years ago."

And he goes off toward the old man's house. There he finds him again,
sitting in the same chair, reading a book.

"But, how . . . ?"

"Fried."

¡Ojo!

- **Dios** or **Dios mío** is very commonly used in Spanish and is not
  considered blasphemous or offensive. Also used frequently is **¡Ay,
  Dios santo!,** *My goodness* (holy God). Similarly, in many countries people say **¡Jesús!,** as well as the more common **¡Salud!**

(Health!), after a sneeze. (For three sneezes, you might hear
¡Jesús, María y José!)

- **Emocionado(-a)** means *excited;* **excitado(-a)** usually refers
  to sexual excitement.

- **Hacerse** often means *become,* as in **hacerse rico(-a),
  famoso(-a),** etc.

- **Cincuentón** or **cincuentona:** For ages above forty **(cuarentón,
  cuarentona),** the **-ón** or **-ona** ending is used to emphasize age.

Vocabulario del capítulo

¡Ay, bendito!	(Blessed one!) Bless my soul!, used to express sympathy, common in Puerto Rico
bien educado(-a)	well brought up
¿Cachas?	(present) Do you catch the drift? Get it?
¿Cachaste?	(past) Did you catch the drift? Got it? (**tú** forms)
¡Chanfle!	Good grief! (used to express surprise or when there is a problem)
los chismorreos	gossip
Chócala.	(Hit it.) Put it here (**tú** form, said with a handshake).
¡Cielo verde!	(Green sky!) Holy smoke!, used to express that something is surprising or unusual
cincuentón, cincuentona	fiftyish (the **-ón** is an augmentative, emphasizing age)
¡Claro!	Sure! Clearly! Of course!
la comay (comadre)	("co-mother" of one's child) close female friend
¿Cómo diré?	How shall I put it (say this)?
¿Cómo está la movida?	How's the action?
Destápate (tú).	(Uncork yourself.) Open up.

¡Diantre(s)! o ¡Dianche!	(Devil!) Holy smoke!, used to express surprise or dismay
éjele	hey (interjection like **oye**, listen)
emocionado(-a)	excited
Eres como arroz blanco: te veo hasta en la sopa.	(You're like white rice: I see you even in the soup.) I see you (**tú** form) everywhere.
esfumarse	to disappear into thin air
Está que arde.	(It's burning.) It's at fever pitch.
estrellar (contra)	to crash (against), fall and see stars
excitado(-a)	aroused, excited (usually sexually)
extrañado(-a)	surprised, perplexed
Fíjese (usted), Fíjate (tú).	Just imagine.
la grosería	("gross" thing, expression, etc.) vulgarity
hacerse + adj.	to become + adj.
¡Híjole!	Wow! (expression of surprise), Darn!
¡Huy!	Wow! (expression of surprise), Ouch! (expression of pain)
Imagínese (usted); Imagínate (tú).	Just imagine.
joder	to screw, bother, trick, or "bug" someone; to break (something), commonly used but vulgar
jodido(-a)	(past participle of **joder**) screwed, messed up, commonly used but vulgar
una mala nota	(a bad note) an unpleasant thing or person, bad news
metiche	nosy
montar un cotorreo	to start a gab session
nítido(-a)	(clear, bright) great, perfect, correct, very acceptable
No puede ser.	It can't be.

las palabrotas	swear words (**-ota** is an augmentative form added to **palabra**, *word*)
platicar	to talk, chat
pleno(-a)	whole, complete; **en plena calle** in the middle of the street; **en pleno invierno** in the middle of winter
ponerse a + inf.	(to set or put oneself to doing something) to begin to (do something)
puto(-a)	(pimp or whore) blasted, damn (vulgar); **la puta máquina** the blasted machine; **no hacer ni puto caso** not to pay any damn attention
¡Qué barbaridad!	(What barbarity!) Good grief!
¡Qué bárbaro!	(How barbarous!) Good grief!
¿Qué notas me cuentas?	(What notes are you telling me?) What news can you tell me?
¡Rayos!	(Lightning rays!) Good grief!, Blast! (a bit old-fashioned, used to express surprise or when there is a problem); **¿Qué rayos pasa?** What the dickens is happening?
realizar	to make real or concrete, as a plan
romper (con alguien)	to break up (with someone)
sacar los trapos al sol	(to take the rags/clothes out into the sun) to give someone the low-down, air the dirty laundry
Sales hasta en la sopa.	(You [**tú**] turn up even in the soup.) I see you everywhere.
salir embarazada	to be (turn out) pregnant
Se comió el sanduche antes del recreo.	(The sandwich was eaten before recess.) Something was enjoyed before it should have been.
Se comió la torta antes de la fiesta.	(The cake was eaten before the party.) Something was enjoyed before it should have been.

ser el as de la baraja	(to be the ace of the deck) to make oneself scarce
tener éxito	(to have success) to be successful
To'el tiempo pa'lante.	(All the time forward.) Onward and upward.
total que	(total that) so, in short
el vejete	old man
¿Viste?	(Did you [**tú**] see?) See?
Y de la vida, ¿qué más?	(And of life, what more?) What else is happening in your life?
ya tú sabe'	you know (already)

¡A USTED LE TOCA!

A. En otras palabras. For each underlined word or expression, give a synonymous word or expression, choosing from the following:

rompimos	**nítida**	**extrañado**	**no puede ser**
notas	**se ponen**	**platicar**	**esfumado**
plena	**total**	**imagínate**	**sales hasta en la sopa**
qué bárbaro			

Dos amigos, Juan y José, se ven en <u>medio de la</u> (1) calle y <u>empiezan</u> (2) a <u>hablar</u> (3). "<u>¡Eres como arroz blanco!</u> (4)" dice José. "¿Cómo está la movida?" "<u>Chévere</u>" (5), contesta Juan, "y tú, ¿qué <u>noticias</u> (6) me cuentas?" "Pues, <u>fíjate</u> (7) que mi esposa y yo <u>nos separamos</u> (8). Ella se ha <u>desaparecido</u> (9)", dice Juan. "<u>¡Imposible!</u>" (10), responde José, <u>muy sorprendido</u>, (11) "Ustedes eran una pareja perfecta." <u>Así</u> (12) que pasan un buen rato hablando hasta que por fin Juan dice, "Tengo una cita a las tres. Nos vemos otro día, ¿eh?" "Sí, hombre, hasta luego. Híjole, <u>¡qué extraño</u> (13)!" se dice José a sí mismo.

B. ¿Qué falta? Complete the expressions on the left, then match them to the English equivalents on the right.

__1. sacar los ____ al sol   a. to start a gab session
__2. ser el as de la ____   b. to become rich
__3. montar un ____   c. to enjoy something prematurely
__4. comer la ____ antes de   d. to be very nosy
    la fiesta   e. to make oneself scarce
__5. salir hasta en la ____   f. to seem to be everywhere
__6. estar ____ arde   g. to bring out the dirty laundry
__7. ____se rico   h. to be at fever pitch
__8. ser muy ____

C. Amigos falsos. The following are false cognates; that is, they do not mean what an English speaker might think they mean. Give a definition in English for each word.

1. embarazada   _____

2. grosería   _____

3. excitado   _____

4. éxito   _____

5. sopa   _____

6. bien educado   _____

7. realizar   _____

D. Sinónimos. Match the synonyms.

__1. comay   a. ¡Diantre!
__2. anciano   b. ¿Viste?
__3. ¡Rayos!   c. groserías
__4. palabrotas   d. muy mal (vulgar)
__5. jodido   e. vejete
__6. ¿Cachaste?   f. comadre

E. En una situación informal, ¿qué dice usted . . . ?

1. antes de dar la mano _____
2. para saber si alguien entiende lo que usted dice _____
3. para describir una situación explosiva _____
4. para expresar sorpresa (tres expresiones) _____
   a. _____
   b. _____
   c. _____

. CAPÍTULO 8 .

¡Juntos pero no revueltos!

EXPRESSING LOVE AND AFFECTION
·
USING TERMS OF ENDEARMENT
·
USING THE TELEPHONE

▌CONVERSACIÓN 1

Un apartamento elegante en Montevideo, Uruguay. Suena el teléfono.

JIMENA   **Aló.** Residencia Martínez.

NACHO   Hola, **mi negra,** ¿cómo estás? Aquí estoy en Caracas, **mi bomboncito,** pero estoy pensando sólo en **vos** . . . en tu cuerpo que asesina . . . , en tu lindo pelo . . .

JIMENA   **Ignacio,** ¿cuántas **copas has tomado?** ¿Por qué me **llamás a larga distancia** para decirme tonterías?

NACHO   Jime, **tesoro,** no te pongas así. ¿Sabés que estoy loco por **vos?**

JIMENA   ¡Qué noticias! Pensaba que éramos amigos, nada más. ¿Y por qué este cambio? ¿Por qué ahora me querés?

NACHO   ¡Ay, **mi reina**! Pues . . . . , este . . . , sos tan hermosa. **Te quiero** por tu cara preciosa . . .

¡Mi bomboncito! ¡Mi tesoro! ¡Mi reina!

An elegant apartment in Montevideo, Uruguay. The telephone rings.

JIMENA   Hello. Martínez residence.

NACHO   Hi, sweetie (my black one), how are you? Here I am in Caracas, honey pie (my little piece of candy), but I'm thinking only about you—about your killer body . . . your lovely hair . . .

JIMENA   Nacho, how many drinks have you had (wineglasses have you taken)? Why are you calling me long distance to tell me nonsense?

NACHO   Jimena honey (little Jimena), darling (treasure), don't get like that. Do you know that I'm crazy about you?

JIMENA   News to me. I thought we were just friends. And why this change? Why do you love me now?

NACHO   Oh, sweetheart! Well . . . uh . . . you're so beautiful. I love you because of your lovely (precious) face . . .

JIMENA   ¡Qué maravilla! ¿Me querés por mi cara? ¿Es que no tengo personalidad? Para vos yo soy una linda cara y nada más, ¿verdad?

NACHO   Claro. Digo, ¡no! ¡Ajá! Ahora **caigo**. Querés pelear y plantarme para salir con otro. **Me estás poniendo los cuernos, ¿verdad, mi santa?**

JIMENA   ¡Cálmate, Nacho! ¿Cómo puedo ponerte cuernos cuando no somos novios? Acordate de nuestro lema: "**Juntos pero no revueltos: ¡nada de celos!**" **Tengo que cortar.** Me están **llamando en otra línea. Besos y abrazos. ¡Chau, chau!**

———■———

¡Ojo!

- **Juntos pero no revueltos** means *together but not romantically involved*. Literally, the second word, **revueltos**, means *mixed* or *scrambled together*, as in **huevos revueltos** (scrambled eggs).

- **Aló** or **Hola** are the usual ways of answering the telephone in many places. In Mexico most people say **Bueno** (Good), in Cuba or Miami, **Oigo** (I'm hearing), and in Spain, **Diga** (Tell) or **Dígame** (Tell me).

- **Mi negra** or **mi negro** (literally, *my black one*) is a common equivalent for *sweetie* or *darling*, whether the loved one is dark-skinned or not. Other terms of endearment are **gordo(-a)** (fatty, chubby), **flaco(-a)** (skinny), and **chato(-a)** (pug-nosed). These may sound rude to English speakers, but they express admiration, love and affection in Spanish.

- **Mi bomboncito** (my little piece of candy) is typically Uruguayan, but many love expressions are universal, such as: **tesoro** (treasure), **mi amor** or **amorcito** (my love, my little love), **mi vida** (my life), **mi cielo** (my heaven), **corazón** (heart), **mi corazoncito** (my little heart), **mi dueño(-a)** (my owner).

JIMENA   How marvelous! You love me for my face? So, I don't have a
          personality? For you I'm a pretty face and nothing more, right?

NACHO   Naturally. I mean, no! Aha! Now I catch on (fall down)! You
          want to fight and break up with me so you can go out with
          someone else. You're cheating on me (putting the horns on
          me), right, my dear (my saint)?

JIMENA   Calm down, Nacho! How can I be betraying you (putting
          horns on you) when we aren't going together? Remember our
          motto: "Together but not involved (scrambled, stirred up)—no
          jealousy!" I have to hang up (cut). They're calling me on
          another line. Hugs and kisses (kisses and hugs)! Bye, bye!

"Es tan buen mozo que se me caen las medias cuando lo miro."
(See page 126.)

- **Vos** is the familiar *you* in Uruguay and Argentina, instead of **tú.** Most present-tense and command forms of verbs used with it are altered, generally carrying the stress on a different syllable: **llamás** instead of **llamas, no me regañés** instead of **no me regañes, querés** instead of **quieres, salís** instead of **sales.** "You are" becomes **vos sos** instead of **tú eres.** (*Vos* is also used in various ways in Central America and several other regions.)

- **Ignacio** is the full name and **Nacho,** the nickname **(el apodo).** (See page 100 for more on nicknames.)

- **Te quiero** is *I love (want) you* and often suggests physical desire, although it can mean more than that. **Te amo** means *I love you* in a more spiritual way.

- The verb **caer** means *to fall,* but it's slang for *to catch on* or *to get it.*

CONVERSACIÓN 2

Jimena contesta la llamada de la otra línea.

JIMENA **Aló,** residencia Martínez.

LORENA Hola, **querida.** Soy Lorena. ¿Cómo andás, **che?**

JIMENA **Lo mismo de siempre.** Nacho me pegó **un golpe de telé-fono** desde Caracas.

LORENA **¿Te llamó por cobrar?**

JIMENA No, pero estaba **tomado** y ahora dice que me quiere. No sé si realmente habla **en serio.** Luego **se agarró una rabieta** y yo corté.

LORENA ¿Por qué salís con él?

JIMENA Me cae bien. Es gordito, pero simpático, y tiene **plata.** Mis **veteranos** creen que **es un buen partido.** Pero te cuento un secreto, nena. Ahora pienso mucho en Martín Vargas. Es un **churro bárbaro,** tan musculoso, y siempre me **está haciendo ojitos** en el gimnasio.

- To put horns on a person **(ponerle los cuernos)** is to cheat on that man or woman with another lover. This derives from the medieval idea of the "cuckold" who sprouted horns when his wife deceived him.

- **Besos y abrazos** (Kisses and hugs) is a common way of signing off on the phone or in a letter. The order is reversed from that of the English *hugs and kisses,* as is often the case, e.g., **ir y venir** (*going and coming* instead of *coming and going* as in English), **de los pies a la cabeza** (*from the feet to the head* instead of *from head to toe*), **blanco y negro** (*white and black* instead of *black and white*).

- **Chau** is taken from the Italian *ciao.* It is a very popular way of saying good-bye.

Jimena answers the call on the other line.

JIMENA   Hello. Martínez residence.

LORENA   Hi, Jimena dear. It's Lorena. How are you doing, girl?

JIMENA   The same as usual. Nacho called (hit me with a telephone blow) from Caracas.

LORENA   Did he call collect?

JIMENA   No, but he'd been drinking and now he says he loves me. I don't know if he's really serious or not. Later he threw a fit (he grabbed himself a rabies attack) and I hung up (cut).

LORENA   Why do you go out with him?

JIMENA   I like him (he falls well to me). He's a bit chubby, but very nice, and he has money (silver). My folks (veterans) think he's a good match. But I'll tell you a secret, kid (little girl). Lately I'm thinking a lot about Martín Vargas. He's a cool dude (savage fritter), so well built, and he's always flirting with (making little eyes at) me in the gym.

LORENA   Pues, olvídalo, **flaca.** Yo he salido con Martín.

JIMENA   Ay, ¡**tenés mucha suerte,** Lorena!

LORENA   ¡Hombre, **todo lo contrario!** Es un **tipo** "distinto", como quien dice.

JIMENA   No comprendo. Claro que Martín es distinto. Es tan buen mozo que **se me caen las medias** cuando lo miro. ¿Qué pasó entre ustedes?

LORENA   Pues, mucho **besuqueo** y después nada. Llegó la hora de las confesiones y resulta que Martín **juega para el otro equipo.** El verdadero amor de su vida es . . . ¡José!

JIMENA   ¡**La pucha!** ¡Mejor me quedo con mi gordo simpático!

————■————

¡Ojo!

- The word **querido(-a)** (dear) is often used casually between women or between a man and a woman, as in English.

- **Che,** a term of address used frequently between friends in Uruguay and Argentina, cannot be exactly translated. It means roughly *buddy, friend, man, girl, kiddo.* Other groups have different terms used in similar ways. (See page 160.)

- **Un golpe de teléfono** (a blow with the telephone) is slang for a *phone call* in Uruguay and Argentina.

- **Llamar por cobrar** is *to call collect.* The common way to say this in Spain is **llamar a cobro revertido** and in many places they say **llamar con cargo revertido.**

- **Una rabieta** is a *fit* or a *tantrum* and originally derives from the word for rabies attack. *To throw a fit or tantrum* is **darse** or **agarrarse una rabieta.**

- **Mis veteranos** in Uruguay and Argentina is slang for *parents,* since they are older and so have obviously survived some of the wars of life.

LORENA	Well, forget him, my dear (skinny)! I've gone out with Martín.
JIMENA	Oh, you are really lucky (you have a lot of luck), Lorena!
LORENA	Man, just the opposite! He's a "different" guy (type), as they say.
JIMENA	I don't understand. It's obvious (clear) that Martín is different. He's so handsome that I go crazy (my stockings fall down) when I look at him. What happened between the two of you?
LORENA	Well, a lot of smooching and then nothing. The moment of truth (confessions) came and it turns out that Martín is gay (plays for the other team). The true love of his life is—José!
JIMENA	Darn! I'd better stay with my nice chubby guy!

———■———

- **Churros,** popular throughout the Spanish-speaking world, are breakfast fritters made from deep-fried bread dough, dipped in sugar and served with hot chocolate or coffee. In the Southern Cone and Mexico, a **churro(-a)** means a good-looking person, but in some places, it has a crude meaning. **Bárbaro(-a)** means literally *savage, barbarian* but by extension has come to mean *super, marvelous.*

- The normal way of saying *to be very lucky* is **tener mucha suerte** (to have a lot of luck), but in Uruguayan slang it is **tener mucho culo** (to have large buns, ass), which is vulgar but often used among friends.

- In Uruguay or Chile a woman can express the attraction she feels toward someone by saying **Se me caen las medias (los calzones).** *My stockings (or pants) are falling down.*

- The English word *gay* and the cognates **homosexual** and **lesbiana** are used in Spanish to refer to homosexuals. Indirect ways of saying this include the following: **juega para el otro equipo** (he/she plays for the other team), **es distinto(-a)** (he/she is different). **Marimacho** means a masculine woman and can mean a lesbian. The feminine form *marimacha* is used for *lesbian* in some parts of the U.S. and Latin America. The word **maricón** means homosexual but is somewhat derrogatory and roughly equivalent to *queer*. **Maricona** is used in Chile and some other places for lesbian and is derogatory. In Costa Rican slang, a homosexual is a **playo** and a lesbian, a **tortillera** (the latter is also used in Spain).

- Just as *Darn!* is a euphemism for the stronger word *Damn!*, **La pucha!** is a softened form of ¡**La puta!** (the whore!) and is often used in the Southern Cone to express surprise or displeasure. (See page 166 for more on using strong language to express emotions.)

Vocabulario del capítulo

Aló or **Hola**	(Hello) common ways of answering the telephone
amorcito(-a)	(little love) sweetheart
el apodo	nickname
besos y abrazos	(kisses and hugs) hugs and kisses
el besuqueo	smooching
Bueno	(Good) normal way of answering the telephone in Mexico
Caigo	(I fall) I understand.
chato(-a)	(pug-nosed) affectionate nickname
chau, chau	bye-bye (used most in Southern Cone)
che	friend, pal (Uruguay, Argentina)
churro(-a) bárbaro(-a)	(savage fritter) good-looking man or woman
corazón	(heart) darling
Diga, Dígame	(Tell, Tell me) normal way of answering the telephone in Spain

en serio	seriously
Es un buen partido.	He (She) is a good match (for marriage).
flaco(-a)	(skinny) affectionate nickname
un golpe de teléfono	(a blow with the telephone) phone call
gordo(-a), gordito(-a)	(fat; chubby) honey, dear
hacer ojitos	(to make little eyes) to flirt
Juega para el otro equipo.	He/She is homosexual (plays for the other team).
juntos pero no revueltos	together but not romantically involved (mixed up)
llamar a larga distancia	to call long distance
llamar en otra línea	to call on another line
llamar por cobrar	to call collect
lo mismo de siempre	the same as always
el maricón	a somewhat derogatory way of saying homosexual
la maricona	a somewhat derogatory way of saying lesbian
el marimacho	a masculine woman or lesbian
mi amor	my love
mi bomboncito	(my little piece of candy) darling love
mi cielo	(my heaven) sweetheart, darling
mi corazoncito	(my little heart) sweetheart
mi negro(-a)	(my black one) sweetheart, darling
mi vida	(my life) sweetheart, darling
Oigo	(I'm hearing) normal way of answering the phone among Cubans
la plata	(silver) money
ponerle los cuernos	(to put the horns on him/her) to cheat on one's lover or spouse
¡La pucha!	softened form of **¡La puta!**, equivalent to *Darn it!*

querido(-a)	dear
la rabieta	(rabies attack) fit, tantrum
Se me caen las medias (los calzones).	My stockings (pants) are falling down.
Te amo.	I love you (in a spiritual way.)
Te quiero.	I love (want) you (sometimes physically).
tener mucha suerte	(to have a lot of luck) to be very lucky
Tengo que cortar.	I have to hang up (the phone).
tesoro	(treasure) sweetheart, darling
el tipo	(type) guy, fellow
todo lo contrario	(all the contrary) just the opposite
tomado(-a)	drunk (Latin America)
tomar una copa	to have a drink (wine glass)
los veteranos	(veterans) parents (Uruguay and Argentina)
vos sos	you (familiar) are (instead of **tú eres**) in Uruguay, Argentina, Central America, and some other places. (For more on **vos,** see p. 124.)

¡A USTED LE TOCA!

A. ¿Qué falta? Fill in the word that's missing from each phrase, using one of the words from this list: **besos, cobrar, copas, cuernos, rabietas, medias, ojitos**. (One word from the list will not be used.)

1. Creo que tienes otro amante, querida. ¡Me estás poniendo los _____!

2. Cuando Margarita piensa en su novio, se le caen las _____.

3. Adiós, amorcito. ¡ _____ y abrazos!

4. Bárbara tiene interés en Lalo. Siempre le hace _____.

5. Estás borracho. ¿Cuántas _____ has tomado?

6. No tengo plata. Voy a llamar por _____.

B. Palabras revueltas. Unscramble the letters of the words to reveal the phrase that answers each question.

1. All the girls want to marry Daniel. What is he?

   NU   ENUB   DORPATI

   _____   _____   _____

2. Someone's at the door and you have to hang up the phone. What do you say?

   GONET   EUQ   TARROC

   _____   ____   _____

3. A lot of men want to go out with Amalia but she always says no. Why?

   AUGJE   RAAP   LE   TOOR   QEOPUI

   _____   _____   __   _____   _____

4. The phone rings in Madrid, and a Spanish man answers it. What does he say?

   MEDAGI

   _____

5. The phone rings in Guadalajara, and a Mexican woman answers it. What does she say?

   NUBOE

   _____

6. Your Spanish-speaking sweetheart complains that you never use terms of endearment. What could you call him or her?

   IM   ROAM

   __   _____

C. Dos modos de hablar. Match the standard word or expression you would use in the office with the slang that you might use in the café with your friends.

En la oficina
__1. borracho
__2. comprendo
__3. hombre atractivo
__4. llamada
__5. padres

En el café
a. caigo
b. veteranos
c. golpe de teléfono
d. churro
e. tomado

D. ¿Qué dice Ud? What could you say in Spanish in the following situations?

1. You're on the telephone with the operator (**operadora**) in Mexico and want to call long-distance collect to your parents.

   _____

2. You have a sweetheart and want to express your love for him (or her) in Spanish with several terms of endearment.

   _____

3. You are writing a letter (or e-mail note) to your good friend in Latin America and it's time to sign off and say good-bye.

   _____

VOCABULARY AND CULTURE

TALKING ABOUT SEX:
GREEN STORIES AND NATURAL CHILDREN

A big revelation for many English speakers is the general absence in
Spanish culture of the Puritanic attitude associating sex with filth or treat-
ing it as a legal or business matter. This shouldn't be so surprising, of
course, since the ancestors of present-day Latin Americans weren't Puritans
at all, but conquistadors and explorers who had crossed the sea in search of
adventure and natives who in earlier times were living in a pre-industrial,
non-Christian world of nature.

These historical origins may explain in part the different emphasis in
the two languages in many terms used for jokes, stories, and books with sexual themes. In Spanish they are not generally referred to with the word
sucio (dirty), but rather with the word **verde** (green). Green is the color of
life, hope, and nature, and does not imply repugnance as the word *dirty* does.
In Spanish, an elderly man who is still chasing after women is not con-
demned as "a dirty old man" as he is in English, but simply called "a green
old man," **un viejo verde.** Jokes with sexual themes are "dirty jokes" in
English but are just called **chistes verdes** (green jokes) in Spanish. "Dirty
stories" and "dirty books" are **historias verdes** (green stories) and **libros
verdes** (green books). These terms refer to their sexual content, but without
the negative judgment implied in the English designations.

Another contrast is evident in the English usage of business or legal
terms. In English, a love relationship between unmarried persons is *an
affair* or *love affair,* but in Spanish it is **una aventura** or **una aventura
amorosa.** A child born from such an affair (out of "wedlock") is called *an
illegitimate child,* but in Spanish, this child is **un hijo (una hija) natural** (a
natural child).

Whether the baby is **un hijo natural** or not, the common Spanish
expression **dar a luz** for *to have a baby* or *to give birth* is certainly one of
the most beautiful and poetic of any language. To say that Elena had a
baby at six this morning, you say in Spanish: **Elena dio a luz a las seis
de la mañana.** Literally, the idiom means *to give to light,* so, *Elena gave (a
baby) to light at six A.M.*

Comprensión. Circle the answer that best completes each statement.

1. The ancestors of present-day Latin Americans were
   a. Puritans
   b. explorers and adventurers
   c. natives who lived close to nature
   d. both *b* and *c*

2. Jokes about sex in Spanish are most often called
   a. **chistes sucios**
   b. **chistes verdes**
   c. **chistes naturales**
   d. **chistes grandes**

3. The Spanish word **aventura** often means
   a. an illegitimate child
   b. an unfortunate accident
   c. a business appointment
   d. a love affair

4. A synonym for **dar a luz** is
   a. **tener un bebé**
   b. **llegar temprano**
   c. **estar contenta**
   d. **trabajar por la mañana**

CHISTE

LA LEY DEL AJO

Según un chiste mexicano, hay una regla muy importante para la vida y para el amor: la ley del ajo. Va así. La palabra **ajo** en español tiene dos sílabas: *A–JO,* de modo que la Ley del a-jo es *¡Aguantarse y **JO**derse!*

THE GARLIC LAW

According to a Mexican joke, there is a very important rule for life and love, "The Garlic Law." It goes like this. The word **ajo** in Spanish has two syllables: A–JO, so the Garlic Law is *¡**A** **guantarse** (Put up with it) and **Jo***

derse (Get screwed)!

Un Malentendido Regional (A Regional Misunderstanding)

Un elogio de doble sentido

Un funcionario mexicano invitó al agregado cultural de Chile a una cena en su casa. La esposa del mexicano sirvió una comida muy sabrosa y el chileno quería elogiarla. Viendo que había en el comedor muchos adornos de cerámica (que en Chile se llaman "chiches"), el visitante le dijo a su anfitriona—¡Qué lindos chiches tiene Ud.! La señora se puso roja de los pies a la cabeza y salió corriendo del salón. En la jerga de México, la palabra "chiches" quiere decir *tetas*.

A compliment with a double meaning

A Mexican government official invited the cultural attaché from Chile to a dinner in his home. The Mexican's wife served a very tasty meal and the Chilean wanted to compliment her. Seeing that there were many ceramic decorations (which in Chile are called **"chiches"**) in the dining room, the visitor said to his hostess, "What lovely **chiches** you have!" The lady turned red from head to toe and ran out of the room. In Mexican slang, the word **chiches** means *tits*.

. CAPÍTULO 9 .

¿Quién es ese tipo, el palancón?

DESCRIBING PEOPLE

CONVERSACIÓN 1

En una fiesta en Quito, Ecuador. David no conoce a mucha gente y le hace preguntas a su amigo Eduardo.

DAVID   Oye, Eduardo, ¿quién es ese tipo que está allí, el **palancón** con barba?

EDUARDO   ¿Ése? Se llama Enrique. Es **supercoco,** un verdadero **nerdo.**

DAVID   ¿Y la chica que habla con él?

EDUARDO   ¿Marisela? Esa chica es una **zanahoria;** sólo va de la casa al colegio y del colegio a la casa.

DAVID   ¿Y quiénes son esas personas que están sentadas allí en el sofá?

EDUARDO   Son los dueños de la **home.** Su hija Marta es la que cumple años. Ella es un poco **plástica,** pero es generosa y muy divertida.

DAVID   **¡Epa, epa!** ¿Quién es esa **loca superbuena,** la de pelo largo?

ES SUPERCOCO. ES UNA ZANAHORIA.

At a party in Quito, Ecuador. David doesn't know many people and he is asking his friend Eduardo questions.

DAVID   Hey, Eduardo, who's that guy there, the tall one (like a long bar) with a beard?

EDUARDO   That one? His name is Enrique. He's supersmart (super coconut), a real nerd.

DAVID   And that girl who's talking to him?

EDUARDO   Marisela? That kid's a real innocent (carrot); she just goes from home to school and school to home.

DAVID   And who are those people sitting there on the sofa?

EDUARDO   They're the owners of the home. Their daughter Marta is the one having a birthday. She's a little artificial (hypocritical, "plastic"), but she's generous and a lot of fun.

DAVID   Wow! Who's that great (supergood) chick (crazy one), the one with long hair?

EDUARDO   Se llama Claudia. Está con el **chicle** de Javier—ése, sí, que es **pegajoso.** Vamos a rescatarla y te la presento.

DAVID   **¡Bacán!**

———————■———————

¡Ojo!

- **Palancón** is from **palanca,** *lever or bar.* The **-ón** (**-ona** in the feminine) is used to indicate increased size. Similar are **narizón,** *big nose,* **orejón,** *big ears,* **panzón,** *big stomach, potbellied.*

- **Supercoco:** a **coco,** *coconut,* refers to one's head, so a person who is **muy coco** or **supercoco** is very brainy. The feminine form is also **coco.**

- **Nerdo** is of course from the English *nerd.* In some areas **cuadernícolas** (a very serious student who studies a lot) is used; the word comes from **cuaderno,** *notebook.* Someone who reads constantly is a **comelibros;** a bookworm is a **ratón de biblioteca** (library rat) or a **polilla de biblioteca** (library moth).

- **Zanahoria:** In Ecuador, Venezuela, and Colombia a **zanahoria,** *carrot,* is a young person (male or female) who is innocent and

▌ Conversación 2

En la misma fiesta. Los papás de Marta hablan.

SRA. SÁENZ   No puedo creer que Martita ya cumple 18 años. Parece que fue ayer que sólo era una **guagua,** ¿no?

SR. SÁENZ   Así es. ¡Martita!

MARTA   ¿Sí, papá?

SR. SÁENZ   Está muy animada la fiesta. Dime, ¿quién es esa mujer **estrafalaria,** con collares y pulseras? Parece gitana. ¿La conocemos?

EDUARDO   Her name is Claudia. She's with that pest (chewing gum) Javier—he sticks like glue (he's sticky). Let's rescue her and I'll introduce you.

DAVID   Fantastic!

———■———

not socially active, not "with it." In Spain, people say **Está muy verde,** *He or she is very green.*

- **La home:** particularly in the slang of young people, English words are creeping into the Spanish language; most young people see American movies or TV and many travel abroad to areas where they use English.

- **¡Epa, epa!** is used to express surprise or shock.

- **Pegajoso(-a)** means *sticky.*

- **Bacán** or **bac** is like **bacanal** (pertaining to Bacchus, god of wine) and just means *fantastic, exciting, fun.* The word is used in Ecuador, Puerto Rico, and Colombia (**bacano**). (In Spain, one hears **fetén.**)

At the same party. Marta's parents are talking.

MRS. SÁENZ   I can't believe little Marta is already 18 years old. It seems like only yesterday she was a baby.

MR. SÁENZ   That's how it is. Martita!

MARTA   Yes, Dad?

MR. SÁENZ   The party's very lively (animated). Tell me, who is that outlandishly dressed woman, with the necklaces and bracelets? She looks like a Gypsy. Do we know her?

Marta	¿La de la falda anaranjada? Se llama Rosa García.
Sr. Sáenz	**Si se quema la casa, no pierde nada,** ¿verdad?
Marta	Pero es **muy buena gente,** Papá.
Sr. Sáenz	**Ajá.** Y ese tipo que te hablaba hace poco, ¿quién es?
Marta	¿Rodolfo? Es un **remo.** Un **aprovechado,** quiero decir. Pero es muy divertido.
Sr. Sáenz	Y ese chico que te gustaba . . . este . . . Víctor . . . ¿está aquí?
Marta	Dijo que estaba cansado, que iba para su casa a **planchar la oreja.** Pero no lo creo. Ay, **santo que no me quiere, basta con no rezarle,** ¿eh?
Sr. Sáenz	No te preocupes, m'hija. Hay muchos jóvenes aquí. Bueno, Matilde, ¿vamos a **menear el bote**?
Sra. Sáenz	Sí, Oscar, **pongámonos las pilas** y bailemos.

———■———

¡Ojo!

- A **guagua** can refer to a bus (in the Caribbean) or a baby (Ecuador, Chile). One story has it that Chileans living in Cuba used the expression **ir de guagua** meaning *to be carried (to go as a baby)*. From that, the expression began to be used for *to be carried by bus,* and before long **guagua** was used for *bus.* A baby can also be **una criatura** (a creature); **criar** means *to bring up (children) or to breed (animals).*

- **Estrafalario(-a)** refers mainly to bizarre dress rather than behavior.

- **Si se quema la casa** . . . In other words, the person is so over-dressed that he or she appears to be wearing all their worldly goods: jewelry, etc.

MARTA   The one in the orange skirt? Her name is Rosa García.

MR. SÁENZ   If the house burns down, she won't lose anything, will she?

MARTA   But she's a very nice person, Dad.

MR. SÁENZ   Uh-huh. And that guy who was talking to you a little while ago, who is he?

MARTA   Rodolfo? He's a bit of a sponge (oar). A moocher, I mean. But he's a lot of fun.

MR. SÁENZ   And that boy that you like, uh . . . Víctor . . . is he here?

MARTA   He said he was tired and was going home to bed (to iron his ear—i.e., lie down). But I don't believe him. Ay, "saint that doesn't like me, it's enough not to pray to him," eh?

MR. SÁENZ   Don't worry, dear (my daughter). There are a lot of young people here. Well, Matilde, shall we dance (rock the boat)?

MRS. SÁENZ   Yes, Oscar, let's get going (put in our batteries) and dance.

———■———

- **Es muy buena gente** is a commonly used expression to describe a person who is nice, kind, or trustworthy.

- A **remo,** literally *oar,* is someone who doesn't want to do his part but expects others to do things for him, a *sponge,* someone who wants a free ride. In some areas, such as Colombia, **lanzado(-a)** is used with this meaning (although **lanzado** in most countries just refers to someone who is aggressive). In Argentina, **un piola** is used for a *sponge,* while in Mexico it's an **abusivo(-a)** or **abusón (abusona).** **Un(a) aprovechado(-a)** is another term for an opportunist or *sponge.*

- **Planchar la oreja:** *to sleep (iron one's ear):* in Ecuador, young people also say **meterse en el sobre,** *to put oneself in one's envelope,* meaning *to go to bed,* e.g., **Voy a meterme en el sobre.**

- **Menear el bote,** literally *to move the boat,* means *to dance.* In Spain people say **mover el esqueleto,** *to move one's skeleton,* and in Mexico, people say **sacarse la polilla** (to get the moths off); e.g., **Vamos a sacarnos la polilla.**

- **Ponerse las pilas,** *to get with it or to get going,* means literally *to put in one's batteries.* It can be used to try to hurry someone up: **¡Ponte las pilas y vámonos!**

CHISTES

EN LA CANTINA

Un borracho entra en una cantina en El Salvador y grita—¡Tragos para todos! Así que todos van a la barra y piden un trago. El borracho le dice al cantinero que se sirva uno también. El cantinero, un **chaparro** con bigote, lo hace y le dice que van a ser 400 pesos. A lo que el borracho contesta:

—Yo no traigo nada de **feria.**

—¿**Cómo que** nada de feria? ¡**Pasmado**! ¡**Pinche briago pelado**! —grita el cantinero y lo patea fuera del bar.

Al rato entra el borracho otra vez y dice: —Tragos para todos.

—A lo que el cantinero contesta: —¿Y querrás que me sirva yo uno también?

—¡N'ombre! ¡Te pones muy **enojón** cuando tomas!

IN THE BAR

A drunk goes into a bar in El Salvador and yells, "Drinks for everyone!" So everyone goes to the bar and orders a drink. The drunk tells the barman to serve himself one also. The barman, a short guy with a mustache, does it and says that it will be 400 pesos. To which the drunk replies: "I have no money." "What do you mean no money? Idiot! Despicable penniless drunk!" yells the barman and kicks him out of the bar.

A little while later the drunk comes in again and says, "Drinks for everyone!" To which the barman replies: "And you probably want me to serve myself one also?" "No, man! You get very hostile (angry) when you drink!"

¡Ojo!

- **Feria,** *change,* is one of many slang words for money in Mexico and Central America; its standard meaning is *fair;* **un día feriado** is a *day off.*

- **¿Cómo que . . . ?** is commonly heard, meaning *What do you mean . . . ?* **¿Cómo que "No"? ¿Cómo que tienes hambre? ¿Cómo que perdiste el dinero?**

- **Pinche** is a general insult, as in: **pinche viejo,** *base or despicable old man;* **pinche máquina,** *blasted machine.*

- **Briago(-a),** *drunk,* is a term used in Mexico and Central America. **Bolo(-a)** is also used with this meaning in Central America. In Colombia the slang term for *to be drunk* is **estar geto(-a),** and in Venezuela, Argentina, Uruguay, Central America, and Mexico it's **estar pedo(-a).**

- **Pelado(-a),** from **pelar** (to peel, skin, or shave), can mean *bald, smooth,* or, colloquially, *broke, without money.* In Argentina, people say **estar seco(-a),** literally, *to be dry.* See page 229 for other terms related to this topic.

- **Enojón:** the **-ón** ending is used to show an increased level or degree. The feminine ends in **-ona,** without the accent. Similarly, an **asustón** is a "fraidy-cat," a **faltón** (from **faltar**) is someone who doesn't do what is supposed to be done, a **mandón** (from **mandar**) gives a lot of orders, a **comilón** is someone who eats a lot, a **dormilón** is someone who sleeps a lot, a **llorón** is a crybaby or whiner, etc.

Tin-Glao (Costa Rica)

—Piensa que soy su mamá . . .

DOS ESPAÑOLES, EN LA CALLE

—**Joer,** hay que ver cómo es esta juventud. Ojo a ese **espantapájaros**: palancón, **manudo,** con pantalones, el pelo muy corto . . . ¡y esas orejas! **Parece Volkswagen con las puertas abiertas.** ¿Podría usted decirme si es un tío o una tía?

—Pues es una chica.

—Y usted, ¿cómo lo sabe?

—Porque es mi hija.

—Huy, ¡perdón! ¡No sabía que usted fuera su padre!

—Soy su madre.

Atracción fatal...

cursi

Rosa

| cursi *corny, very sentimental*

TWO SPANIARDS, ON THE STREET

"Damn, look at what these young people are like. Get a load of that scarecrow: like a long, skinny bar (lever), with giant hands, pants, very short hair . . . and those ears! Looks like a Volkswagen with the doors open. Can you tell me whether it's a man (uncle) or a woman (aunt)?"

"It's a girl."

"And how do you know?"

"Because she's my daughter."

"Oh, sorry! I didn't know you were her father!"

"I'm her mother."

¡Ojo!

- **Joer** is a short form of **joder.** This expletive is very common in Spain and other places. See page 239 for further explanation.

- **Manudo:** the **-udo** ending expresses an exaggerated size or amount. Other examples: **barba** *beard,* **barbudo** *with a heavy or thick beard;* **pata** *foot (of an animal, furniture, or colloquially, people),* **patudo** *with big feet or long legs* (See Chapter 2, page 22).

- **Un tío:** As you saw in Chapter 4, **un tío (una tía)** is very common in Spain meaning *man (woman)* or *guy (girl).*

VOCABULARIO DEL CAPÍTULO

abusivo(-a)	someone who takes advantage of others, sponge (Mexico: **abusón, abusona**)
Ajá.	Uh-huh. I see.
un(a) aprovechado(-a)	someone who takes advantage of others; an opportunist
asustón (asustona)	"fraidy-cat"
¡Bacán! ¡Bac!	Great! Fantastic! (Ecuador, Puerto Rico, Colombia [**bacano**])
barbudo	bearded, with a heavy beard
el briago, la briaga	drunkard (Mexico, Central America)
buena gente	(good people) nice, kind person or people
chaparro(-a)	short (Mexico, Central America)
el chicle	(chewing gum) someone hard to get rid of, pest
coco	(coconut) smart, intelligent
el comelibros	(bookeater) bookworm
comilón, comilona	gluttonous
¿Cómo que . . . ?	What do you mean . . . ?
¿Cómo que perdiste el dinero?	What do you mean you lost the money?
la criatura	(creature) baby
el cuadernícolas	very serious student who studies a lot, from **cuaderno,** notebook

cursi	corny, too cute or sentimental
dormilón, dormilona	someone who sleeps a lot
enojón, enojona	someone hostile or angry
¡Epa, epa!	interjection expressing surprise or shock
el espantapájaros	scarecrow
estar bolo(-a)	to be drunk (Central America)
estrafalario(-a)	strange, weird (usually referring to dress)
faltón, faltona	someone who doesn't do what they are supposed to do
la feria	(fair or day off) money (Mexico, Central America)
la guagua	baby (Ecuador, Chile); bus (Caribbean)
la home	home (from the English influence)
joer from **joder**;	interjection used in Spain, something like *Damn!*
lanzado(-a)	someone who takes advantage of others (Colombia, Spain) or who is simply aggressive
llorón, llorona	crybaby, whiner
un loco (una loca)	guy (girl) (Ecuador, Colombia, Venezuela)
mandón, mandona	someone who likes to give orders, bossy person
manudo(-a)	having large hands
menear el bote	to dance (literally, *to rock or move the boat*)
narizón, narizona	having a big nose
el nerdo	nerd
orejón, orejona	having big ears
palancón, palancona	very tall (from **palanca,** *a lever or stick*)
panzón, panzona	having a large stomach
parece Volkswagen con las puertas abiertas	(looks like a Volkswagen with the doors open) someone with very large ears
pasmado(-a)	foolish, stupid

pegajoso(-a)	sticky, referring also to someone who is hard to get rid of or shake off
pelado(-a)	penniless, broke (from **pelar,** *to peel;* can also mean *bald, smooth*)
pinche	blasted, damn (**pinche viejo, pinche máquina,** etc.) (Mexico, Central America)
planchar la oreja	(to iron one's ear) to go to bed (Ecuador, Venezuela, Colombia)
plástico(-a)	(plastic) artificial, hypocritical
ponerse las pilas	(to put in one's batteries) to get with it, get going
el remo	(oar) sponge, leech (Ecuador)
Santo que no me quiere, basta con no rezarle.	(Saint that doesn't like me, it's enough not to pray to him.) There's no need to bother with someone who doesn't care about me.
Si se quema la casa, no pierde nada.	If the house burns down, he or she won't lose anything (because they are wearing so much jewelry or finery on their person).
la zanahoria	(carrot) young person who is innocent, not socially active or "with it" (Ecuador, Venezuela, Colombia)

¡A USTED LE TOCA!

A. ¿Qué es? Give a word or phrase that best fits each description. Choose from the following: **chaparro, chicle, cursi, estrafalario, pelado, plástico, supercoco, zanahoria.**

1. Alma es muy inteligente. _____

2. Carlos nunca tiene dinero. _____

3. Pepe es muy bajo. _____

4. Juana es joven y no sale mucho. _____

5. Iris lleva ropa rara o extravagante. _____

6. Gloria es muy pero demasiado
   sentimental. _____

7. Luis es muy "pegajoso"; no
   deja a la gente en paz. _____

8. Mimi es hipócrita, no muy
   natural. _____

B. Características. What characteristic is very prominent in someone who is:

Physical characteristics

1. palancón   *height*_____

2. narizón   _____

3. orejón   _____

4. panzón   _____

5. barbudo   _____

6. manudo   _____

7. patudo   _____

Other characteristics

8. comilón		*gluttonous*
9. llorón		_____
10. mandón		_____
11. enojón		_____
12. dormilón		_____
13. faltón		_____
14. asustón		_____

C. Sinónimos. Match the synonyms.

__1. remo	a. dinero
__2. guagua	b. tonto
__3. feria	c. un tío
__4. bacán	d. briago
__5. geto	e. aprovechado
__6. pasmado	f. comelibros
__7. un loco	g. criatura
__8. cuadernícolas	h. fantástico

D. ¿Qué falta? Complete the sentences on the left, then match them to the English equivalents on the right.

__1. Ana es muy buena ____, muy simpática.

__2. ¡Pongámonos las ____!

__3. Si se quema la casa, no ____ nada.

__4. ¡Vamos a ____ el bote!

__5. ¡____, epa! Ojo a ese tipo allí.

__6. Tengo sueño. Voy a planchar la ____.

__7. Santo que no me quiere, ____ con no rezarle.

a. No sense praying to a saint that doesn't care for me.

b. Let's rock the boat (dance)!

c. Wow! Look at that guy there!

d. Let's get with it (Put on the batteries)!

e. I'm tired. I'm going to catch some Zs (iron my ear).

f. If the house burns down, he/she won't lose anything.

g. Ana is a very good person, very nice.

E. Mi hermano. Miguelito is talking about his brother. Give an opposite description by substituting antonyms for the underlined words. Antonyms: **abusivo, chaparro, comilón, faltón, mandón, panzón, pasmado.**

Mi hermano Antonio es <u>alto</u> y rubio. Es muy <u>obediente y servil</u>. Siempre (Nunca) cumple con sus promesas porque es muy <u>responsable</u>. Es <u>delgado</u> y <u>no come mucho</u>. Es muy <u>generoso y altruista</u>. ¡Qué hermano más <u>coco</u>!

. CAPÍTULO 10 .

¡Qué cochinadas hacen!

USING EXPLETIVES AND SWEAR WORDS FOR AFFECTION, SURPRISE, OR DISPLEASURE
·
COMMUNICATING IN SLANG ACROSS TWO DIFFERENT DIALECTS

CONVERSACIÓN 1

El hombre de negocios mexicano, Memo González, se encuentra de visita en Buenos Aires, Argentina, y llega a la casa de su antiguo colega, Uriel Linotti. Lida, la esposa de Uriel, lo recibe.

MEMO   ¡Mire nomás, qué buena **botana** prepararon!

LIDA   ¿Botana? Ah, la palabra mexicana para decir las **picadas.** Se llaman picadas porque son para picar.

MEMO   Si Ud. lo dice . . . Aquí siempre **me hago bolas** con el lenguaje.

LIDA   ¡Ay, no diga Ud. eso! Se oye horrible. Aquí en nuestro país tenemos una obsesión nacional con la palabra *bolas.* La usamos de mil maneras. Siéntese, amigo. Pronto vendrán Uriel y los **pendejos.**

MEMO   ¿**Mande**? ¡Qué barbaridad! ¿Dijo usted "pendejos"?

¡QUÉ COCHINADAS HACEN!
TODO LO HACEN POR DEBAJO DE LA MESA.

The Mexican businessman Memo González is visiting in Buenos Aires, Argentina, and arrives at the home of an old colleague, Uriel Linotti. Uriel's wife, Lida, greets him at the door.

MEMO   Look at that, what a nice **botana** (hors d'oeuvres) you prepared!

LIDA   **Botana?** (Hors d'oeuvres?) Ah, the Mexican word for **picadas** (appetizers, literally, *cut or chopped-up pieces*). They are called **picadas** because you pick at them.

MEMO   Whatever you say (if you say it). I always get confused (get balled up) here with the language.

LIDA   Oh, don't say that! It sounds horrible. Here in our country we have a national obsession with the word *balls.* We use it in a thousand ways. Sit down, my friend. Uriel will come soon with the **pendejos** (vulgar expression in Mexico, but common word for kids in Argentina).

MEMO   Excuse (Command) me? Good lord! Did you say *pendejos?*

LIDA Sí, hombre, pendejos son los chiquilines, los **pibes. Es un problema mayúsculo** si no hay nadie aquí para recibirlos. El **bondi** llega a las cinco.

MEMO ¿El bondi? ¿Te refieres al camión escolar? Pero, dime, ¿realmente les dicen "pendejos" a los niños? En México, "pendejo" suena muy **pelado.** Es un insulto.

LIDA Escuche. Uds. los mexicanos y nosotros los **porteños** hablamos el **castellano** a nuestro modo. Sabe Dios cuál es más correcto. Hablando de otra cosa: dígame, ¿cómo van las cosas en México ahora? ¿Qué tal el gobernador de su provincia?

MEMO No tenemos provincias en México, tenemos estados. El gobernador de mi estado es un ladrón y sus amigos también. ¡Qué cochinadas hacen! **Todo lo hacen por debajo de la mesa;** y aquí en Argentina, ¿qué tal?

LIDA Aun peor. Aquí el gobernador es un **boludo** que no sabe hacer nada. Dicen que acepta coimas. La situación **está por el suelo.**

MEMO ¿**Coimas**? Ah, sí, la plata pagada por los favores. En México, igual. Muchos problemas se solucionan con **la mordida.** Pero ¿no habrá noticias mejores que ésas?

LIDA **Por supuesto que sí.** ¡Hoy ganó **Boca Juniors**! ¡Viva el fútbol!

———— ■ ————

¡Ojo!

- **¡Que cochinadas hacen!** What (pig acts) dirty tricks they do! This is an insult that is not vulgar and can be said in almost any company to indicate strong disapproval of someone's actions.

- **Botana** is the typical Mexican word for hors d'oeuvres or appetizers, while the Argentine word is **picadas.** Here is a good

LIDA Right, man, the **pendejos** are the kiddies, the children. It's a major (capital letter) problem if there's no one here to greet them. The **bondi** (*school bus* in Argentina) arrives at five.

MEMO The **bondi?** Are you referring to the **camión escolar** (scholarly truck, school bus in Mexico)? But tell me, do you really say **pendejos** for children? In Mexico, **pendejo** sounds very vulgar (peeled, bald). It's an insult.

LIDA Listen. You Mexicans and we Argentines from Buenos Aires (port dwellers) speak Spanish (Castilian) in our own fashion. God knows which is more correct. Changing the topic: tell me, how are things going in Mexico now? What's the governor of your province like?

MEMO We don't have provinces in Mexico, we have states. The governor of my state is a thief and his friends are too. What dirty tricks (pig acts) they do! Everything is done behind closed doors (under the table). And here in Argentina, how's it going?

LIDA Even worse. Here our governor is a dope (jerk with weighty balls) who doesn't know how to do anything. They say he takes bribes. The situation is the pits (down on the ground).

MEMO **¿Coimas?** Oh, right, money paid in exchange for favors. In Mexico it's the same. A lot of problems are solved with the **mordida** (*bite, bribe* in Mexico). But isn't there any better news than this?

LIDA Of course there is. The Boca Juniors won today! Hooray for soccer!

———■———

example of the regional variety of Spanish. In Chile they say **cosas para picar,** in Spain **tapas,** and in Venezuela **pasa palos**, meaning food to help pass drinks (into the digestive system), since **palos** is slang for *alcoholic drinks.*

- Sometimes this regional variety leads to misunderstandings. The common Mexican expression **me hago bolas** (I get confused) sounds crude to Lida because the words **bolas** and **pelotas** (balls) are endowed in Argentina with a secondary meaning referring to body parts. (See *Vocabulary & Culture* for this chapter.)

- **Pendejos** is said quite innocently in Argentina to mean *children* (with the literal meaning of pubic hair), but in Mexico it is a vulgar insult in certain situations. In Colombia **pendejo** is not an offensive term and just means *silly,* as in the expression, **No seas pendejo** (Don't be silly). (See *Vocabulary & Culture* in this chapter.)

- **¿Mande?** is often used in Mexico and some parts of Central America when someone doesn't quite hear or understand what you've said. This is the **Ud.** command form of the verb **mandar** (to order, command) and so sounds servile to Argentine ears where it is more customary to say **¿Cómo?** (literally, *How?*) when you don't understand.

- **Pibes** is the most common **argentinismo** for children or youngsters.

- People who live in Buenos Aires are **porteños** and are generally considered a breed apart from other Argentines, loved and admired by some who consider them sophisticated and lively and intensely disliked by others who consider them snooty and condescending.

- **Castellano** is the way many people in Latin America say *Spanish,* although they also understand **español**. The origin is the word for *Castilian,* referring to the central plateau region of Spain whose dialect evolved into modern Spanish. Most Spaniards do not say **castellano,** preferring **español**.

- Insults. Every country has its national insult (often used to describe politicians or the players on a rival soccer team), and Argentina's is **boludos,** which is rather vulgar, but not terrible. In Mexico it's **pendejos** and in Chile, **huevones,** but there are many others. Indeed, Spanish is most varied and expressive in this department. (See *Vocabulary & Culture* in this chapter for more about the meanings and uses of these and other "off-color" words.)

- **Soborno** is the standard Spanish word for *bribe*, but some countries have their own terms: **coima** in Argentina and **mordida** *(bite)* in Mexico.

- **¡Por supuesto!** (literally, *taken as supposed*) is one of many ways of saying *Of course!* and is very common in Latin America. **¡Claro!** (Clear!) is also frequent, and **que sí** or **que no** can be added to both: **¡Por supuesto que sí! ¡Por supuesto que no! ¡Claro que sí! ¡Claro que no!** (Of course it is! Of course I do, you will, etc. Of course not!) In Spain, **desde luego** is often used for *of course,* but **que sí** and **que no** are not added to it.

"Vos y yo siempre lo pasamos bomba, ¿no?" (See page 158.)

CONVERSACIÓN 2

Una hora más tarde, entra Uriel y se abraza con su amigo.

MEMO   **Pinche cabrón argentino,** ¿cómo estás?

URIEL   **Recopado** ahora que vos estás aquí, **che.** Vos y yo siempre **lo pasamos bomba,** ¿no? Desde que dejaste nuestra oficina, **no es lo mismo.**

MEMO   No me digas. ¿**Echas de menos** a tu **cuate** mexicano?

URIEL   Así es. Pero, dime, ¿qué tal tu jefe en México?

MEMO   **Muy especial. Abusadísimo** para los negocios y **muy picudo** con el gobierno. Maneja mil negocios bien y siempre se lo ve **tan fresco como una lechuga.** Eso sí, tiene un genio **de la chingada,** pues nos da unas **regañadas** tremendas . . .

URIEL   Es igual que Virgilio, ¿lo recuerdas? Ese tipo **tenía unas tablas increíbles.** Además, **tenía los pantalones bien puestos** cuando nos defendía delante de los gerentes. ¡**Cómo armaba escándalos!**

MEMO   Hombre, éste es mucho peor. Nos llama a todos **una bola de pendejos.** Si no hemos cumplido con la expectativa de venta, se pone **fúrico.** Nos grita, "**¡Me están chingando!**" **Nos mienta la madre. Y agarra a toditos por parejo**—a sus directores, a los gerentes, a los empleados— ¡a todos!

URIEL   ¿A hombres y mujeres?

MEMO   No, claro que no. No hay mujeres en ventas a esos niveles.

URIEL   Parece que las cosas no han cambiado tanto; ¡qué joda!

MEMO   **Pues, ya ves,** así es.

One hour later, Uriel comes in and greets his friend with a hug.

MEMO   You damn Argentine son of a gun (kitchen-working old goat), how are you?

URIEL   Super, now that you're here, buddy (**che**). You and I always tear up the town (spend it like a bomb), don't we? Since you left our office, it's just not the same.

MEMO   You don't say. Do you miss your old Mexican pal (twin)?

URIEL   I sure do. (So it is.) But tell me, how's your boss in Mexico?

MEMO   A real case (very special). Very sharp (extremely abused) for business and really in (picked) with the government. He's managing a thousand different businesses just fine and yet he always appears (is seen) as fresh as a daisy (a lettuce). One problem, though (that, yes), he has a damn rotten (of the great violated one) temper, because he gives us tremendous tongue lashings.

URIEL   He's just like Virgil, remember? That guy (type) was an ace (had some incredible boards). Besides, he sure had a lot of guts (had his pants well-placed) when he defended us against (in front of) management. How he raised a fuss (armed scandals)!

MEMO   Man, this guy is a lot worse. He calls us all a bunch (ball) of bastards. If we haven't reached our sales target (expectation), he gets furious. He screams at us, "You're messing with me!" He insults us in the worst way ("mentions the mother" to us). And to every single one, he rips into us the same way: directors, managers, employees—everybody!

URIEL   Both men and women?

MEMO   No, of course not. There aren't any women at those levels in sales.

URIEL   It seems that things haven't changed that much, by damn!

MEMO   Right you are. (Well, you already see.) They sure haven't. (So it is.)

——————■——————

¡Ojo!

- **Cabrón** (or **Pinche cabrón**) is strong language and can be a very vulgar insult, but as is evident in the dialogue, it can also be used among friends for affection. (See *Vocabulary and Culture* in this chapter for explanation about the meaning of these and other strong terms.)

- **Recopado** is a term used currently in Argentina to describe a feeling of contentment. It probably derives from the word **copa,** which means *wine glass* and by extension *a drink (alcoholic)* and also refers to a gold cup or trophy (**la copa de oro**) won at certain sports events such as **El mundial** (The World Soccer Championship) so important in the Spanish-speaking world. To be **recopado(-a)** suggests plenitude, that your cup is full.

- **Che** is the universally recognized trademark of intimacy in Argentine and Uruguayan speech. It is used among friends, and roughly translates as *old buddy*. In a similar way, Mexican men use **cuate** (twin) or **'mano** (short for **hermano,** *brother*), and women use **'mana,** Cubans use **chico** or **chica,** Venezuelans, Ecuadorians, and Colombians use **pana** for both men and women, and Costa Rican men use **maje** (dummy).

- **Lo pasamos bomba** in Argentina means *to have a heck of a good time.* The word **bomba** means *bomb* or *pump* in standard Spanish. More universal ways of saying *we have a good time* are: **Lo pasamos bien, lo pasamos regio, pasamos un buen rato, nos divertimos mucho.**

- **Echar de menos** (literally, *to throw for less*) is the standard way of saying *to miss* (in the sense of feeling lonely for someone).

- **Muy especial** (very special) can be said instead of making a negative comment about another person.

- **Abusadísimo** (literally, *very abused*) is a compliment, meaning *very clever or sharp,* especially with reference to business. **Picudo** is also positive, but it refers to someone having good contacts or connections with powerful people. Both of these are **mexicanismos.**

- **Tener unas tablas** (boards) **increíbles** means to have all the requisite experience and skills for a particular job.

- **Tener los pantalones bien puestos** (to have his or her pants put on well) is a common way of saying *he (she) has a lot of guts or nerve.*

- **Fúrico** is used in Mexico, but in most other places they say **furioso**.

- **Chingar** is an innocuous word in some countries that just means *to rip or tear,* e.g., **El mantel está chingado** *(The tablecloth is torn)* and in Spain means to get sulky or to be in bad mood. However, it is a very strong and vulgar insult in Mexico. It means *to bother or harm* but with the strength of the "f" word in English. Curiously, the derivative expression **chingón** is a compliment meaning *extremely astute and effective.* (See *Vocabulary & Culture* in this chapter for more discussion on these terms.)

- **Mentar (ie) la madre** (to mention the mother) to someone is to insult him or her very badly. Simply the words **"tu madre"** are considered extremely provocative and aggressive. This is discussed in *Vocabulary & Culture* in this chapter.

- **Pues, ya ves** (literally, *Well, you already see*) means roughly that you're right, that you "got it" (have understood something).

VOCABULARIO DEL CAPÍTULO

abusado(-a), abusadísimo(-a)	sharp, clever (Mexico)
armar escándalo	to raise a fuss
el boludo	vulgar term for a lazy dope (Argentina)
el bondi	school bus (Argentina)
la botana	appetizers (Mexico)
el cabrón	bastard (male goat, vulgar)
el castellano	the Spanish language
el chico, la chica	friend (Cuba)

chingar	vulgar f-word in Mexico; to rip or tear (Argentina), to get sulky or bad-tempered (Spain)
chingón	extremely clever (Mexico)
¡Claro que sí! **¡Claro que no!**	Of course it is. Of course not.
la cochinada	(pig act) dirty trick
las coimas	bribes (Argentina, Uruguay)
la copa	wine glass, (alcoholic) drink, trophy
echar de menos	to miss (throw for less) someone or something far away
Es un problema mayúsculo.	It's a major (capital letter) problem.
Está por el suelo.	It's in the pits (down on the floor).
los huevones	vulgar term for *lazy dopes* (Chile, Mexico, Central America)
Lo pasamos bomba.	We have a good time (spend it bomb). (Argentina)
maje	(dummy) friend (male) (Costa Rica)
¿Mande?	What? Pardon me? (when you haven't understood) (Mexico)
Me hago bolas.	I get confused, mixed up (make balls to myself). (Mexico)
mentar la madre (ie)	(to mention the mother) to insult someone by inferring that his mother is not pure
la mordida	(bite) bribe (Mexico)
el Mundial	world soccer championship
No es lo mismo.	It's not the same.
pasa palos	(drink passers) appetizers (Venezuela)
los pendejos	kids (Argentina); vulgar for *jerks* (Mexico, Central America)
los pibes	kids, young people (Argentina)
las picadas	appetizers (Argentina)

picudo(-a)	well-connected and clever (Mexico)
¡Por supuesto!	Of course!
por parejo	equally
los porteños	people from Buenos Aires
pues, ya ves	well, you're right (you got it)
recopado(-a)	super, fantastic (filled with many trophies)
la regañada	scolding, bawling out
el soborno	bribe
tan fresco como una lechuga	as fresh as a daisy (lettuce)
las tapas	appetizers (Spain)
tener los pantalones bien puestos	to be brave, have guts (well-placed pants)
tener unas tablas increíbles	to have good preparation (boards) (Argentina)
Todo lo hacen por debajo de la mesa.	They do everything in a corrupt manner (under the table).

¡A USTED LE TOCA!

A. ¿Qué quiere decir? Match each word in boldface with its definition.

___ 1. **abusadísimo**

___ 2. **castellano**

___ 3. **¿cómo?**

___ 4. **pues, ya ves**

___ 5. **el Mundial**

___ 6. **porteño**

___ 7. **recopado**

___ 8. **soborno**

a. dinero pagado por favores

b. alguien que vive en Buenos Aires

c. muy listo para los negocios (mexicanismo)

d. el campeonato (*championship*) de fútbol

e. muy contento (argentinismo)

f. no comprendo lo que Ud. dijo

g. otra manera de decir "español"

h. has comprendido la situación

B. ¿Dónde estamos, en Argentina o en México? Put *A* or *M* in front of each statement to tell where it is being said. Then write a translation of the boldfaced words (in standard Spanish or English) in the blanks following them.

1. __ Los **pibes** (____) están en la escuela hasta las cuatro.
2. __ Ese policía está hablando mucho porque quiere una **mordida** (____).
3. __ ¡Ay, mi **cuate** (____)! Esos chistes son muy **pelados** (____).
4. __ Vamos, **che** (____). El **bondi** (____) ha llegado.
5. __ Nuestros hijos **lo pasan bomba** (____) con Uds.
6. __ Siempre **me hago bolas** (_____) con las calles de esta ciudad.
7. __ Espera, Conchita, te voy a preparar una deliciosa **botana** (____).
8. __ En la mesa hay bebidas y **picadas** (____) para todos.
9. __ ¿**Mande**? (____) ¿Puedes repetir lo que dijiste?
10. __ En ciertas oficinas los empleados buscan **coimas** (____).

C. Completar la frase. Complete the idioms in boldface with the appropriate word or phrase.

1. Mi primo es muy valiente. Tiene los pantalones _____.
2. Carlos está pasando el año en Sevilla. ¡Cómo **lo echo** _____!
3. Amigos, tenemos un problema enorme. **Es un problema** _____.
4. Hay una crisis económica. **La situación está** _____.
5. Acepto tu invitación. ¡**Por supuesto** _____!
6. Es necesario llamar la atención del público. Es necesario **armar** _____.
7. Nélida tiene mucha energía. Tiene dos trabajos pero siempre parece **tan fresca** _____.
8. Héctor va a ser un jefe magnífico. **Tiene unas tablas** _____.
9. Esos congresistas no son honestos. **Todo lo hacen** _____.

D. ¡Insultos y palabrotas! (Insults and Swear Words) Choose the best way to finish each statement.

1. In many Spanish-speaking countries, one of the worst insults is to **mentar**
   a. **el padre**
   b. **la madre**

c. **el suelo**

d. **la copa**

2. Although the word **pinche** only means *kitchen helper* in Spain and certain other countries, it is a strong swear word in

a. **Argentina**

b. **Ecuador**

c. **México**

d. **Venezuela**

3. A word that is a strong insult in Mexico and Central America is **pendejos,** but in Argentina, it simply means

a. **actores**

b. **niños**

c. **trabajadores**

d. **doctores**

4. On the other hand, a vulgar word in Argentina that is not bad in Mexico is

a. **bondi**

b. **pelado**

c. **coimas**

d. **bolas**

5. A common verb that in Spain means *to take* or *to catch* but in several regions in Latin America is very vulgar is

a. **coger**

b. **mandar**

c. **tomar**

d. **recibir**

E. Reacciones. React to the following situations in Spanish, using expressions from this chapter.

1. An announcement has just been made that government officials have mismanaged the state pension fund and most of the money is gone.

_____

_____

2. Your friend asks you what your angry boss says at the sales meeting.

_____

_____

3. An old friend comes over and greets a male friend with some colorful language to show affection.

_____

_____

Vocabulary and Culture

The Varying Uses of Spanish Swear Words

Just as in English, most swear words in Spanish have multiple uses. Indeed, in many parts of the Hispanic world, swearing has been developed to such an expressive degree that its skillful use can be described as challenging or poetic. Only a few highlights of this vast topic will be presented here, relating to Latin America, and on page 238, relating to Spain.

Swear words are variously used as ironic metaphors of affection, offensive insults, general terms of condemnation, or simply as a way of letting off steam, depending on the circumstances. A Mexican woman may start out a conversation with her sister or best friend like this: **¿Qué tal, pendejita?** Close male friends who have been separated for years (or hours) may greet each other with: **¡Pinche cabrón!** (Mexico), **¡Boludo!** (Argentina), or **¡Huevón!** (Chile), to name just a few possibilities. These terms must be used with care, for they can be vulgar in many circumstances. Shouted to a passing driver on the street or addressed to a stranger in a bar, they could provoke a fight and even lead to serious consequences.

Swearing by What We Hold Most Sacred   Swear words are commonly called **groserías** or **palabrotas (palabra** + augmentative ending **-ota,** literally, *big heavy words*) in Spanish, although they are known by other names too: **garabatos** (graffiti terms) in Chile and **lisuras** (smoothies) in Peru. They are powerful words that pack a wallop and perhaps that is the explanation of their contradictory usage: at times of strong emotion, either negative or positive, people call on these terms to make an impression. The designation *swear words* in English can be explained by recalling that traditionally we *swear* by what we consider most sacred—on the Bible, the Koran, or on our mother's grave. Therefore, these same objects relating to religion, parentage, our body, or sex are also potent ways to insult someone if we really want to offend.

Female Relatives and Sex   Female relatives are a sacred topic in most cultures. The simple words **¡Tu madre!** (Your mother!) are extremely insulting in many countries, where this usage is referred to as **mentar la madre** (mentioning the mother). The phrase implies a calling into question of your mother's "honor." The insinuation is expressed directly in the complete phrase, **tu puta madre,** since the word **puta** means *whore.* This insult dates from medieval times, when the very worst thing to be was "illegitimate," and by impugning the honor of someone's mother, you inferred he or she was a bastard, an **hijo(-a) de puta.** Nowadays, in more enlightened times, these expressions retain their force in most contexts, but, as illustrated in the dialogues, they are also used in a joking or affectionate way among friends. Sex in general is considered sacred, and so the verb expressing the sexual act is powerful and can also express the worst abuse. Of course, this word (the famous "f" word in English) varies depending on the particular region under discussion. Common ones include the following: **joder** (in most places, although in some countries this word often means simply *to bother* or *annoy*), **chingar** (Mexico), **coger** (many parts of Latin America, but in Spain and some other places this verb just means *to take or catch*).

Words relating to religion are also employed in swearing, but this usage is very developed in Spain and so is discussed on pages 239 and 240.

The Expressive Power of Body Parts   Parts of the body, especially the sensitive ones, are expletives in Spanish, used as an outlet for strong emotions such as surprise, displeasure, frustration, or even affection. The most universal ones are **coño** (with many variations) for the female organ, and **verga** and **carajo** for the male part. These words are commonly used as expletives but are vulgar, being roughly equivalent to *God dammit!* or *Oh, f . . . !* There is also a great variety of terms for testicles, said in many expressive or insulting ways. These are referred to as **huevos** (eggs) in Mexico (with the feminine variant, **huevas,** in Chile), **bolas** or **pelotas** (balls) in Argentina and Uruguay, and **cojones** in Spain and other places. (See page 239.) Insulting terms built from these words abound. They usually imply that a person possesses these appendages in such a large and weighty form that he or she (yes, they also apply to women) has been rendered completely useless and incompetent. **Huevón** in Mexico and Chile, and **boludo** in Argentina and Uruguay, are examples. The stupid things done by such people are referred to as **huevadas** or **boludeces**.

Bathroom Talk   Of course, a number of bathroom expressions also form part of Spanish swearing, just as they do in English. **¡Mierda!** (Shit) is a common expletive and **Vete a la mierda** (Go to shit) is roughly the equivalent of the English phrase, *Go to hell!* The verb for this is **cagar,** and it is often used for *to make a mistake,* e.g., **Cagué en la entrevista** (I messed up in the interview) or *to treat someone very badly,* e.g., **Esos malvados me cagaron** (Those nasty guys messed me up).

Euphemisms to the Rescue!   If you need to vent rage or frustration and don't want to offend, the best recourse is to use a euphemism, one of those expressive little words or phrases that almost—but doesn't quite—say anything vulgar. In English you might say *Darn!* or *Shoot!* (instead of *Damn!* or *Shit!*). In Spanish you can say **¡Caramba!** or **¡Caray!** (instead of **¡Carajo!**), **¡La pucha!** (instead of **¡La puta!**) or **¡Miércoles!,** *Wednesday!* (instead of **¡Mierda!**).

Selecciones. Choose the correct option to finish each statement.

    1. In Peru, a synonym for **palabrotas** is
        a. **malvadas**
        b. **garabatos**
        c. **lisuras**
        d. **negativos**

2. Most swear words relate to what we hold sacred, like religion, parents, body parts, and
    a. male relatives
    b. female relatives
    c. work
    d. money

3. If your Venezuelan friend says to you, **"No me jodas,"** it means
    a. he is insulting you
    b. he is very angry
    c. he doesn't want to be bothered
    d. he doesn't want to see you anymore

4. If a Chilean talks about **huevadas,** he means
    a. favors bought with money
    b. really stupid actions
    c. big parties
    d. a potato omelet

5. If you stub your toe and want a euphemism to use as an expletive, you can say
    a. ¡Lunes!
    b. ¡Martes!
    c. ¡Miércoles!
    d. ¡Jueves!

Some Words Used Differently in Mexico and Argentina

Word	Mexico	Argentina
bomba	pump	pump, fun (*pasarlo bomba*)
camión	bus	truck
chocho	old	happy
forro	gorgeous woman	condom
hacerse bolas	to get confused	(vulgar, refers to testicles)
pendejos	dopes (vulgar)	children
seco	dry, dull (person)	dry, poor (with no money)
torta	sandwich	cake

1.c 2.b 3.c 4.b 5.c

Objects with Different Words in Mexico and Argentina

English	Mexican	Argentine
appetizers	botanas	picadas
bedroom slippers	pantuflas	chinelas
blanket	cobija	frazada
children	chavos	pibes, pendejos
dislike	No me cae bien.	No me banca.
refrigerator	heladera	nevera
fun, to have fun	pasarlo bien	pasarlo bomba
hypocrite	hipócrita	persona que tiene caretos
pen	pluma, bolígrafo	virome, lapicera
"pick up" (someone)	ligarse a	levantarse a
soft drink	refresco	gaseosa
strawberry	fresa	frutilla
subway	metro	subte
terrific	de pelos	recopado
waiter	mesero	mozo

Chistes

Un malentendido regional: ¡Ud. tiene que lavar los trastes!

Una señora mexicana se casó con un porteño y se fue a vivir a Buenos Aires, donde encontraba algunas dificultades con las diferencias lingüísticas. Un día llamó a la mucama y le empezó a explicar las tareas que tuviera que hacer en la casa.

> —Por la tarde—dijo—debe limpiar la mesa después de la comida y luego, Ud. tiene que lavar los trastes.

> La mucama por poco se desmaya y le responde—Está bien, señora, se lo hago a Ud. y a las niñas, ¡pero al señor, no!

A REGIONAL MISUNDERSTANDING:
YOU HAVE TO WASH THE DISHES (BUTTOCKS)!

A Mexican lady married a man from Buenos Aires and went to live in that city, where she encountered some problems with linguistic differences. One day she called the maid and began to explain the tasks that she would have to do in the house. "In the evening," she said, "You should clean the table after dinner and then you have to wash the dishes." (In Mexico **trastes** means *dishes, pots and pans,* but in Argentina it means *bottom* or *buttocks.*) The maid almost fainted and replied, "All right, ma'am, I'll do it for you and the girls, but *not* for the mister!"

———■———

EL PRESIDENTE Y EL PAN ESTADOUNIDENSE

Hace unos años, los mexicanos tenían un presidente que muchos tenían por cobarde. Entonces se circulaba una adivinanza popular:

— ¿Por qué es el presidente como el pan estadounidense?

— Porque es blando, cuadrado y, ¡no tiene huevos!

THE PRESIDENT AND AMERICAN BREAD

Some years ago, the Mexicans had a president who many took for a coward. At that time a popular riddle went around:

— Why is the president like American bread?

— Because he's soft, square, and—he doesn't have eggs (balls)!

REPASO 2

Review of Chapters 6–10

(50 points)

A. Crucigrama. Solve the following crossword puzzle. (1–13)

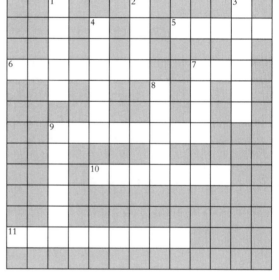

Horizontal:

5. niños, jóvenes (Argentina)
6. salvadoreño
7. amigo(-a) en Argentina o Uruguay; ¡Hola, ____!
9. bajo, no alto
10. come mucho
11. joven inocente, no muy activo(-a) socialmente (Ecuador, Venezuela, Colombia)

Vertical:

1. en México se dice "botana", en Argentina se dice "picadas" y en España, se dice ____
2. costarricense
3. ____ el bote, bailar
4. bebé (Ecuador, Chile); autobús (el Caribe)
7. muy inteligente
8. demasiado sentimental
9. guatemalteco

B. ¿Qué podemos decir de mis amigos y yo? What can we say about my friends and me? Many things. Match each Spanish description to the correct English meaning. (Two English meanings will not be used.)

__ 14. **Tiramos mucho arroz.**

__ 15. **No montamos cotorreos.**

__ 16. **Somos un poco mandones.**

__ 17. **No escuchamos chismorreos.**

__ 18. **Tenemos mucha suerte.**

__ 19. **Echamos muchas flores.**

__ 20. **Nos gusta menear el bote.**

__ 21. **Salimos hasta en la sopa.**

__ 22. **Llamamos por cobrar.**

__ 23. **Somos un poco dormilones.**

__ 24. **A veces decimos groserías.**

a. We give a lot of compliments.

b. We don't listen to gossip.

c. You see us (we turn up) everywhere.

d. We sometimes use swear words.

e. We don't start gab sessions.

f. We criticize a lot.

g. We are somewhat like sleepy-heads.

h. We are hard to get rid of.

i. We call collect.

j. We are moving forward.

k. We are a little bit bossy.

l. We are very lucky.

m. We like to dance (rock the boat).

C. La terminación perfecta. Find the right word from the list to end each sentence. (Two words will not be used.)

lechuga	cuernos	chicle	oreja	revueltos
piola	enojona	medias	partido	baraja
menos	olla	asustón	alma	

25. ¡Qué gusto de verte! Te invitamos a comer a la suerte de la

_____.

26. Tengo mucho sueño. Voy a planchar la _____.

27. Los señores Méndez han perdido mucho dinero. Lo pasan _____.

28. ¡Qué actor más guapo! Se me caen las _____.

29. El doctor Benton tiene amantes. Le pone los _____ a su esposa.

30. Eduardo desapareció. Es el as de la _____.

31. Debes casarte con Humberto, m'ija. Es un buen _____.

32. Mira a la señora Gálvez, ¿no parece tan fresca como una _____?

33. Juan y Anita son sólo amigos, juntos pero no _____.

34. Paquito tiene miedo de todo. ¡Qué _____!

35. Norma y yo nos llevamos bien. Somos amigas del _____.

36. Ahora vivimos lejos de México y lo echamos de _____.

D. Palabras revueltas. Unscramble the words and write the Spanish expressions from the list that are hidden in the mixed-up letters. Two expressions from the list will not be used.

chapada a la antigua   echan mucho relajo
de los pies a la cabeza   juega para el otro equipo
ponte las pilas   se comió la torta antes de la fiesta
es un comelibros   tiene los pantalones bien puestos

37. Martín is always reading. [se nu locrimsebo] ¡ _____!
38. Simón is not afraid of anything. His friends say:
    [neite sol laptanones nieb sotusep] ¡ _____!
39. Tania is a little old-fashioned. She is [apadach a al tugania]

    _____ .

40. Alejandro doesn't like to date women. He . . . [gueja rapa le roto
    ipoque] _____ .
41. Oops! Amalia and her husband just had a baby four months after
    their wedding. It looks as though . . . [es ocimó al ratot nesta ed
    al estifa] _____ .
42. It's time to get going: [nopet sla lisap] _____ .

E. Pero, ¿qué querrán decirme? Choose the correct meaning for the following Spanish words or expressions.

43. A lady walks by, all decked out with lots of jewelry and finery, and
    someone says: **"Si se quema la casa . . ."**
    a. There's a big problem here.
    b. She's wearing everything she owns.
    c. She isn't very generous to others.

44. A Mexican friend refers to his fax machine as **esa pinche
    máquina** and you know he means that his fax machine is . . .
    a. reliable
    b. dreadful
    c. fantastic

45. An employee warns his boss he is going to **sacar los trapos al sol** about the bribe situation. What's he going to do?

    a. spill the beans

    b. keep quiet

    c. quit his job

46. A friend is going to introduce you to her **veteranos.** You will meet her . . .

    a. classmates

    b. cousins

    c. parents

47. In Central America, a person who is **bolo** is someone who . . .

    a. is drunk

    b. cheats at cards

    c. has good luck

48. A man tells you he is a **zapallo,** so you know he is from . . .

    a. Venezuela

    b. Lima

    c. Guatemala

49. A buddy comes up to you and says, **"¡Chócala!"** which means you ought to . . .

    a. eat chocolate

    b. shake or hit hands

    c. tell your story

50. A man who is **orejón** . . .

    a. gets mad easily

    b. has big ears

    c. talks all the time

. CAPÍTULO 11 .

¡*Déjate de cuentos!*

EXPRESSING DISAGREEMENT

▌ CONVERSACIÓN 1

*María Carmen, una chica venezolana, **surfea** la Red y se encuentra en un **cuar-to de discusión** sobre el cine. El tema es el director español Pedro Almodóvar. José es de Venezuela también y Juan es de Honduras.*

JUAN   ¿Han visto *Mujeres al borde de un ataque de nervios?* Es una película vieja pero estupenda. Almodóvar es un genio.

JOSÉ   Un genio loco, quizás. Para mí sus películas son morbosas y neuróticas. *Kika,* por ejemplo. **¡Qué tonterías! Puras vainas, sin ton ni son.**

JUAN   **¿Se te cruzaron los cables?** Es una película muy buena, muy optimista.

JOSÉ   ¿Optimista? ¿En qué forma? Es violentísima.

JUAN   Pues, es verdad que Kika sufre toda clase de horrores, pero nunca pierde su inocencia, su optimismo . . . Y es muy chistoso el diálogo.

¿SE TE CRUZARON LOS CABLES?

María Carmen, a Venezuelan girl, is surfing the Net and finds herself in a chatroom about the movies. The theme is the Spanish director Pedro Almodóvar. José is also from Venezuela and Juan is from Honduras.

JUAN   Have you seen *Women on the Verge of a Nervous Breakdown*? It's an old movie, but it's great. Almodóvar is a genius.

JOSÉ   A crazy genius maybe. To me his movies are morbid and neurotic. *Kika*, for example. What foolishness! Complete nonsense (Pure husks), without rhyme or reason (without tone or sound).

JUAN   Are you crazy? (Did your cables get crossed?) It's a very good movie, very optimistic.

JOSÉ   Optimistic? In what way? It's very violent.

JUAN   Well, it's true that Kika suffers all kinds of horrors, but she never loses her innocence, her optimism. And the dialogue is very funny.

JOSÉ   ¿Chistoso? **¡Qué ridículo!** Es un diálogo muy pesado, sin gracia.

MARÍA   Chicos, **basta ya.** A mí me gustaría cambiar de tema porque vi
CARMEN   una película buenísima anoche, de María Luisa Bemberg . . .

JUAN   Está bien. **Me sacaste de onda,** José. Mira, **ciberamigo, en
un ratito** te voy a **emailear** una crítica de las películas de
Almodóvar que encontré en la Red y vas a ver lo popular que
son en todas partes.

—————◼—————

¡Ojo!

- **Surfear la Red (Internet)** is becoming a common pastime
  among Hispanics as it is with other groups. (The word **navegar**
  is also used, *to navigate*.) The slang terminology involved is heavily anglicized, as in many other parts of the world; for instance:
  hacer un download, hacer un backup, cliquear en *(to click
  on),* **el mouse, el CD-ROM,** etc.

- **¡Puras vainas!** The word **vaina** means *case* or *husk* but figura-
  tively means *problem, bother,* or *nonsense.* In Colombia, people say
  ¡Pura chepa! or **¡Pura leche!** In Venezuela, **vaina** often just
  means *thing.*

- **Sin ton ni son** means *without tone or sound.* Also used: **No tiene
  pies ni cabeza,** *It has neither feet nor head*—that is, one can
  make no sense of it.

CONVERSACIÓN 2

En una tienda de aparatos electrónicos en Caracas, Venezuela.

JUAN   Mire ese televisor. A ver, ¿cuánto vale?

JOSEFINA   **Vaya uno a saber.** Ya tenemos televisor.

JUAN   Pero no como éste, con pantalla grande.

JOSÉ	Funny? How ridiculous! It's a very boring (heavy) dialogue, with no wit (grace).
MARÍA CARMEN	Guys, enough already. I'd like to change the subject because I saw a very good movie last night, by María Luisa Bemberg . . .
JUAN	All right. You knocked me out of kilter (took me out of my sound wave), José. Look, cyberfriend, in a little while I'm going to e-mail you a review of Almodóvar's movies that I found on the Net and you'll see how popular they are everywhere.

———◼———

- **¿Se te cruzaron los cables?** *Are you crazy? (Did your cables get crossed?)* Another example: **Se me cruzaron los cables con tanto trabajar.** *So much work made me crazy.*

- **Me sacaste de onda:** *You took me out of my sound wave*—that is, upset me in some way. In Venezuela or Ecuador, one might hear **Me cortaste la nota** (You cut off my news or note).

- **En un ratito: un rato** is *a time, a while;* the diminutive **un ratito** means *a short time.*

- **Emailear** is pronounced with the English sounds of *e-mail.* **Mandar por correo electrónico** is the standard Spanish term. An *e-mail address* is **una dirección electrónica** (or **una casilla electrónica**). Also common is **faxear, el fax.**

In an electronics store in Caracas, Venezuela.

JUAN	Look at that TV set. Let's see—how much does it cost?
JOSEFINA	Who knows? (How is one going to know . . .) We already have a TV set.
JUAN	But not like this one, with a big screen.

JOSEFINA   El que tenemos funciona bien, Juan.

JUAN   **No hablas en serio,** ¿verda'? Ese aparato ni tiene control remoto . . .

JOSEFINA   Vámonos Juan, que quiero mirar los **CD-ROMs** para los niños. No necesitamos otro televisor.

JUAN   Un momento . . . ¿dónde diablos puse mis tarjetas de crédito? Cariño, ¿me prestas tu tarjeta Visa?

JOSEFINA   **Ni a la fuerza,** hombre. **Ni hablar.**

JUAN   Josefina, préstame tu tarjeta. Tendré que volver aquí mañana si no. Necesitamos otro televisor . . . el que tenemos **no sirve.**

JOSEFINA   **Déjate de cuentos,** Juan. Si tú crees que yo voy a comprar este televisor, **¡estás soñando con pájaros preñados!**

———————■———————

¡Ojo!

- **Vaya uno a saber:** also, **A saber** or **Sabe Dios,** *God knows.*

- **Ni a la fuerza:** The expression **a la fuerza** (literally, *by force, against my will*) is very common: **Tuve que acompañarlos a la fuerza.** *I had to go with them even though I didn't want to (feel like it).* Alternative expressions for **Ni a la fuerza** are: **Ni a palos,** *Not even with blows;* **Ni loco(-a),** *Not even crazy,* and, in Venezuela, **Ni de vaina.** A similar expression with a more general meaning is **¡Naranjas!** *No!,* used in many parts of Latin America. In Spain, people sometimes say **¡Naranjas de la China!**

- **Déjate de cuentos:** also, **Ya está bien de cuentos,** *Enough stories.*

JOSEFINA   The one we have works fine, Juan.

JUAN   You're not serious, are you? That thing (apparatus) doesn't even have a remote control . . . .

JOSEFINA   Let's go, Juan, I want to look at CD-ROMs for the kids. We don't need another TV.

JUAN   Just a minute . . . . Where in the devil did I put my credit cards? Sweetheart (Affection), will you lend me your Visa card?

JOSEFINA   Not on your life (Not even by force). Don't even think (talk) about it.

JUAN   Josefina, lend me your card. I'll have to come back here tomorrow if you don't. We need another TV . . . the one we have is no good (doesn't serve).

JOSEFINA   Enough of your stories (Stop with your stories), Juan! If you think that I'm going to buy this television set, you're crazy (dreaming of pregnant birds)!

————■————

CHISTES

¡QUÉ ANTIPÁTICO!

Un tipo muy **antipático** está de visita en Ecuador, y va a la Catedral de Quito a visitar la tumba del general Antonio José de Sucre, líder revolucionario en la Guerra de Independencia.* Allí hay un guía que lo explica todo:

—Y éste es el gorro que Sucre usó en la batalla de Pichincha.

———

*Sucre, born in Venezuela, became the first president of the Republic of Bolivia; the Battle of Pichincha liberated Ecuador from Spain in 1822 in the War of Independence.

—**¡Qué va!** No tenía gorro Sucre—dice el hombre.

—Y éste es el sable que Sucre usó en la batalla de Pichincha.

—**¡Pura paja!** No tenía sable Sucre.

—Y éste es el poncho que Sucre usó cuando cruzó los Andes.

—**No juegue,** chico, que Sucre no tenía poncho.

Y así molesta el hombre durante todo el tur . . . hasta que llegan a la tumba de Sucre.

—Y éstas son las cenizas de Sucre . . .

—**No voy a tragarme esa guayaba,** que no fumaba pa' nada Sucre.

HOW DISAGREEABLE!

A very disagreeable fellow is visiting Ecuador, and he goes to the Cathedral of Quito to visit the tomb of General Antonio José de Sucre, a revolutionary leader in the War of Independence. A guide is explaining everything there:

"And this is the cap that Sucre used in the battle of Pichincha."

"Oh, come on! Sucre didn't have a cap," says the fellow.

"And this is the saber that Sucre used in the battle of Pichincha."

"Hogwash! (Pure straw!) Sucre didn't have a saber."

"And this is the poncho that Sucre used when he crossed the Andes."

"Don't kid around (play), Sucre didn't have a poncho."

And so the fellow annoys people during the entire tour . . . until they arrive at Sucre's tomb.

"And these are Sucre's ashes . . . ."

"I'm not swallowing that one (that guava)! Sucre didn't smoke."

¡Ojo!

- **¡Qué va!** is very common, meaning *Oh, come on!*
- **¡Pura paja!** means literally, *Pure straw!*
- **Una guayaba** is a guava, a tropical fruit.

———————■———————

EL MENDIGO

Un **maestro** va caminando por una calle de Madrid cuando **se topa con** un mendigo.

—¡Una limosnita, por el amor de Dios!

—De seguro la querrás para ir a beber.

—**De ninguna manera,** señor, yo no bebo.

—Entonces para ir a malgastar con las mujeres, **donde te dicen** *hijito* **sin conocerte.**

—**Al contrario,** señor, yo no hago eso.

—Entonces para ir a **jugarte la pasta.**

—Tampoco, señor. ¡Yo soy un tipo honrado!

—Pues vente a mi casa. ¡Le voy a enseñar a mi **jefa** cómo acaba un hombre honrado!

THE BEGGAR

A fellow is walking down a street in Madrid when he comes across a beggar.

"Alms, for the love of God!"

"You probably want it to go drinking."

"No way, sir, I don't drink."

"Then to waste on women, at the bordellos (where they call you *my son* without knowing who you are)."

infame canalla *disgusting (infamous) pig*

"On the contrary, sir, I don't do that."

"Then to gamble (bet your money) with."

"Not that either, sir. I'm an honorable man!"

"Then come home with me. I'm going to show the missus (my boss) how an honorable man ends up."

¡Ojo!

- A **maestro(-a)** is a *master* or, commonly, a *schoolteacher,* but a **maestro** can refer to any older (adult) person.

- **Toparse con** is *to bump into or come across.* **Topar** can also mean to end in: **Esa calle topa con el parque.**

- **Donde te dicen** *hijito* **sin conocerte** (where they call you *my son* without knowing you) refers to a **burdel** (bordello, house of prostitution).

- **Jugar** is the common word for *to gamble* as well as *to play*. In Spain, **la pasta** is slang for *money*. **Chiviar,** *to gamble with dice,* is a slang term used in Mexico and Central America.

- **Mi jefa:** There are various slang words for one's spouse; two common ones are **jefe (jefa)** and **viejo (vieja). Mi viejo(-a)** can be used whether the spouse is young or old and is not as pejorative as "my old man (lady)."

VOCABULARIO DEL CAPÍTULO

al contrario	on the contrary
antipático(-a)	disagreeable, unpleasant
¡Basta ya!	Enough already! That's enough!
el CD-ROM	CD-ROM
el ciberamigo, la ciberamiga	cyberfriend
chiviar	to gamble, play dice (Mexico, Central America)
cliquear	to click (e.g., on a computer mouse)
el cuarto de discusión	chat room
de ninguna manera	no way, in no manner
Déjate de cuentos. (Ya está bien de cuentos.)	Enough of your stories.
la dirección (casilla) electrónica	e-mail address
donde te dicen *hijito* **sin conocerte**	(where they call you *my son* without knowing you) bordello
emailear; el email	to e-mail; e-mail
faxear; el fax	to fax; fax

hacer un download o un backup	to download or back up
el jefe (la jefa)	(boss) husband (wife)
jugar to bet; **jugarse la pasta**	to bet one's money (paste) (Spain)
el maestro	(teacher, master) middle-aged or older man, guy
Me sacaste de onda.	You knocked me out of kilter, threw me off. Also: **Me cortaste la nota.** (You cut off my note.)
el mouse	mouse (computer)
¡Naranjas!	(Oranges!) No!
Ni a la fuerza.	(Not even by force.) Not on your life. No way.
Ni a palos.	(Not even with blows of a stick.) No way.
Ni loco(-a).	(Not even crazy.) No way.
Ni hablar.	Don't even think (talk) about it.
¡No habla(s) en serio!	You're not serious (talking seriously)!
No juegue (usted). No juegues (tú).	Don't play around.
No sirve.	It's no good. It doesn't work (serve).
No tiene pies ni cabeza.	(It has neither feet nor a head.) It makes no sense.
No voy a tragarme esa guayaba.	I'm not going to swallow that nonsense (guava).
Pura paja.	(Pure straw.) Complete nonsense.
Puras vainas.	(Pure husks.) Complete nonsense.
Puros disparates.	Complete nonsense.
¡Qué invente!	Bologna!
¡Qué ridículo!	How ridiculous!
¡Qué tontería(s)!	What nonsense!
¡Qué va!	Oh, come on!
ratito: en un ratito	in a little while

Sabe Dios.	God knows.
¿Se te cruzaron los cables?	(Did your cables get crossed?) Are you crazy?
sin ton ni son	(without tone or sound) without rhyme or reason
soñar (ue) con pájaros preñados	(to dream of pregnant birds) to be crazy, thinking of the impossible
surfear la Red (Internet)	to surf the Net
toparse con	to bump into, run into, come across
Vaya uno a saber. A saber.	Who knows?
la vieja	(old woman) wife, girlfriend
el viejo	(old man) husband, boyfriend

¡A USTED LE TOCA!

A. Al contrario. Disagree, using an expression with an opposite meaning. There may be more than one possibility.

1. ¡Qué simpático! —Al contrario, es muy _____.
2. De alguna manera vas a ir, ¿verdad? —No, no voy a ir _____.
3. Es muy lógico, ¿no? —¿Cómo que lógico? Sin _____.
4. Lo vas a ayudar, ¿no? —¿Yo? No lo ayudo ni _____.
5. Habla en broma *(joking)* siempre. —Pero esta vez habla _____.
6. No es urgente mandar ese fax, ¿verdad? Lo haremos mañana. —No, prometí que lo mandaríamos en un _____.
7. Todavía funciona bien ese televisor, ¿no? —¿Éste? No, no _____ para nada.

B. En otras palabras. Julia and Eduardo are trying to decide what to watch on TV. Replace the underlined words in their conversation with synonyms. Choose from the following.

naranjas	**sabe Dios**	**ni hablar**
no tiene pies ni cabeza	**maestro**	**se me van a cruzar los cables**
	puras vainas	

JULIA
(*entrando*)
¿Qué pasa, Eduardo? Ese programa, ¿qué es?

EDUARDO
Se llama *Invasión de los tomates gigantes.*

JULIA
¿Cómo? ¿Hablas en serio?

EDUARDO
Lo estaba viendo, pero en realidad <u>es ridículo</u> (1). <u>Puros disparates.</u> (2) Tú, ¿qué quieres ver?

JULIA
No sé.

EDUARDO
Sale la película *Drácula* ahora. Es buenísima.

JULIA
¿Buenísima? Es muy larga. Si paso dos horas viendo esa tontería, <u>me voy a volver loca</u> (3). *(leyendo del periódico)* ¿Qué tal esta biografía de Friedrich Nietzche? ¿Te interesa?

EDUARDO
<u>¡No!</u> (4) <u>De ninguna manera.</u> (5)

JULIA
Okei, okei. Pues aquí dice que sale un programa que se llama *Colombo.*

EDUARDO
¿De qué se trata? *(What is it about?)*

JULIA
<u>A saber.</u> (6) Creo que trata de un <u>señor</u> (7) que es detective.

EDUARDO
Bueno, vamos a verlo.

C. Cognados. ¿Cómo se dice . . . ?

1. to surf _____

2. to click _____

3. to fax _____

4. to e-mail _____

5. to download _____

6. to make a back up _____

D. ¡Falta algo! Complete the expressions on the left, then match them to their English equivalents on the right.

___1. ¡Estás soñando con _____
   preñados!

___2. De vez en cuando me _____
   con Enrique en el Café Sol.

___3. ¡Qué va! No voy a _____me
   esa guayaba.

___4. ¡ _____ ya! Déjate de cuentos.

___5. Lo siento, pero me sacaste
   de _____ .

___6. No voy a _____me la pasta
   en eso.

a. I'm sorry, but you rattled me
   (knocked me out of kilter).

b. Oh, come on! I'm not swallowing that one.

c. That's enough! Stop with your
   stories.

d. I'm not going to bet on that.

e. You're crazy!

f. From time to time I bump into
   Enrique in the Café Sol.

E. Responda, por favor. React to the following, using different expressions from this chapter.

1. El mundo es plano *(flat).*   _____

2. El gobierno de este país es
   perfecto.   _____

3. Batman es una verdadera
   persona.   _____

4. Las vacas vuelan *(fly).*   _____

Cuente usted conmigo

....

GIVING ENCOURAGEMENT, ADVICE, AND EMOTIONAL SUPPORT
•
EXPRESSING SYMPATHY

| CONVERSACIÓN 1

Dos estudiantes "ticos" de la universidad de Costa Rica comen **"casados"** *en una* **"soda"** *de San José.*

NIDIA . . . unas vacaciones estupendas. **¡Pura vida!** Y después me acosté y dormí **a lo chancho chingo.**

JUAN ANTONIO Y yo **no pegué los ojos en toda la noche.**

NIDIA Juan, ¿qué le pasa? Pensaba que algo andaba mal. Ud. parece **más serio que un burro en lancha.**

JUAN ANTONIO La verdad es que me dejó Irene sin avisarme ni nada, **¿diay?**

NIDIA ¡Qué mala nota!

JUAN ANTONIO Y me siento fatal, abandonado, como si estuviera **en un callejón sin salida.**

MÁS SERIO QUE BURRO EN LANCHA.

Two "Tico" students from the University of Costa Rica are eating a dish called "married people" in a cafe (soda) in San José.

NIDIA   . . . a wonderful vacation. Superfantastic! (Pure life!) And afterward I went to bed and slept like a rock (like a long-tailed pig).

JUAN ANTONIO   And I couldn't sleep a wink the whole night.

NIDIA   Juan, what's the matter (what's happening to you)? I thought something was wrong (was walking badly). You really look down (more serious than a donkey in a rowboat).

JUAN ANTONIO   The truth is that Irene left me without telling me in advance or anything. Ay, but what can be done?

NIDIA   What an awful thing to do! (What bad news!)

JUAN ANTONIO   And I feel lousy (fatal), abandoned, as if I were at the end of my rope (on a dead-end street).

NIDIA   ¡Hombre, **no es para tanto! Se le fue la pajarita,** ¿y qué? **Al mal tiempo, buena cara.** Ya conocerá a otra chica, una buena chica que lo sepa apreciar . . .

JUAN ANTONIO   ¡Eso será **cuando la rana eche pelos!** Soy **más feo que mandado a hacer.**

NIDIA   No diga eso. Ud. es inteligente y **resimpático** y está sobresaliendo en sus estudios . . .

JUAN ANTONIO   Por eso precisamente me dejó mi amorcito. Dijo que trabajo demasiado y yo le respondí que ella no trabaja lo suficiente. Luego, **se armó la gorda.** Y ahora **paso las noches en vela,** llorando y dejando mensajes en el contestador de la mamá de Irene. **¡Qué perra vida!**

NIDIA   Ánimo, amigo. Ud. vale mucho. Todo va a mejorar. Ya verá. **Cuente Ud. conmigo.**

————■————

¡Ojo!

- **Cuente Ud. conmigo** Count on (with) me. Many Spanish expressions are similar to English ones except for slight differences in the prepositions or adverbs. Another example is *to depend on* which in Spanish is used with **de** (of) instead of *on:* **Jorge depende de su familia.** George depends on his family.

- **Ticos** is the popular term for Costa Ricans. It may derive from their frequent use of **-ico** (instead of **-ito**) for a diminutive ending for words with the stem ending in *t,* e.g, **¡Un momentico, por favor!** (Just a little moment, please!)

- A **casado** (married person) is a typical Costa Rican dish of rice, beans, meat or fish, and salad, and perhaps derives its name because all these foods are combined or "married" together on one plate.

- **Sodas** are Costa Rican cafés that offer daily specials at very reasonable prices and usually without charging tax.

NIDIA   Man, things aren't that bad (it's not for so much)! Your sweetie flew the coop (your little bird left you) and so what? When the going gets tough, the tough get going (to bad weather, a good face). You'll soon meet another girl, a good girl who will know how to appreciate you . . .

JUAN ANTONIO   It'll be a cold day in July when that happens (that will be when the frog grows hair). I'm as ugly as a toad (than if I'd been designed for the purpose of being ugly).

NIDIA   Don't say that. You are intelligent and very charming ("re-empathetic") and you are doing very well (coming out above) in your studies.

JUAN ANTONIO   That's exactly why my sweetie pie (little love) left me. She said I work too much, and I said she doesn't work enough. Then there was a big blowup (the fat one got armed). And now I spend my nights awake (on watch), crying and leaving messages on Irene's mother's answering machine. What a crummy (dog's) life!

NIDIA   Courage, my friend. You are a wonderful person (you are worth a lot). Everything's going to get better. You'll see. Count on me.

———■———

- **¡Pura vida!** is probably the most famous *"tiquismo"* and is the Costa Rican standard sign of approval ("super, great, cool"), the equivalent of **chévere** in the Caribbean and other parts of Latin America.

- **¿Diay?** is a *tiquismo* that expresses a sort of fatalistic acceptance of bad times, rather like: *"Ay, but what else can you expect?"*

ESO SERÁ CUANDO LA RANA ECHE PELOS.

- **En un callejón sin salida** literally means *in an alley with no way out* and is a common way to express the feeling of hopelessness.

- **Al mal tiempo, buena cara** is an example of the many proverbs commonly quoted in everyday speech by Costa Ricans.

Since the word **tiempo** means *time* as well as *weather,* it applies to many occasions.

- **Más feo que mandado a hacer** suggests that someone or something is uglier than if he or it had been designed for the very purpose of being ugly.

- **Simpático** is that often-used Spanish word that means so much more than its usual translation of *nice.* It refers to someone who posseses the trait of **simpatía,** that quality of openness to others so admired in Latin cultures. It is a false cognate because it does not mean *sympathy* but is closer to the idea of *empathy.* (For expressing sympathy, see below, in notes following the second conversation.) The prefix **re-** is an intensifier (See *Vocabulary & Culture*) so **resimpático** means *very empathetic.*

CONVERSACIÓN 2

Tres semanas más tarde en la misma soda.

JUAN ANTONIO   Hola, Nidia. **¡Qué dicha** que Ud. llegó! **La vida me sonríe.** Hace tiempo que quiero darle las gracias por el apoyo y los consejos que me dio. Necesitaba mucho desahogarme aquella tarde. Muchas gracias.

NIDIA   **Con mucho gusto.** Me alegro de que le haya servido el **desahogo.** ¿Ud. ya anda mejor?

JUAN ANTONIO   Mucho mejor, **gracias a Dios.** Ahora **me doy cuenta** de que Irene estaba **más loca que una cabra. Más vale solo que mal acompañado,** como dicen. Pero, Nidia, ¿por qué parece tan triste?

NIDIA   Pasó algo horrible, Juan Antonio. Se nos murió mi **abuelito** Gabriel la semana pasada en un accidente de automóvil en esa carretera tan **feota** del norte.

Three weeks later in the same café (soda).

JUAN ANTONIO   Hi, Nidia. How great (what bliss) that you've come! My lucky day (Life is smiling on me). For quite a while I've been wanting to thank you (it makes time that I want to give you the thanks) for the support and advice you gave me. I really needed to unload on (to unsuffocate myself with) someone that afternoon. Thank you.

NIDIA   You're entirely welcome (with much pleasure). I'm happy that the unloading (unsuffocation) helped (served) you. Are you doing better now?

JUAN ANTONIO   Much better, thank God. Now I realize (give myself an account) that Irene was as mad as a hatter (crazier than a goat). Better alone than with someone not good for you (badly accompanied), as they say. But, Nidia, why do you look (appear) so sad?

NIDIA   Something horrible happened, Juan Antonio. My dear grandfather Gabriel died in a car accident on that awful rotten (big ugly) highway in the North.

JUAN ANTONIO **¡Achará!** ¡Qué difícil para usted y su familia! Un hombre tan bondadoso y trabajador, **tan bueno como el pan.** Nidia, **la acompaño en su dolor.** Permítame **darles el pésame** a Ud. y a su familia.

NIDIA Gracias. Mamá **está destrozada.** Estamos todos tristísimos, sobre todo Ana María aunque es tan **chiquitica.**

JUAN ANTONIO **Estoy con ustedes,** de veras. **Lo siento muchísimo. Cuente conmigo para cualquier cosa.** Si necesitan **el carro,** por ejemplo . . .

—■—

¡Ojo!

- **¡Qué dicha!** and **por dicha** (What luck!, by luck) both use the rather old-fashioned word **dicha,** which literally means *bliss* or *good fortune.*

- **Con mucho gusto** is a way of saying *You're welcome* in Costa Rica, after someone thanks you. The idea is that you did the favor with great pleasure.

- **Desahogo** and the corresponding verb **desahogarse** don't have exact equivalents in English but in general they relate to letting off steam by venting your inner feelings with a friend. (See the *Vocabulary & Culture* in this chapter for more about these unique terms.)

- **Gracias a Dios** *(Thank God)* is a common phrase added to expressions of good luck or fortune, just as **si Dios quiere** *(if God wills)* is often added when making plans for the future.

- **Feo(-a)** literally means *ugly* but is used by Costa Ricans to refer to anything in really bad shape. The augmentative endings **-ote**

JUAN ANTONIO   What a shame! How difficult for you and your family! Such a kind and hard-working man, as good as gold (bread). Nidia, I am sorry you are going through this. (I accompany you in your pain). Please accept my sympathy (permit me to give the "it weighs on me") for you and your family.

NIDIA   Thank you. Mom is devastated (broken in pieces). We are all very sad, especially Ana María, although she is so very young.

JUAN ANTONIO   I feel so bad for (I am with) all of you, truly. I am extremely sorry (I feel it very very much). Count on (with) me for anything at all. If you need the car, for example . . .

—■—

(**-ota**) emphasize this more, so **feota** means "big ugly" or really terrible. (See *Vocabulary & Culture.*)

- **¡Achará!** is a *tiquismo* for **¡Qué lástima!** *(What a pity!)*

- **Dar el pésame** (literally, *to give the "it weighs on me"*) means to express one's sympathy to someone who has suffered a loss. Common expressions for this occasion are: **Lo (La, Te) acompaño en su (tu) dolor** (I accompany you in your pain), **Permítame darle el pésame** (Allow me to express my sympathy), **Estoy con ustedes** (I am with you), **Lo siento muchísimo** (I feel it very much), **Cuente conmigo para cualquier cosa** (Count on me for anything).

- **Chiquitica** (so very tiny) is an example of the typical *Tico* use of **-tico(-a)** at the end of words ending in **-ito(-a)** to signal smallness or affection.

- **El carro** is the usual way of saying *car* or *automobile* in Costa Rica. **El auto** or **el coche** are used in many countries. Cubans generally say **la máquina**.

VOCABULARIO DEL CAPÍTULO

el auto	car
chiquitico(-a)	very very tiny (Costa Rica and some other areas of the Caribbean)
feote(-a)	very ugly or very rundown (**-ote[-a]** augmentative)
¡Achará!	What a shame! (Costa Rica)
Al mal tiempo, buena cara.	(To bad weather, a good face.) When the going gets tough, the tough get going.
el carro	car (Central America, Mexico)
casado	(married person) Costa Rican dish of rice, beans, meat or fish, and salad
el coche	car
con mucho gusto	(with great pleasure) you're welcome (Costa Rica)
cuando la rana eche pelos	(when the frog sprouts hair) the twelfth of never, when hell freezes over
Cuente Ud. conmigo.	Count on (with) me.
dar el pésame	to express one's sympathy (give the *it weighs on me*) in case of death or misfortune
darse cuenta	to realize (give oneself account)
desahogarse	(undrown oneself) to get rid of worry by talking with a friend about a problem
el desahogo	(undrowning) outpouring of feeling with a friend
destrozado(-a)	broken up, upset
¿diay?	but what can one do? (Costa Rica)
dormir a lo chancho chingo	to sleep like a rock (long-tailed pig)
en un callejón sin salida	in a hopeless situation (blind alley)
estar más serio que un burro en lancha	to look worried (more serious than a donkey in a rowboat)
Estoy con ustedes.	I am with you. (expressing sympathy)

gracias a Dios	thank God
Lo (La) acompaño en su dolor.	Please accept my condolences. (I accompany you in your pain.)
Lo siento muchísimo.	I am very very sorry. (I feel it very very much.)
la máquina	car (Cuban); machine
Más vale solo que mal acompañado.	Better alone than badly accompanied.
más feo que mandado a hacer	uglier than if one were designed for that purpose
más loco(-a) que una cabra	crazier than a goat
no es para tanto	it's not as bad as all that (for so much)
no pegar los ojos en toda la noche	to not sleep a wink (glue the eyes) the whole night
pasar las noches en vela	to spend sleepless nights (on watch)
¡pura vida!	(pure life) fantastic, wonderful! (Costa Rica)
¡Qué dicha!	What luck (bliss)! (Costa Rica)
¡Qué perra vida!	What a horrible (dog's) life!
resimpático	very nice (empathetic)
Se armó la gorda.	(The fat one got armed.) There was a big blowup.
Se le fue la pajarita.	Your lover (The little bird) flew the coop (went away from you).
la simpatía	openness and interest in others
una soda	café that sells reasonably priced food (Costa Rica)
los ticos	slang term for Costa Ricans
¡Un momentico, por favor!	Just a little moment, please! (**-tico** diminutive typical of Costa Rica)
La vida me sonríe.	What a stroke of luck (Life is smiling on me).

¡A USTED LE TOCA!

A. Completar las frases. Choose the correct way of finishing each sentence.

1. Juana estaba tan triste que
   no pegó los ojos . . .
2. Tenemos que ser valientes.
   Al mal tiempo . . .
3. ¡Pobrecito! Ese perro **es**
   más feo que . . .
4. Extraño *(I miss)* tanto a Tomás
   que **paso** las noches . . .
5. ¡Hoy tengo buena suerte!
   La vida . . .
6. José vive solo, pero **más**
   vale solo que . . .
7. Oí que su padre se murió, Sr. López.
   Lo acompaño . . .
8. ¡Qué noticias más tristes!
   Lo siento . . .
9. Soy su amiga, de veras.
   Cuente Ud. . . .

a. **buena cara**
b. **conmigo**
c. **en su dolor**
d. **en toda la noche**
e. **en vela**
f. **mal acompañado**
g. **mandado a hacer**
h. **me sonríe**
i. **muchísimo**

B. Tiquismos. Choose the correct words or phrases from the list of standard expressions to replace the Costa Rican slang in boldface.

¿qué se puede hacer?	**¡fantástico!**	**el café**	**postre**
¿no es verdad?	**de nada**	**dinero**	**costarricenses**
plato de arroz y	**miguita**	**simpatía**	**auto**
otras cosas	**estudiantes**	**pequeñito**	**¡qué sorpresa!**
¡qué lástima!			

1. Es demasiado **chiquitico** (_____) para tener **carro** (_____).
2. **Con mucho gusto** (_____), mi amigo, no hay problema.
3. Sí, es un choque muy grande para mí, **¿diay?** (_____)
4. **¡Pura vida** (_____)! Los **ticos** (_____) ganaron el partido.
5. ¿Quieres comer un **casado** (_____) en **la soda** (_____) de enfrente?
6. **¡Achará** (_____)! Se le rompió el brazo.

C. Palabras revueltas. Unscramble the letters to get each message.

1. Zoila's ready to explode. She needs **nu gadhoseo.**   _____
2. We thought she didn't catch on, but **es oid tancue.**   _____
3. When she complained to the boss, **es móra al ragdo.**   _____
4. She lost her job. **¡Charáa!**   _____
5. Her husband took it hard and now **táse zootadresd.**   _____
6. At least he has a good salary. **¡équ chadi!**   _____

D. ¡Faltan los animales! Some names of animals are missing. Choose the correct animal for each expression and match it to its meaning.

burro	cabra	elefante	pajarita	pollo	serpiente
caballo	chancho	gato	perra	rana	vaca

1. **más loca que una** ____   a. my lover has gone
2. **dormir a lo** ____ **chingo**   b. when hell freezes over
3. **qué** ____ **vida**   c. completely off her rocker
4. **se me fue la** ____   d. how terrible things are
5. **más serio que un** ____   e. sleep like a baby
   en lancha   f. very worried
6. **cuando la** ____ **eche pelos**

E. ¿Qué dice Ud.? What could you say in the following situations? Try to use as many of the expressions from this chapter as possible.

1. Your friend Margarita comes to see you and tells you that her father has just died. She is crying and feels sad and alone.

   _____

   _____

2. You are working in Costa Rica and your co-worker Paco invites you out for a drink. You like him a lot and think highly of him. He tells you that his wife wants a divorce and he is miserable.

   _____

   _____

Vocabulary and Culture

Superlatives, Diminutives, Augmentatives—and More!

Built into every language is a program of unique characteristics for the articulation of meaning, just as every instrument possesses its own strengths and limitations and so produces music which is distinct from all others. Spanish has a special strength for expressing the minute nuances of emotion and feeling.

Cranking Up the Intensity with Superlatives and Re-que-te   English speakers often laugh when they hear a reference to the former dictator of Spain as "**Generalísimo** Francisco Franco" because the title sounds so exaggerated, but the superlative **ísimo(-a)** endings are common in Spanish. To say that a woman is very beautiful you can say she is **muy hermosa** (very beautiful), **muy muy hermosa** (very very beautiful), or **extremadamente hermosa** (extremely beautiful), but using the absolute superlative intensifies the quality even more: she is ¡**hermosísima!** (In popular speech you sometimes hear "**hermosisisisísima**" when the speaker gets carried away and goes on repeating syllables for even greater emphasis.) Similarly, an important book is **importantísimo,** and if you want to say you are sorry, you can say that you feel it very very very much: ¡**Lo siento muchísimo!** There is no equivalent for this kind of intensity in English.

Adverbs are also capable of extension to the absolute superlative: a restaurant may be **cerquísima** (very very close by) or **lejísimos** (very very far away), or a dancer can be described as **riquísimamente vestida** (very very richly attired). There is something emphatic and expressive about Spanish superlatives. As if this weren't enough, three prefixes **re-, que-,** and **te-** also can be used singly or together to emphasize. Nidia tells her friend Juan Antonio that he is "**resimpático,**" meaning *very* or *truly* nice or charming. In other circumstances or in a different mood, she might call him **retesimpático** or **requetesimpático** (very very very charming), using all three. A problem may be **redifícil** (really difficult), a person **rebuena** (truly good), and someone can do something **rebien** (very well), or perhaps **requete mal** (really very truly badly). Many and varied are the ways of adding emphasis in Spanish.

Diminutives for Affection and Emotional Nuance   Another expressive feature of Spanish is the great variety of diminutive endings, such as **-ito/-ita, -cito/-cita, -illo/-illa, -ico/-ica,** etc. These are called diminutives, since they indicate small size, e.g., **el librito** (the little book), **la mesita** (the small table), but in addition they often express the feelings of the speaker toward the object. Diminutives can also be combined in endless ways to emphasize the smallness even more: **un poco** (a little), **un poquito** (a very little bit), **un poquitito, poquitico,** or **poquitín** (a very tiny little bit). Often, these endings suggest love or terms of endearment: **amiguito** (dear friend), **hijita** (darling daughter), **amorcito** (sweet love), and are added to first names as a sign of affection, corresponding to the English **ey** or **ie: Juanito** (Johnny), **Carlitos** (Charley), **Susanita** (Susie).

Besides affection, a broad range of emotional nuance is implied by diminutives. If you go swimming and the water is just the right temperature, a diminutive can show your pleasure, **¡Está fresquita!** (It's deliciously cool, from **fresco**). Or it can signal your urgency, **Tenemos que salir ahora mismito** (We have to leave this very minute, from **ahora mismo**). Paradoxically, diminutives occasionally indicate contempt, disdain, or pity, especially the **-illo** form: **hombrecillo** or **hombrecito** (puny little man), **su talentico** (her sparse talent), but this is not a very common use.

Augmentatives for the Nastier Side   To imply the more negative qualities, Spanish supplies a gamut of augmentative endings, such as, **-ón/-ona, -ote/-ota, -acho/-acha.** The first has the general tendency of simply increasing size. For example, an **hombre** is a man and an **hombrón** a big man; a **mujer** is a woman and a **mujerona** a large woman; a **silla** is a chair and a **sillón** an armchair; a **casa** is a house and a **caserón** a mansion.

Most other augmentatives usually (but not always) imply negative feelings on the part of the speaker and suggest something is ugly, clumsy, grotesque, or in bad condition. That's why an old beaten-up purse (**bolsa**) is a **bolsota**; swear words or "bad words" (**palabras**) are called **palabrotas**; a boring old book (**libro**) is a **librote**; a run-down house (**casa**) is a **casucha**; and someone who looks a dreadful mess is **feote**, from the word for *ugly* (**feo**).

Some Words Not Easily Translated   Certain words in Spanish illustrate a special concern with emotional states. The noun **desahogo** and the verb **desahogarse** refer to an outpouring of repressed emotions. These words don't have exact equivalents in English. **Ahogarse** means *to suffocate or drown,* so **desahogarse** means *to undo the sensation of "drowning" in anguish and confusion* by having a **desahogo** with a friend. Words exist in a particular culture because they reflect people's habits, but it also works in reverse: people tend to act in a certain way if a word exists for the action. So perhaps Hispanic people tend to **"desahogarse"** more than their English-speaking counterparts.

Spanish has many synonyms, and often the difference between them is an affective one. **Casa** and **hogar** both mean *home,* but the first word refers to the physical house, and **hogar** to the fireplace or hearth and so has a much more emotional tone. **Cama** and **lecho** both mean *bed,* but the first word is a piece of furniture and the second has an emotional association, such as a **lecho matrimonial** (marriage bed) or a **lecho de muerte** (death bed). **Cara** and **rostro** both mean *face,* but the second is more poetic. Among the best-known examples are the two different ways to say *I love you* in Spanish: **te quiero** and **te amo,** the first often for physical, carnal love (also meaning "I want you"), and the second for the more spiritual (the one you would say to God).

Selecciones. Choose the correct option to finish each statement.

1. A woman described as **hermosísima** is
    a. somewhat beautiful
    b. beautiful
    c. very very beautiful
    d. not beautiful

2. If a deal (**trato**) is **requetemalo,** it is
    a. pretty bad
    b. bad
    c. very very very bad
    d. not bad

3. Diminutive endings like **–ito** or **–ico** usually indicate small size and
    a. affection
    b. hatred
    c. indifference
    d. ignorance

4. Augmentative endings such as **-ón, -ota,** and **-ucho** often imply clumsiness, ugliness, and
   a. grey color
   b. smallness
   c. good condition
   d. large size

5. You would probably need a **desahogo** after
   a. a night of heavy drinking
   b. winning a prize
   c. going through a bad experience
   d. getting a job

6. The difference between **te amo** and **te quiero** is that the first expression is
   a. more sensual
   b. more spiritual
   c. more beautiful
   d. more sincere

LOS ANIMALES EN LOS REFRANES TICOS

Many Costa Rican proverbs (**refranes**) include references to animals. See if you can tell which *Tico* proverbs and expressions below correspond to the English proverbs or explanations on the right. Answers are on page 267.

Refranes ticos	Refranes o explicaciones en inglés
1. A todo perro flaco, se le pegan las pulgas.	A. *You can dress someone up but it doesn't change what he or she is.*
2. Aquí hay gato encerrado.	B. *Even a fish doesn't get in trouble if it keeps its mouth shut.*
3. Deja de hacer chanchadas.	C. *When you're down and out, you get even more troubles.*
4. En boca cerrada no entran moscas.	D. *What the heck do I (does he or she) know about that subject?*

1. c 2. b 3. c 4. b 5. c

5. Hijo de tigre, tigre serás.	E. *A bird in the hand is worth two in the bush.*
6. La mona aunque se vista de seda, mona se queda.	F. *There's something rotten in the state of Denmark.*
7. Más vale pájaro en mano que cien volando.	G. *He (She) blends right in.*
8. Parece lora en mosaico.	H. *Stop doing dirty tricks!*
9. ¿Qué sabe un chancho de aviación?	I. *Like father, like son. (Like mother, like daughter.)*

CHISTES

¡UN POCO DE APOYO, QUERIDO!

Una mujer entrada en años se corta el pelo con la idea de lucir más joven. Luego, no está muy segura del resultado, y busca apoyo emocional de su marido. Le dice:

—Oye, querido, ¿verdad que con el pelo corto, ya no tengo el aspecto de una vieja?

—Es cierto, querida. Ahora tienes el aspecto de un viejo.

A LITTLE SUPPORT, DEAR!

A woman getting up in years gets her hair cut with the idea of looking younger. Afterwards, she's not very sure of the result and looks for some reassurance from her husband. She says to him:

"Listen, dear. Isn't it true that with my hair short, I don't look like an old woman any more?"

"That's true, dear. Now you look like an old man."

¿POR QUÉ, MAMÁ? ¿POR QUÉ?

Una chica que ha tenido bastante experiencia con los hombres se prepara para su matrimonio y tiene dudas respecto al vestido de novia. Busca consejos de su mamá, y le dice:

—Mamá, ¿por qué las mujeres, cuando se casan, usan el vestido blanco?

La mamá comprende sus dudas y le responde:

—Mira, hijita, las mujeres usan el vestido blanco porque es el día más feliz de su vida.

—Pero, entonces—pregunta la chica—¿por qué los hombres se visten de negro?

WHY, MAMA, WHY?

A girl with a good deal of experience with men is getting ready for her wedding and has some doubts about the wedding dress. She seeks advice from her mother and says to her:

"Mom, why do women wear a white dress when they get married?"

The mother understands her doubts and answers:

"Look, dear, women wear white dresses because it's the happiest day of their lives."

"But, then," asks the girl, "why do men wear black?"

. CAPÍTULO 13 .

¡Estoy hasta la madre!

EXPRESSING ANGER

▊ CONVERSACIÓN 1

*En Puebla, México. Cuando Miguel llega a la casa, su esposa, Blanca, está **como** **agua para chocolate** y tiene **una cara de teléfono ocupado**.*

BLANCA   ¡Otra vez llegas tarde! ¿Dónde **carajo** estabas?

MIGUEL   Lo siento, mi amor. Salí tarde del trabajo.

BLANCA   **Ya me encabronaste.** Vienes tarde todos los días ahora. La comida ya está fría.

MIGUEL   No **te sulfures.** ¿Por qué andas tan **brava**?

BLANCA   Mira, pasé **todo el santo día** limpiando esta casa. Y ¿para qué? . . . si ustedes me la dejan mugrosa un ratito después. Tiras la ropa por todas partes, me ensucias la alfombra con tus zapatos lodosos, **quieres que te reciba como si fueras el rey . . . Me tienes harta . . .** un día voy a reventar, por tu culpa. Te lo digo en serio: ¡**estoy hasta la madre!**

COMO AGUA PARA CHOCOLATE

In Puebla, Mexico. When Miguel comes home from work, his wife, Blanca, is boiling over (like water for [hot] chocolate) and has a face like a busy telephone.

BLANCA   You're late again! Where the devil were you?

MIGUEL   I'm sorry, love. I got off work late again.

BLANCA   Now you've really ticked me off! You get home late every day. The food is cold.

MIGUEL   Don't get so steamed up. Why are you so angry?

BLANCA   Look, I spent the whole live-long day cleaning this house. And for what?. . . if (since) you all get it dirty a little bit later. You throw your clothes everywhere, you dirty the rug with your muddy shoes, you expect me to greet you as if you were the king . . . . You've got me fed up; one day I'm going to explode (crack) and it'll be your fault. I'm telling you seriously: I'm up to here (to the mother)!

MIGUEL   Yo no quiero **broncas** . . . Es que tú te enojas por **una media cosita.**

BLANCA   ¿Una media cosita? Cuando llegas tan tarde, para mí es **una gran cosota.**

MIGUEL   **No se puede contigo. Está cabrón.** Pero discúlpame, mi reina, discúlpame. Mañana vamos a comer a un restaurante y después iremos a bailar, ¿está bien?

———————■———————

¡Ojo!

- **Carajo** (vulgar, referring originally to the male sex organ) is used in many circumstances: **¿Qué carajo hacías? ¿Cuándo carajo volviste? ¿Con quién carajo estabas?** It can also be used to express disgust or annoyance, for example at a situation that is difficult to resolve: **¡Carajo! ¡Caray!** and **¡Caramba!** are euphemisms, forms that are less strong.

- **¡Ya me encabronaste!** *Now you've really made me furious!* **Encabronado(-a)** means *angry* and is used in Mexico, Central America, the Caribbean, and many South American countries.

- **Bravo** is used to describe a fierce, angry bull at the bullfight, the **toro bravo.** It means *brave* as well as *angry.*

▌CONVERSACIÓN 2

En el aeropuerto de México, D.F. Guadalupe habla con un empleado de una aerolínea.

EMPLEADO   Lo siento, señorita, pero todos los asientos se encuentran ocupados.

GUADALUPE   ¿Cómo? No puede ser. Tengo un boleto con asiento reservado.

MIGUEL   I don't want any problems (fights). You get angry over every little thing (half a little thing).

BLANCA   Every little thing? When you get home this late, for me it's a big deal.

MIGUEL   Things are impossible with you. It's unbearable. But forgive me, my dear (my queen), forgive me. Tomorrow let's eat out in a restaurant and then let's go dancing, okay?

———■———

- **Hasta la madre: la madre** (mother) has a multitude of meanings. A **madre** can be a thing of little value: **Me importa madre; puras madres. Darle en la madre** or **romperle la madre** is to hurt someone where they are vulnerable (emotionally or physically), and **¡Ni madre!** means *No way!* Alternatives to **hasta la madre** are **hasta las cejas** (eyebrows) and **hasta la coronilla** (crown of the head).

- A **cabrón** (literally, *a male goat*) can be someone deceived by his or her spouse or someone generally unbearable, as you saw in Chapter 10. The feminine **cabrona** is used occasionally. It serves as a general insult, somewhat like bitch or s.o.b. **Está cabrón** means the situation is difficult, **insoportable** or unbearable. A **cabronada** is a dirty trick.

In the airport in Mexico City. Guadalupe is talking to an airline employee.

EMPLOYEE   I'm sorry, miss, but all of the places are taken.

GUADALUPE   What? It can't be. I have a ticket with a reserved seat.

EMPLEADO   Sí, señorita, pero usted ha llegado tarde y . . .

GUADALUPE   ¿Tarde? Tarde llegará su abuela, señor. Son las ocho y
                quince y el avión no sale hasta las nueve y media.

EMPLEADO   Efectivamente. Siempre les aconsejamos a nuestros pasajeros
                que lleguen con hora y media de anticipación.

GUADALUPE   Mire usted. **Yo no estoy jugando.** Tengo que llegar a una
                cita de trabajo esta tarde.

EMPLEADO   **Tranquilícese,** señorita. ¿Qué quiere que yo haga?

GUADALUPE   Compré mi boleto hace dos meses. Quiero que usted no
                me siga **fregando** y me dé mi asiento, pasmado.

EMPLEADO   Calma, señorita, calma. Le advierto que usted **se está
                pasando de la raya.**

GUADALUPE   ¿Cómo se atreve usted? Yo soy la cliente. Los clientes siem-
                pre tenemos razón.

EMPLEADO   Sí, de acuerdo. A veces los clientes no tienen cortesía, **ni
                pizca de educación.** A veces son **nacos.** Pero sí, ¡tienen
                razón!

GUADALUPE   Usted es el naco. Está portándose muy **pelado** conmigo.
                No me muevo de aquí hasta que usted no me resuelva este
                problema.

EMPLEADO   Francamente, señorita, me importa madre lo que usted
                piense o haga.

GUADALUPE   **¡Esto es el colmo! Hijo de su . . .** lo voy a denunciar.
                ¡Váyase a la porra!

—————■—————

¡Ojo!

- **Fregar** (literally, to scrub) means *to mess up, ruin, jerk around,* but
  it can also be vulgar, meaning *to screw;* it is less strong than
  joder, which you saw in Chapter 7.

EMPLOYEE   Yes, miss, but you arrived late and . . .

GUADALUPE   Late? Your grandmother will arrive late, sir. It's 8:15 and the plane doesn't leave until 9:30.

EMPLOYEE   Indeed. We always advise our passengers to arrive an hour and a half early.

GUADALUPE   Look. I'm not fooling. I have to be at an appointment for work this afternoon.

EMPLOYEE   Calm down, miss. What do you want me to do?

GUADALUPE   I bought my ticket two months ago. I want you to stop jerking me around and give me my seat, idiot.

EMPLOYEE   Calm down, miss, calm down. I'm warning you that you're out of line (passing the line).

GUADALUPE   How dare you? I'm the customer. The customer is always right.

EMPLOYEE   Yes, okay. Sometimes the customers have no manners (courtesy), not a pinch of upbringing. Sometimes they're jerks. But yes, they are right!

GUADALUPE   You're the jerk. You're behaving shamelessly (with me). I'm not moving from here until you solve this problem (for me).

EMPLOYEE   Frankly, miss, I don't give a damn (it doesn't matter mother to me) what you think or do.

GUADALUPE   This is the last straw (the brim, limit). Son of a gun . . . I'm going to report you. Go to the devil!

———■———

- **Pelado(-a)** (literally, bald or peeled) is used to mean *broke* or *penniless,* as you saw in Chapter 9; in Mexico, it can also mean *shameless.*

- **Naco(-a)** originally was used in Mexico to refer to an ignorant peasant, someone who could not function in society, often a person of dark skin. It has lost classist or racist connotations now and just means *uneducated jerk*. Some say it came from **totonaco,** an Indian tribe.

- **Hijo de su** is a less offensive form of **hijo de su puta madre,** a strong insult; also used is **hijueputa (hijo de puta).**

- **¡Váyase a la porra!: ¡Porra!** is an interjection used to express disgust or annoyance. **Váyase** is the **usted** form; **Vete** would be the **tú** form. A stronger term is **¡Váyase al diablo** *(devil)!* or sometimes **¡Váyase al infierno** *(hell)!* An even stronger term is **¡Váyase a la mierda!** (literally, *go to shit*)

CHISTES

¿QUÉ PASA?

Dos compás van por primera vez a un partido de fútbol y no entienden ni jota de lo que pasa. Después de un rato ven que toda la gente está **puteando** al árbitro:

—¡Cabrón!

—**¡Malnacido!**

—**¡Qué pendejada!**

Uno de los dos amigos le pregunta al otro:

—Oye, ¿a quién le están diciendo eso?

—Al de negro.

—¡Ah, no me extraña! Lleva media hora en el campo y todavía no ha toca'o bola.

WHAT'S HAPPENING?

Two friends go to a soccer game for the first time and don't understand a thing going on. After a while they notice that everyone is insulting the referee:

"Jackass (Male goat)!"

"S.o.b. (Badly born)!"

"What stupidity!"

One of the two friends asks the other:

"Hey, who are they saying that to?"

"To the guy in black."

"Oh, I'm not surprised. He's been on the field for a half hour and hasn't even touched the ball."

¡Ojo!

- **Putear,** from **puta,** *whore,* means *to call someone offensive names.* Also used is **echar putadas.**

- **Malnacido(-a)** refers to possible illegitimate birth (not to birth defects).

- **¡Qué pendejada!:** a **pendejada** is like a **tontería** (from **tonto**), a kind of *goofing or clowning around, a silly or stupid thing to do, a trick.* **Pendejear** and **tontear** are similar, meaning *to behave in a foolish or stupid way,* but **tontear** is a milder (less vulgar) term. As you have seen in Chapter 10, **pendejo** is used as a general insult in the masculine or in the feminine (**pendeja**), meaning something like *idiot;* the literal meaning is *pubic hair.*

SAN FELIPE Y EL COLO-COLO

En un partido muy importante entre dos equipos de fútbol chilenos, San Felipe y el Colo-Colo, el árbitro favorece el Colo-Colo y por fin el Colo-Colo gana. Los sanfelipeños, muy enojados, entran al campo de juego para liquidar al árbitro.

—**¡Cretino!**

—**¡Ya te pasaste!**

Unos días después, el árbitro golpea las puertas de una nube y le recibe un señor con barba y túnica blanca.

—San Pedro, gusto en conocerlo. Yo soy el árbitro.

—¿Cuál árbitro?

—El árbitro asesinado en el estadio de San Felipe. Es que yo
   quería, San Pedro, preguntarle dónde voy a vivir acá en el cielo.

—No, mi amigo, tú te vas derecho **al infierno.**

—San Pedro, apiádese de mí. No quiero irme al infierno.

—**Derecho al infierno contigo.** Además, **pa' que sepas,**
   huevón, yo no soy San Pedro. Yo soy San Felipe.

San Felipe and the Colo-Colo

In a very important game between two Chilean soccer teams, San Felipe
and Colo-Colo, the referee favors Colo-Colo, and Colo-Colo finally wins.
The San Felipeños, very angry, go onto the field to liquidate the referee.

"Idiot!"

"Now you've gone too far!"

After a few days, the referee knocks on the doors of a cloud and a man with a beard and white tunic receives him.

"San Pedro (St. Peter), nice to meet you. I'm the referee."

"What referee?"

"The referee who was assassinated in San Felipe Stadium. San Pedro, I wanted to ask you where I'm going to live here in heaven."

"No, my friend, you're going straight to hell."

"San Pedro, take pity on me. I don't want to go to hell."

"Straight to hell with you. Moreover, so that you know, you no-account (stupid person), I'm not San Pedro. I'm San Felipe."

¡Ojo!

- **Cretino(-a),** like *cretin* in English, comes from the word **cristiano(-a),** or *Christian;* poor souls who needed to be cared for because they were mentally incapable. It's a strong word; there are many less offensive terms like **bobo, tonto,** and so on.

Vocabulario del capítulo

la bronca	fight, argument
la cabronada	(vulgar) dirty trick
carajo	(vulgar), used as an interjection to express disgust or annoyance; **caray** and **caramba** are euphemisms
como agua para chocolate	(like water for chocolate) at the boiling point, because of either anger or passion (Mexico)
cosa: una media cosita	(half a little thing) every little thing
una gran cosota	a big deal
cretino(-a)	idiot
darle en la madre, romperle la madre	to hurt someone where they are vulnerable (emotionally or physically)
Derecho al infierno contigo.	Straight to hell with you.
encabronado(-a)	(vulgar) angry (Mexico, Central America, Puerto Rico, many South American countries)
Está cabrón.	(vulgar) It's unbearable.
estar hasta la madre	(vulgar); also, **hasta las cejas** (eyebrows), **hasta la coronilla** (crown of the head) to be up to here, fed up; to have "had it"
¡Esto es el colmo!	This is the last straw (the brim, limit, culmination)!

fregado(-a)	useless, messed up, ruined
fregar (ie)	(to scour, rub [the wrong way]) to mess up, ruin, jerk around
harto(-a)	fed up
el hijo de su (puta madre)	(vulgar) son of a gun (of a bitch); also **el hijueputa**
la pendejada	(vulgar) silly or stupid thing to do; trick
madre: me importa madre	(vulgar) I don't give a darn
¡Ni madre!	No way!
puras madres	things of little value
malnacido(-a)	(badly born) s.o.b.
el naco (la naca)	jerk (Mexico)
ni pizca de educación	not a pinch of good manners (upbringing)
No se puede contigo.	Things are impossible with you (**tú**).
No te sulfures (tú).	Don't get so steamed up.
pa' (para) que sepas	just so you (**tú**) know
pasarse de la raya	to be out of line (go over the line)
pelado(-a)	penniless, broke (see Chapter 9); also, shameless (Mexico)
pendejear	(vulgar) to behave in a foolish or stupid way
¿Por qué andas tan bravo(-a)?	Why are you (**tú**) so angry?
putear, echar putadas	(vulgar) to insult with offensive names
Quieres que te reciba como si fueras el rey.	You (**tú**) want me to welcome you as if you were the king.
tener una cara de teléfono ocupado	(to have a face like a busy telephone) to be angry
todo el santo día	the whole live-long day
tontear	to behave in a foolish or stupid way

Tranquilícese (usted). **Tranquilízate (tú).**	Calm down.
¡Váyase (usted) a la porra! ¡Vete (tú) . . . !	Go to the devil!
¡Ya me encabronaste (tú)!	(vulgar) Now you've really got me furious!
¡Ya te pasaste (tú)!	You've gone too far (passed yourself)!

¡A USTED LE TOCA!

A. Responda, por favor. Circle the appropriate response.

Modelo:

¿Qué te pasó?
    a. Me importa madre.
    ⓑ Tuve una bronca con mi jefe.
    c. Sí, para que sepas.

1. ¿Dónde carajo estabas?
    a. Tranquilízate. No te sulfures.
    b. Andábamos bravos.
    c. Puras madres.

2. ¡Esto es el colmo!
    a. Deja de putear.
    b. ¿Qué te pasa?
    c. ¿Dónde demonios está el colmo?

3. No se puede contigo.
    a. Sí, nos llevamos bien.
    b. También estoy harto.
    c. Están fregados.

4. ¡Me robaron la cartera!
    a. ¡Qué huevón!
    b. Vete a la porra.
    c. ¡Qué cabronada!

B. For each pair of expressions, tell which is "stronger" in tone.

1. a. Me tienes harta. b. Estoy hasta la madre.
2. a. Cretino. b. Tonto.
3. a. Está cabrón. b. Está mal.
4. a. Déjame en paz. b. Al infierno contigo.
5. La situación está . . . a. fregada. b. jodida.
6. a. ¿Por qué andas tonteando allí? b. ¿Por qué andas pendejeando allí?

C. ¡Falta algo! Complete the expressions on the left, then match them to the English equivalents on the right.

___1. todo el _____ día   a. because of every little thing

___2. una cara de teléfono _____   b. to be out of line

___3. como agua para _____   c. the whole live-long day

___4. por una media _____   d. at the boiling point

___5. darle en la _____   e. to hit someone hard

___6. pasarse de la _____   f. an angry face

D. En otras palabras. Martín runs into a friend on the street in Los Angeles, California. For each underlined word or expression, give a synonymous word or expression, choosing from the following:

bravo	**hasta la madre**	**pizca**
fregada	**naco**	**tranquilízate**

MARTÍN ¿Qué pasa, José?

JOSÉ Estoy <u>hasta las cejas</u> (1).

MARTÍN ¿Por qué andas tan <u>enojado</u> (2)?

JOSÉ Ahorita me paró un policía.

MARTÍN ¿Por qué?

JOSÉ Me preguntó dónde vivía, por qué estaba allí . . . Me paró por nada, el hijo de su.

MARTÍN <u>Cálmate.</u> (3) Está <u>muy mal</u> (4) la situación, pero ¿qué se puede hacer?

JOSÉ El <u>idiota</u> (5) me encabronó de veras. No tenía ni <u>un poquito</u> (6) de educación.

E. ¿Cómo se dice . . . ? You're having a disagreement with someone. Tell him or her:

1. "Calm down!" _____

2. "Things are impossible with you." _____

3. "I've really had it." _____

4. "This is the last straw!" _____

5. "You've gone too far." _____

. CAPÍTULO 14 .

Se me antojan unas tapas

EXPRESSING LIKES AND DISLIKES, TASTES AND PREFERENCES
·
STARTING A CONVERSATION
·
CHANGING THE SUBJECT

▌ CONVERSACIÓN 1

La mejillonera, un bar en Madrid, España, a las siete de la noche.

AURELIO   Tres **finos,** por favor. ¿Qué hay de **tapas**? *(El **mozo** indica un grupo de platos diversos.)*

PAMELA   ¡Ay, qué rico! **Se me hace la boca agua. Me encantan** los gorriones en adobo. ¿No quieres **probarlos,** Gloria?

GLORIA   *(Haciendo una mueca.)* **No seas pelmaza,** mujer. Ya sabes que soy vegetariana **a rajatabla.** No aguanto la carne y menos la de pajarillos. Sólo la idea **me da asco.**

AURELIO   Pero qué **finolis** te oigo hoy. ¡Yo te he visto devorar unos mejillones tan vivos que gritaban en protesta desde el plato!

Soy vegetariana a rajatabla

The Lady Mussel Catcher, a bar in Madrid, Spain, at seven o'clock in the evening.

AURELIO   Three cream sherries (fine ones), please. What do you have for appetizers (covers)? *(The waiter points to an assortment of varied dishes.)*

PAMELA   Oh, how delicious! My mouth is watering (My mouth is turning into water). I love (am enchanted by) marinated sparrows. Don't you want to try them, Gloria?

GLORIA   *(Making a face [grimace].)* Don't be a pain (squashed mass of garbage), dear (woman). You already know that I'm a dyed-in-the-wool (to table-breaking) vegetarian. I can't stand meat and even less that from little birds. The very idea makes me sick.

AURELIO   How high and mighty you seem (so super-refined I hear you) today. I've seen you devour mussels so alive that they were screaming in protest from the dish!

GLORIA   Claro. Hace muchos años cuando era joven e ignorante como **vosotros** . . . Además, los animales del mar no me parecen tan hermanos. Pero los de la tierra . . . ¿Y tú no tienes alergias, Aure?

AURELIO   **Estoy hasta el gorro** con alergias. No quiero pensar en ellas. **A mí se me antoja** una tortilla española.

PAMELA   **¿No os apetecen** estas **patatas bravas**? Están **sabrosas**.

AURELIO   ¡Demasiado **picantes**! Prefiero la comida **suave,** como las **patatas pobres**.

GLORIA   Muy apropiado, hombre.

AURELIO   ¿Qué insinúas? Esta noche traigo mucha **pasta**. ¡Soy millonario!

GLORIA   Vale, tío, vale. Está bien. Porque yo **no tengo ni una perra.**

———————■———————

¡Ojo!

- **Se me antojan unas tapas** means *I have a taste (hankering, yen) for tapas* (the assorted appetizers the Spanish serve with wine or cocktails). The person referred to changes with the pronoun since literally **tapas** is the subject and the meaning is "the tapas are fancying themselves to me (you, him, her, us, them)." **Se me (te, le, nos, les) antojan.**

- A **fino** refers to a particular type of sherry (**jerez**), the strong wine from the region of that name in the south of Spain. The name *sherry* comes from the mispronunciation several centuries ago by the English families who came there and set up vineyards but who could not quite get their tongues around the Spanish *j*. The only true sherry comes from **Jerez de la frontera** (as it is properly called), although imitations are produced in California, Australia, and many other parts of the world.

GLORIA   Sure (Clear). Many years ago (it makes many years) when I was young and ignorant like you two . . . Besides, sea creatures (the animals from the sea) don't seem to me like brothers and sisters. But land creatures (those from the land) . . . And don't you have allergies, Aure?

AURELIO   I'm sick and tired of (up to the cap with) allergies. I don't want to think about them. What I have a craving for (to me is appearing appealing) is a Spanish omelet.

PAMELA   Wouldn't either of you like (to both of you aren't they appetizing) some of these *patatas bravas* (ferocious potatoes)? They are tasty.

AURELIO   Too hot (stinging)! I prefer mild food, like these *patatas pobres* (poor potatoes).

GLORIA   Very appropriate, man.

AURELIO   What are you insinuating? Tonight I have lots of dough. I'm a millionaire!

GLORIA   Right (it's valid), fella'. That's good. Because I don't have a red cent (I don't have even one dog) . . .

———■———

- **Tapas** are the wonderful assortment of appetizers generally offered free when you order a drink in bars in Spain at the hour of the **paseo** (stroll), usually around 7:00 P.M. They include diverse forms of seafood, meats, and vegetables.

- **Mozo(-a)** is a common term for *waiter* in Spain, as is **camarero(-a).** The word **mesero**, so often employed in Mexico and certain other countries, is not often used in Spain.

- **Se me hace la boca agua** (literally, my mouth is becoming water) is very close to the English phrase *My mouth is watering* and implies that you find the food in front of you very inviting.

- **Me encanta** (literally, *it enchants me*) is a common way to express a liking for something.

- To try for the first time is **probar (ue).** This applies to food, clothing, a sport, etc.

- **No seas pelma** means *Don't be a pain (idiot or a dolt)* and an even stronger form is **No seas pelmazo** which means very **pelma.** This would be translated as **No seas pesado** (heavy, weighty) in most parts of Latin America, and this idiom also is used in Spain. Literally, **pelmazo** means the undigested food that lies heavily in your stomach, or a squashed mass that looks like that.

- The expression **a rajatabla** literally means *to (the point of) board breaking* and evokes the image of someone pounding a fist on the table and breaking the boards. It can be translated as *at any cost, fanatically,* or in other ways.

- **Asco** is nausea or stomach upset. If something gives it to me (**me da asco**), then it means that it turns my stomach.

- **Fino** means *refined, very fine or correct.* **Finolis** is closer to the idea of *finicky,* or *over-refined, exaggeratedly correct.*

- **Como vosotros** in this case means *like both of you.* **Vosotros** is the subject pronoun used in Spain for the intimate plural (two or more friends or children), and in this case it includes both a male and a female. The **-os** form would also be used for a group only of males, but **vosotras** would be used for two or more females.

- **Hasta el gorro** (up to my cap) means *fed up.*

- **Antojos** are cravings or hankerings. **Antojarse** means to provoke a craving in someone (**a alguien**) and, like **gustar,** is used with the indirect object pronouns (**me, te, le, nos, os,** and **les**) to refer to the person. **Se me antojan unas aceitunas** is trans-

CONVERSACIÓN 2

El mismo bar, una hora más tarde.

AURELIO   **Me apetecen** más aceitunas.

PAMELA   Para mí, nada. **Estoy satisfecha.**

lated as *I have a craving for some olives,* but literally it means *The olives are provoking a craving in (to) me.*

- **Apetecer** is a common verb in Spain, also used much in the same way as **gustar**. So a Spaniard may ask, **¿Te apetece** (instead of **te gustaría**) **ir al cine?** (*Does it appeal to you* instead of *would you like*) to go to the movies? The question **¿Os apetecen las patatas?** means literally *To both of you are the potatoes appetizing?* which is to say *Do you feel like having some potatoes?* Notice the indirect object **os,** which corresponds to **vosotros** and is used primarily in Spain. **¿Os gusta el vino?** would mean *Do you (both, all) like the wine?*

- **Patatas** is used for *potatoes* in Spain; **papas** in Latin America. **Patatas bravas** are made with cayenne pepper, which makes them spicy "wild" (**bravas**), whereas **patatas pobres** are made with oil and salt and pepper, humbler or "poor" ingredients.

- **Picante,** the Spanish word for *hot,* in the sense of spicy, comes from the verb **picar,** *to sting* or *to bite,* e.g., **Los insectos nos pican** (*Insects bite/sting us*) and means *stinging, biting.* It has nothing to do with heat because *hot,* referring to temperature, is **caliente.** The opposite of (spicy) hot in English is *mild* and in Spanish the opposite of **picante** is **suave** (smooth, soft). The opposite of **caliente** is, of course, **frío.**

- To say you are without a cent in Spain, you can say you are **boquerón** (a type of little sardine) or that you don't have a **perra** (dog) or **gorda** (fat one), two ways of referring to the ten-cent piece. A variant: **Estoy sin blanca** (I'm without a white one) which may refer to an ancient copper coin called a **blanca.**

The same bar, one hour later.

AURELIO   I feel like having (to me appear appetizing) more olives.

PAMELA   Nothing for me. I'm full (satisfied).

Gloria	**Mirad** al tío con el Walkman®. **Tiene careto** y está fumando un pitillo tras otro como una chimenea. ¿Qué **os** parece? **Tiene pinta** de traficante de drogas.
Aurelio	A mí me parece **ordinario.**
Pamela	A lo mejor **está fumando porros.**
Aurelio	No, hombre. Ahora no se hace en público. Se ha pasado de moda. **¡Cuidado!** Se nos acerca.
el desconocido	Buenas tardes. Muy **ricas** las tapas que se sirven aquí, ¿no es verdad?
Aurelio	**Ricas, sí, sabrosas.**
Gloria	**Fenomenales.**
el desconocido	Soy del norte, de Santander. Por eso no conozco bien lo bares de Madrid. *(Saca su **cajetilla** y mira por todos lados nerviosamente.)*
Gloria	Algunos son **buenos** y otros **son antros.** Hay de todo. Puedes fumar **si te apetece.** No nos **molesta** en absoluto. Oye, compañero, estamos **picados de la curiosidad.** Sabes que estábamos tratando de adivinar **a qué te dedicas . . .**
el desconocido	Ah, ¿sí? Y, ¿qué **pensabais?**
Pamela	**Bueno, pues** . . . comerciante, pensábamos.
el desconocido	Psiquiatra. Pero, **cambiando de tema:** ¿qué **opináis vosotros** de la música que tocan esta noche?

— ■ —

GLORIA   Look at the guy (uncle) with the Walkman®. He looks like death warmed over (has a white-faced mask) and he's chain smoking like a chimney. What do you all think about him? (What does he seem like to you all?) He looks like (has paint of) a drug trafficker.

AURELIO   I think he looks (seems) common (ordinary).

PAMELA   Maybe (to the best) he's smoking joints.

AURELIO   No, kid (man). It isn't done in public now. It's out of (has passed from) fashion. Watch out (Care)! He's coming over (he's approaching us).

STRANGER   Good evening. The appetizers are really delicious (rich) here, aren't they?

AURELIO   Right, delicious (rich), tasty.

GLORIA   Fantastic (phenomenal).

STRANGER   I'm from the north, from Santander. That's why (for that) I don't know Madrid bars (the bars of Madrid) very well. *(He takes out his cigarette pack and looks around [on all sides] nervously.)*

GLORIA   Some are good and some are dives. There's a bit of everything. You can smoke if you like (if it is appetizing to you). It doesn't bother (molest) us at all (in absolute). Listen, friend, we are dying of (itching with) curiosity. You know, we were trying to guess what you do for a living (what you dedicate yourself to).

STRANGER   Oh, yeah? And, what did you think?

PAMELA   Ummm . . . uh . . . businessman, that's what we thought.

STRANGER   Psychiatrist. But, on a different topic (changing theme), what do you all think of the music they are playing tonight?

———■———

¡Ojo!

- **Estoy satisfecho(-a)** (literally, *I am satisfied*) is the usual way to say *I am full* (and don't want any more). A frequent mistake made by English speakers is to say **estoy lleno(-a),** the direct translation of *I am full,* and this presents a rather comical or unpleasant picture to many Spanish speakers, of a person being puffed up with food. However, some Hispanics say **Me llené** or **Estoy lleno** to mean *I've had enough food.*

- **Mirad** is the imperative for the plural intimate *you* (**vosotros**) form of the verb **mirar.** It means *Look!* and corresponds to **Miren Uds.** in Latin America where there is no plural intimate form of *you.*

- **Tener careto** (to have a white-faced mask) means *to look really bad* because of lack of sleep, excessive problems, etc.

- **Pitillo** is another word for **cigarrillo** (cigarette).

- **Tener pinta de** means *to look like* or *to have the appearance* (literally the "paint") *of* (someone or something).

- **Ordinario** and **común** are misleading, since their connotations in Spanish are almost the opposite of those of their English cognates. In English, an *ordinary person* is an average "everyday Joe" and this is not negative, but in Spanish, **una persona ordinaria** is someone who looks uneducated and poorly dressed. **Ordinario** can also mean *tacky,* as in the Chilean expression **más ordinario que traje de baño de lana** (*tackier than a wool bathing suit*). Conversely, in English if you say someone looks "common," this has a negative meaning and suggests he or she is poorly dressed and uneducated, whereas in Spanish, **la persona común** is the average ordinary person we all identify with.

- **Porros** is the word for marihuana joints. In Mexico it is common to say **toques** (touches).

- Words for describing foods that appeal to you include the following: **comida rica** (literally, *rich,* but not in the sense of heavy as in English, simply good-tasting), **sabrosa** (tasty), **fenomenal** (used a lot in Spain as a superlative), and the handy cognate **deliciosa** (delicious).

- **Antro** means a dive or a seedy place.

- **Molestar** is a false cognate that does not mean *to molest,* but only *to bother.*

- **Cambiando de tema** (Changing the subject) is a direct way of changing the topic of conversation. Of course, if you prefer, you can simply begin to talk of something else, especially of something in the surroundings to divert attention immediately.

VOCABULARIO DEL CAPÍTULO

a qué te dedicas	what you do for a living
a rajatabla	(to board breaking) at any cost, fanatical
antojarse (a alguien)	to provoke a craving in someone; **Se me antoja una manzana** I have a taste for an apple.
el antro	dive, seedy place (Spain)
apetecer	to appeal to (to awaken one's appetite) (Spain)
el asco	nausea or stomach upset
asqueroso(-a)	horrible, sickening
la cajetilla	pack (of cigarettes)
caliente	hot (in the sense of temperature)
el camarero, la camarera	waiter, waitress
cambiando de tema	changing the subject (theme)
común	average, ordinary, e.g., **el hombre común** the common man
¡Cuidado!	(Care!) Watch out! Be careful!
Estoy hasta el gorro con . . .	I'm fed up (up to the cap) with . . . (Spain)

Estoy satisfecho(-a).	I'm full (satisfied, in the sense of not wanting to eat any more).
fenomenal	(phenomenal) great, super (Spain)
un fino	a glass of sweet sherry
finolis	exaggeratedly refined, uppity (Spain)
el jerez	sherry wine
Me da asco.	It makes me sick to my stomach (gives me nausea).
Me encanta(n).	(It enchants me/They enchant me.) I love it (them).
el mesero, la mesera	waiter, waitress (Mexico)
molestar	to bother
el mozo	(boy, lad, youngster) waiter
No seas pelma, pelmazo(-a).	Don't be a pain (mass of undigested food). (Spain)
No tengo ni una perra.	I don't have even a cent (dog).
ordinario(-a)	common, low-class, tacky
os	to you (all); object pronoun for **vosotros (-as)** forms, e.g., **¿Os gusta el vino?** *¿Do you (both, all) like the wine?* (Spain)
el paseo	(stroll) walk; customary stroll taken by Spanish and Latin Americans in the late afternoon
la pasta	(dough) money (Spain)
picados de la curiosidad	burning (itching) with curiosity
picante	(stinging) spicy hot
el pitillo	cigarette
los porros	marihuana joints
¿Qué te apetece?	What do you have a taste for? (Spain)
Se me antoja(n) . . .	I have a taste for . . .
Se me hace la boca agua.	My mouth is watering (becoming water).

probar (ue)	(to prove) to try for the first time (food, clothing, a sport, etc.)
si te apetece	if you **(tú)** like (Spain)
sin blanca	(without a white one) broke, without money (Spain)
sin una gorda	(without a fat one) broke, without a cent (Spain)
suave	bland, non-spicy (for food); smooth, soft
tener careto	(to have a white-faced mask) to look awful (from fatigue or worry) (Spain)
tener pinta de	(to have the paint of) to look like
vosotros(-as)	familiar *you* for two or more (Spain)

¡A USTED LE TOCA!

A. Antónimos. Match the words or phrases with their antonyms (opposites).

___ 1. Estoy satisfecho.   a. suave

___ 2. Se me antojan.   b. Estoy sin una gorda.

___ 3. ordinario   c. Me dan asco.

___ 4. antro   d. Tengo hambre.

___ 5. picante   e. lugar muy lindo

___ 6. Tengo mucha pasta.   f. distinguido *(distinguished)*

B. En España, ¿cómo se dice? Fill in each blank with the word or expression from the list that could be used in Spain to convey the same meaning. Some words will not be used.

tiene pinta	**pelmazo**	**vosotros**	**un pitillo**	**boquerón**	**una perra**
os apetece	**tapas**	**finos**	**mozo**	**da asco**	**patatas**

1. Amigos, ¿no les gustaría un poco de vino?
   En España: Amigos, ¿no _____ un poco de vino?
2. Estoy completamente sin lana.
   En España: Estoy completamente _____.

3. Compañeros míos, estas bebidas son para Uds.

En España: Amigos míos, estas bebidas son para _____.

4. La carne con papas está sabrosa.

En España: La carne con _____ está sabrosa.

5. Ay, Ricardo, ¡no seas pesado!

En España: Ay, Ricardo, ¡no seas _____!

6. ¡Mesero! Queremos botana (picadas), por favor.

En España: ¡ _____! Queremos _____, por favor.

7. ¿Pagar la cuenta? No tengo ni un centavo.

En España: ¿Pagar la cuenta? No tengo ni _____.

C. Selecciones. Choose the correct word(s) to complete each statement.

1. A synonym for **pitillo** is
   a. **alergia**
   b. **cigarrillo**
   c. **plato**
   d. **cajetilla**

2. If you say in Spanish that a woman looks **ordinaria,** you are implying that she looks
   a. elegant
   b. well educated
   c. average
   d. lower class

3. If someone has a **careto,** it means he or she looks very
   a. **feliz**
   b. **guapo**
   c. **mal**
   d. **borracho**

4. If you don't like spicy food (**comida picante**), then you should ask for **comida**
   a. **fina**
   b. **brava**
   c. **rica**
   d. **suave**

5. If your Spanish friends call you **finolis,** they are suggesting that
you are
a. putting on airs
b. learning fast
c. very fashionable
d. very sensitive

D. Palabras revueltas. Unscramble the letters to get the message and
write it in the blank to the right.

1. Carlita es una feminista muy
dedicada. Es una feminista . . .
a jabaslatar _____

2. Roberto tiene un trabajo duro
y gana poco. Ya no lo aguanta.
Está . . . **satha le rrogo** _____

3. ¡Qué comida más deliciosa! **Se
me hace . . . al cabo gaau** _____

4. Paco no quiere hablar de la
política. Paco dice: **bimadonac
ed mate . . .** _____

5. Esas bananas están malas. Son
repugnantes. **em nad soca** _____

E. Situaciones. Write in Spanish what you could say in the following
situations, using words and expressions from this chapter.

1. You are in a bar in Madrid with friends and the waiter comes over for
your order.

_____

_____

2. Your friends are all talking about food, so tell something about your food tastes and preferences, and then change the subject.

_____

_____

3. Your friends leave and you stay. There is a pleasant-looking person sitting next to you, and you decide to start a conversation.

_____

_____

Vocabulary and Culture

Colorful Language in Spain

In Latin America, Spaniards from Spain have a certain reputation for being **malhablados,** that is to say, somewhat crude in their speech. This is partly due to misunderstanding, since some words considered strong in many parts of the Hispanic world are quite innocent in Spain. For example, the verb **coger** is a common verb there, meaning _to take_ or _to catch,_ and does not have the secondary meaning as an obscenity (equivalent to the "f" word in English) that it has for many Latin Americans. When it comes to swearing (**maldecir**), Spaniards make the same general references to what is held sacred. (See pages 166–168.) However, they often use different terms and variations.

Variations on the Same Themes   The heritage of the medieval honor code is just as alive (although unconsciously so) in peninsular speech as in other Spanish-speaking countries, accompanied by its preoccupations with legitimacy, matrimonial faithfulness, sex, and the purity of female relatives. The simple form **Tu madre** so common in Latin America does not have much meaning in Spain but the vulgar form, **Tu puta madre,** is used in the same way. Motherhood may be attacked more indirectly by saying, ¡**La madre que te parió!** _(the mother who gave birth to you)._ Part of the insult here is the verb **parir,** generally used for animals, instead of **dar a luz,** the term meaning _to give birth_ for humans. So, really this phrase suggests that the person spoken to (and his mother) are both animals! Common insults include **cabrón** (**cabrona**), which means *goat*. Since goats have horns (**cuernos**), the implication is that the person so designated is a "**cornudo(-a),**" someone who has grown horns because his or her partner is unfaithful. In everyday use, however, the origin is unimportant and anything, such as a locked door or non-functioning cash machine, may be called **cabrona.** The equivalent of the "f" word in Spain (though not as vulgar) is **joder,** and it is sometimes used to mean *to take advantage of,* or by itself simply for emphasis.

The Three C's of Swearing in Spain   The three most frequent swear words, or what are sometimes called "the three *c's* of Spanish swearing," have to do with body parts: **coño** (female part), **carajo** (male part), and **cojones** (testicles). The first two are commonly used (even by grandmothers) and not considered very strong in Spain, being roughly equivalent to *Damn it!* (These generally sound much more vulgar to Latin American ears.) The third term is used extensively, mostly by men, in multiple, inventive ways for many occasions. Recently, a list appeared on the Internet with over forty distinct uses for this very Spanish-from-Spain word. It can express surprise, pleasure, anger, affection, frustration, etc. The adjective **cojonudo** is also common for both the best of things and the worst of things. In a classic film by Spanish director Antonio Trueba, an old man sees the handcuffs on a young war deserter and shouts, **¡Cojonudo!** in surprise and condemnation. Then, when the young man turns out to be a good cook and serves him cod soup, he says, **¡Ésta es la sopa de bacalao <u>más cojonuda</u> que haya probabo!** *(This is the best damn cod soup I've ever tasted!)*

In Spain, the term signifying someone useless and stupid (**pendejo, huevón, boludo** in different parts of Latin America) is **gilipollas** (with the first part meaning *foolish* and the second referring to the male part). This is very common, not too strong, and can be applied to both men and women. The usual bathroom words are also commonly used. (See page 168).

Religious References   Religious references play an even greater role in the idioms and expressions in Spain than in Latin America. God, the saints, and the devil are familiar figures in sayings and comparisons. A man may be referred to, for example, as **el diablo vendiendo cruces** (the devil selling crosses) to indicate that he is a hypocrite, or a grandpa may assert his authority with **Más sabe el diablo por viejo que por diablo** (the devil knows more because he's old than because he's the devil). Many religious words are also used for swearing: **¡Diablos!** (more or less like *Damn it!* or its variant with the same meaning, **¡Diantres!**), **¡Vete al diablo!** (Go to the devil!), and **¡Virgen santísima!** are all rather mild expletives. Much stronger expletives that carry the force of sacrilege (insulting the holy) are **¡Hostias!** (*Hosts!,* which is an attack on the element taken by Catholics to represent Christ's body) or **Me cago en Dios** (literally, I shit on God). To say *damn,* Spaniards use **maldito,** or the milder **condenado,** or even milder yet **bendito** (a euphemism meaning *blessed*). For example, one can say **¡Este maldito (condenado, bendito) auto no arranca!** *This damn (darn, blessed) car won't start!*

Selecciones. Choose the best way to finish the statements.

1. Spaniards have the reputation in Latin America of being **malhablados** partly because
    a. they like to shock people
    b. they use cruder speech forms
    c. they aren't well educated
    d. they use some words differently

2. The insult **¡La madre que te parió!** implies that the person spoken to and his or her mother are
    a. unimportant
    b. unattractive
    c. animals
    d. criminals

3. The strong swear word **cabrón** (goat) suggests a person has **cuernos** (horns), a reference to
    a. immoral actions by that person
    b. unfaithfulness by that person's spouse
    c. violent behavior
    d. slovenly appearance

4. In comparison with their use in Latin America, the words **coño** and **carajo** in Spain are
    a. more vulgar
    b. less vulgar

1. d 2. c 3. b 4. b 5. c 6. a 7. b 8. d

      c. about the same

      d. almost nonexistent

5. The common Spanish swear words **cojones** and **cojonudo** are

      a. insults

      b. compliments

      c. used in many ways

      d. used only by adolescents

6. If someone is called **el diablo vendiendo cruces,** it means he is considered

      a. a hypocrite

      b. very old

      c. evil

      d. smart

7. An insult in Spain which has the force of sacrilege is

      a. **iglesias**

      b. **hostias**

      c. **cruces**

      d. **diantres**

8. A euphemism for **maldito** or **condenado** (damn) is

      a. **malo**

      b. **bueno**

      c. **arranca**

      d. **bendito**

Expresiones con alimentos

Many sayings in Spanish contain references to foods. Match each saying to the English proverb or explanation on the right that has a similar meaning. Answers are on page 268.

Spanish Sayings	English Sayings or Explanations
1. A falta de pan, buenas son tortas.	A. The shrimp that sleeps gets swept away by the current. (The race is to the swift.)
2. Camarón que se duerme se lo lleva la corriente.	B. I'm as bored as an oyster (bored stiff).

3. Está donde las papas queman.	C. On tastes, there is nothing written. (There's no accounting for taste.)
4. La última chupada del mate.	D. If there's no bread, cakes are good. (Something better than expected.)
5. Me aburro como una ostra.	E. Never say, "Of this water, I will not drink." (You never know what you'll have to go through.)
6. No hay que llorar sobre la leche derramada.	F. He's where potatoes burn (at the center of the action).
7. Nunca digas, "De esta agua no beberé."	G. He has horchata (a cold, white summer drink made from the chufa root) for blood. (He's indifferent and slow to react.)
8. No pidas peras al olmo.	H. No use crying over spilled milk.
9. Sobre los gustos, no hay nada escrito.	I. Don't ask for pears from an elm tree. (You can't get blood from a stone.)
10. Tiene sangre de horchata.	J. The last sip of tea (mate). (Good to the last drop.)

Chiste

El presidente que se ganó tres premios Nóbel

Un español estaba de visita en México y se jactaba un poco con su amigo mexicano de un premio ganado recientemente por un escritor español. Entonces, su amigo le respondió:

—Bueno, eso no es nada. Nuestro presidente acaba de ganar tres premios Nóbel.

—¡Pero, hombre!—dijo el español, sorprendido—. ¡No puede ser! Su presidente justamente ha sido bastante tonto. Hizo la devaluación del peso mexicano con consecuencias desastrosas. Ha aumentado mucho la pobreza.

—Es verdad—concedió el mexicano—. Sin embargo, el presidente ha ganado este año tres premios Nóbel.

—¿A ver?—preguntó el español, con tono escéptico.

—Primero—explicó el mexicano—ganó el premio de la física porque hizo lo imposible: hizo "flotar" el peso. Segundo, ganó el premio de la química porque transformó la plata en . . . mierda. Finalmente, el presidente ganó el premio de la literatura.

—¿Por qué?—preguntó el español, riéndose.

—Porque—dijo el mexicano—¡con un solo plumazo nuestro presidente creó más "miserables" que Víctor Hugo!

The President Who Won Three Nobel Prizes

A Spaniard was visiting Mexico and was boasting a little with his Mexican friend about a prize recently won by a Spanish writer. Then his friend replied:

"Well, that's nothing. Our president has just won three Nobel Prizes."

"Good heavens!" said the Spaniard, surprised. "That's impossible! Why, your president has in fact been rather foolish. He devaluated the Mexican peso with disastrous consequences. Poverty has grown considerably."

"That's true," conceded the Mexican. "Nevertheless, the president has won three Nobel Prizes this year."

"And how is that?" asked the Spaniard with a skeptical tone.

"First," explained the Mexican, "he won the prize for physics because he did the impossible: he made *weight* float. (This is a pun because in Spanish **peso** means both the unit of currency and also *weight*.) Second, he won the prize for chemistry because he changed silver (money) into . . . shit. Finally, the president won the prize for literature."

"Why?" asked the Spaniard, laughing.

"Because," said the Mexican, "with one single stroke of the pen, he created more 'miserables' (poor people) than Victor Hugo!" (Victor Hugo is the French author of the famous novel *Les Miserables*.)

. CAPÍTULO 15 .

¡Buen provecho!

ORDERING IN A RESTAURANT OR BAR
•
MAKING A TOAST

CONVERSACIÓN 1

*En **un bar** en Colombia.*

EL CANTINERO   ¿Qué le sirvo, señor?

RAFAEL   **Una fría.**

EL CANTINERO   ¿De cuál quiere?

RAFAEL   **De barril.**

EL CANTINERO   **Un momentico.**

RAFAEL   ¡Ey, Rubén! ¿Qué tal?
(a un amigo)

RUBÉN   Bien. ¿Tú? ¿Cómo está la **media naranja**?

RAFAEL   Está con sus **jefes,** de visita. ¿Y la tuya?

RUBÉN   En casa, con **los chiquitines.** *(El cantinero le da una cerveza a Rafael.)*

RAFAEL   **¡Para las que amamos!**

RUBÉN   **¡Salud!** Al centro y p'adentro.

¡SALUD! ARRIBA, ABAJO, AL CENTRO, P'ADENTRO.

In a bar in Colombia.

WAITER	What can I serve you, sir?
RAFAEL	A beer (cold one).
WAITER	What kind do you want?
RAFAEL	Draft. (From the barrel.)
WAITER	Just a moment.
RAFAEL *(to a friend)*	Hey, Rubén! How are you?
RUBÉN	Fine. And you? How's your better half (half orange)?
RAFAEL	She's with her parents (bosses), visiting. And yours?
RUBÉN	At home, with the kids (little ones). *(The waiter gives Rafael a beer.)*
RAFAEL	For those that we love!
RUBÉN	Cheers (Health)! Bottoms up (to the center and inside)!

(Después de unos minutos.)

EL CANTINERO   ¿Algo más?

    RAFAEL   Sí, tráeme una sopa de pollo, por favor. *(El camarero se la da.)*

    RUBÉN   **¡Buen provecho!** Pues, tengo que irme. Susana me está esperando. Gusto de verte, amigo.

    RAFAEL   **Que te vaya bien.**

———■———

¡Ojo!

- **Un bar** is not just a place to drink; food is served also.

- **De barril** means *on tap,* literally *from the barrel.*

- **Un momentico:** in Colombia and Venezuela, as well as Costa Rica, the **-ico** diminutive form is very common; in most other places, one usually hears -**ito,** as in **Un momentito.**

- **La media naranja,** *half orange,* is one's spouse or sweetheart, male or female.

- **Los jefes** here refers to one's parents. (**El jefe** or **la jefa** can also refer to one's husband or wife, as you have seen.) Commonly, parents are referred to as **los tatas** (**el tata** is *father*), although curiously, the word **tatas** can also be used for one's grandparents, and **tatarabuelos** is great-great-grandparents. In certain Andean countries, **los jamones,** *hams,* is used rather disrespectfully by young people for *parents.* In direct address, **papi** and **mami** are very common.

- **Al centro y p'adentro (para adentro)** is a toast, sometimes said as **Arriba, abajo, al centro y p'adentro,** holding the glass up, down, toward the mouth, and then drinking. A Colombian toast is **¡Fondo blanco!,** used with strong drinks that are supposed to be drunk all at once. In Mexico, a variation of **¡Salud!** is **¡Salucitas!** Another common toast is **¡Salud, amor y dinero!** In Spain or Venezuela, you may hear **Chin chin,** which imitates the sound of glass clinking.

(After a few minutes.)

WAITER   Anything else?

RAFAEL   Yes, bring me some chicken soup, please. *(The waiter gives it to him.)*

RUBÉN   Enjoy your meal ([take] good advantage)! Well, I have to go. Susana is waiting for me. Nice to see you, pal.

RAFAEL   Good-bye. (May all go well with you.)

SOLO EN TWA

Tu amorcito vuela gratis.

PROMOCION 2X1

Ahora, invitar a quien quieras

a USA no te costará nada.

Tu chiquitín vuela gratis.

TWA te regala otro billete

cuando compres el tuyo para

diferentes destinos en USA.

Para más detalles sobre esta

Tu mami vuela gratis.

promoción y nuestras ofertas

de fin de semana, llama a TWA

(91-310 30 94 ó 93-215 84 06),

Si vuelas a USA con TWA
quien tú quieras vuela gratis.

o a tu agencia de viajes.

Puedes dar a quien quieras una

alegría, sin que te cueste nada.

TWA La forma más confortable de volar.

There are several ways to say *kid* in Spanish: **el chiquitín (la chiquitina)** is used in many places.

- **¡Buen provecho!** This courteous phrase is often said to some-one who is about to start eating by someone who is not going to eat. You may also hear **¡Que aproveche!**

CONVERSACIÓN 2

En un restaurante en Bogotá.

EL CAMARERO	**Buenas.** ¿Una mesa para dos?
JOSÉ	Sí.
EL CAMARERO	Por aquí . . . ¿Gustan tomar algo?
JOSÉ	Un vino tinto . . .
EL CAMARERO	¿De la casa?
JOSÉ	**Ey.**
EL CAMARERO	¿Y para la señorita?
JOSÉ	¿Qué clase de jugos hay?
EL CAMARERO	Hay de mango, piña, papaya . . .
ROSA	De mango, pues.
JOSÉ	*(a Rosa, bromeando)* Como eres un **manguito,** ¿eh?

(Media hora despúes.)

JOSÉ	¡Señor!
EL CAMARERO	¿Listos? ¿Qué desean pedir?
JOSÉ	Quisiera el bistec. Viene solo o . . .
EL CAMARERO	Con papas y una ensalada.
JOSÉ	Bien. Que esté bien cocido el bistec, por favor. Y las papas . . . papas fritas.
EL CAMARERO	Así que me **manda a freír papas,** ¿eh? *(riéndose)* ¿Y para usted?

- **Que te vaya bien.** *May all go well with you.* This is said by a person who is not leaving; if you yourself are leaving, the expression is not appropriate, but it may be said to you. The **te** is the **tú** form; for **usted** it is **le** and for **ustedes, les: Que le(s) vaya bien.**

In a restaurant in Bogotá.

WAITER   Afternoon. A table for two?

JOSÉ   Yes.

WAITER   This way. . . . Would you like something to drink?

JOSÉ   A (glass of) red wine.

WAITER   The house wine?

JOSÉ   Yeah.

WAITER   And for the lady?

ROSA   What kind of fruit juices are there?

WAITER   There's mango, pineapple, papaya . . .

ROSA   Mango, then.

JOSÉ   *(to Rosa, joking)* Since you're a **manguito,** ¿eh?

(Half an hour later.)

JOSÉ   Waiter!

WAITER   Ready? What would you like to order?

JOSÉ   I'd like the steak. Does it come by itself or . . . ?

WAITER   With potatoes and a salad.

JOSÉ   Fine. Please have the steak well done. And the potatoes . . . french fries.

WAITER   So you're telling me to get lost (sending me to fry potatoes), huh? *(laughing)* And for you?

ROSA   Para mí, el arroz con pollo.

EL CAMARERO   Sí, señorita.

(Más tarde.)

JOSÉ   ¿Qué tal el pollo, **mona**?

ROSA   **Regio.** Este sitio es **una soda.** ¿Y el bistec?

JOSÉ   Pues, parece que pedí el bistec James Bond.

ROSA   ¿Cómo?

JOSÉ   Frío, duro y con nervios de acero.

———■———

¡Ojo!

- **Buenas** is often used instead of **Buenas tardes/noches.**

- **Ey** is sometimes used to mean **Sí.**

- A **mango** is a good-looking person (male or female) in many countries. **Está hecha un mango** means *She's very beautiful.*

- **¡Señor!**: To call a waiter, you can always use **Oiga, señor(ita)**, but in Mexico, **¡Joven!** is often used, even if the waiter is sixty years old. In other areas, such as Colombia, **joven** is used, but only if the server is young. **¡Amigo!** is used in certain Caribbean areas. (Of course, many times people simply say **¡Camarero(-a)!** or **¡Mozo(-a)!** but this is less polite.)

- **Mandar a freír papas** (to tell someone to get lost): In some countries, such as Spain, the expression is **mandar a freír espárragos** *(asparagus).*

- **Mono(-a)** means *blond(e)* in Colombia; in general, it is used to mean *cute.*

- **Una soda:** in Colombia, **¡Es una soda!** means *It's great (wonderful, terrific)!*

ROSA For me, the chicken with rice.

WAITER Yes, miss.

(Later.)

JOSÉ How's the chicken, **mona**?

ROSA Great. This place is terrific (a soda, soft drink). And the steak?

JOSÉ Well, it looks like I ordered the James Bond steak.

ROSA What?

JOSÉ Cold, hard, and with nerves of steel.

———■———

CHISTES

EN "GRINGOLANDIA"

Un tipo que no sabe nada de inglés está preocupado porque pronto viaja a Nueva York y no sabe ni cómo pedir algo para comer. Le cuenta el problema a un compañero de trabajo.

—No se preocupe uste' . . . Lo único que uste' tiene que hacer es decir bien **rapidingo** "Usted, ¿quién es?", y el gringo le va a entender *steak and eggs,* y eso es carne con huevos.

—Pero si eso es **facilingo,** dice el hombre contento.

Estando ya en "**Gringolandia**", decide poner en práctica sus conocimientos del idioma y entra en un restaurante. El camarero se le acerca y le pregunta: "How can I help you?" Y el tipo contesta rápidamente:

—Y **vos**, ¿quién sos?

IN "GRINGOLAND"

A fellow who knows nothing about English is worried because soon he is traveling to New York and he doesn't even know how to order something to eat. He tells a co-worker the problem.

"Don't worry . . . the only thing you have to do is say 'Who are you?' (**usted** form) very quickly, and the gringo is going to understand 'steak and eggs'; that's steak (meat) and eggs."

"But that's a snap ('very easy')," says the man happily.

Being now in "Gringoland," he decides to put his knowledge of the language into practice. He goes into a restaurant. The waiter comes up to him and asks: "How can I help you?" And the fellow answers quickly: "Who are you?" (**vos** form).

¡Ojo!

- **Rapidingo = rápido; facilingo = fácil.**

- **Vos:** This form originally was between **tú** and **usted** in terms of level of formality. In the sixteenth and seventeenth centuries in Spain, **vos** and **tú** were used interchangeably, but gradually **vos** died out in favor of **tú.** However, **vos** is still used by all social classes in Argentina, Paraguay, Uruguay, most of Central America (Guatemala, Nicaragua, Honduras, El Salvador, and Costa Rica), and areas that were isolated from Spanish rule (away from the influence of the viceroyalty governments). In parts of Colombia, Ecuador, Chile, and one region of Venezuela, **vos** is common. The verb form is very similar to the **tú** form. In the present tense, the endings are **-ás** for **-ar** verbs, **-és** for **-er** verbs, and **-ís** for **-ir** verbs. Stem vowels don't change (e.g., **vos podés**). There are some irregular forms, such as **vos sois** (sometimes pronounced **sos**); you will hear these forms often if you travel around Latin America.

Ni chicha ni limonada

En un café en España.

El camarero   ¿Qué **le pongo** al señor?

El señor   A él una vela, y a mí un café.

El camarero se lo va a hacer y el tío dice:

EL SEÑOR   Que no esté ni muy caliente ni muy frío.

EL CAMARERO   De acuerdo.

EL SEÑOR   En taza ni muy grande ni muy pequeña.

EL CAMARERO   **Como quiera.**

Cuando se lo va a poner:

EL SEÑOR   Y no me lo ponga ni muy dulce ni muy amargo.

EL CAMARERO   Vale.

EL SEÑOR   Y ahora no me eche ni poca ni mucha leche.

EL CAMARERO   ¿Sabe lo que le digo?

EL SEÑOR   No.

EL CAMARERO   Que me parece que le voy a **dar una patada** ni muy alta ni muy baja.

NEITHER **CHICHA** (CORN LIQUOR) NOR LEMONADE

In a café in Spain.

WAITER   What can I put before the gentleman (lord)?

MAN   For him a candle and for me a coffee.

The waiter goes to get it and the guy says:

MAN   Not too hot or too cold.

WAITER   Okay.

MAN   In a cup that's not too big or too small.

WAITER   As you like.

When he goes to put it before him:

MAN   And don't make it too sweet or too bitter.

WAITER	Right.
MAN	And now, don't put too little or too much milk.
WAITER	Do you know what I think (what I'm telling you)?
MAN	No.
WAITER	That it seems to me I'm going to give you a kick that's not too high or too low.

¡OJO!

- **Chicha** is an alcoholic drink usually made from corn. The South American expression **ni chicha ni limonada** means *neither fish nor fowl.*

- **Poner** is often used in restaurants and bars in Spain instead of **servir.**

- **Como (usted) quiera** is a subjunctive form meaning *however you like, as you wish.*

- **Dar una patada** is *to kick.* It comes from **pata,** the leg of an animal, of a piece of furniture or (informally) of a person.

VOCABULARIO DEL CAPÍTULO

¡Arriba, abajo, al centro y p'adentro!	(Up, down, to the center, and inside!) Down the hatch! Sometimes this is just said as, **¡Al centro y p'adentro!**
¡Buen provecho!	([Take] Good advantage!) Enjoy your meal!
Buenas.	(Good) Afternoon/Evening.
Como quiera.	As you like.
el chiquitín, la chiquitina	kid, small child
dar una patada	to (give a) kick
de barril	(From the barrel) Draft (beer)
Está hecha un mango.	(She's become a mango.) She's very beautiful.
Ey.	Yes.

facilingo	very easy
¡Fondo blanco!	(White bottom [of glass]!) Bottoms up!
una fría	(a cold one) a beer
Gringolandia	(Gringoland) the United States
los jamones	(hams) parents (Andean countries)
los jefes	(bosses, chiefs) parents
mandar a freír papas (espárragos)	(to send to fry potatoes [asparagus]) to tell someone to get lost, go to blazes
un manguito	a good-looking person
la media naranja	(half orange) spouse or sweetheart (male or female)
mono(-a)	cute; (Colombia) blond(e)
ni chicha ni limonada	(neither chicha, an alcoholic beverage usually made from corn, nor lemonade) neither fish nor fowl
¡Oiga, señor(ita)!, ¡Joven! ¡Amigo!	(Listen, sir/miss! Young person! Friend!) Waiter! Waitress!
¡Para las que amamos!	For those whom we love!
¿Qué le pongo al señor?	What shall I serve (put before) the gentleman? (Spain)
Que te (le, les) vaya bien.	May all go well with you.
rapidingo	very quick
regio(-a)	great, beautiful (Colombia, Puerto Rico, Ecuador)
¡Salud!	(also, Mexico: **¡Salucitas!**) (Health!) To your health!
una soda	(a soda) terrific, great, wonderful (Colombia)
el tata	father (also **taita**)
los tatas	parents, father and mother (also, grandparents)
Un momentico.	Just a moment. (Colombia, Venezuela, Costa Rica)

¡A USTED LE TOCA!

A. Antónimos. Match the opposites.

__1. Ey.	a. muy malo
__2. de barril	b. una persona fea
__3. regio	c. un horror, cosa fatal
__4. una soda	d. No.
__5. hijos	e. jamones
__6. un mango	f. en botella

B. En otras palabras. The Restrepo family is at a restaurant. Replace the underlined words or expressions with synonyms, choosing from the following:

fondo blanco	**media naranja**	**pongo**	**jefes**
fría	**momentico**	**chiquitines**	**tata**
rapidingo	**mona**		

El sábado pasado fui a un restaurante con mis <u>padres</u> (1), mi <u>esposa</u> (2) y los <u>hijos</u> (3). "¿Alguna bebida para empezar? ¿Qué les <u>sirvo</u> (4)?" preguntó el camarero, un español. "Para mí, una <u>cerveza</u>" (5), le dije, y los otros familiares también pidieron bebidas. "Vale", dijo el mesero, y desapareció. Un <u>momentito</u> (6) después, regresó con las bebidas. Mi <u>padre</u> (7) le dijo a mi hija mayor, "Pero, <u>chula</u> (8), ¡no vas a tomar ese whisky, seguramente!" "Ay, abuelito, y ¿por qué no? ¡<u>Salud!</u> (9)", dijo mi hija, y tomó el whisky <u>muy rápido</u> (10). "¡Dios mío!" dijo mi madre, "¿por qué dejas que tu hija tome bebidas tan fuertes?" "Abuelita, ya no soy niña . . . tengo mis dieciocho años", dijo mi hija, enojada. La verdad es que yo no sé qué hacer cuando hay problemas entre las generaciones, pero creo que es así en todas las familias, ¿no?

C. ¡Brindemos! *(Let's toast!)*

1. Make two very informal toasts, as if with a friend.

_____   _____

2. Make a more formal toast, as if to your boss.

_____

D. ¡Falta algo! Complete the expressions with the name of a food or drink.

1. "Usted no es nada, ni chicha ni _____." *(from a song lyric)*
2. ¡Caray! La Julia se ve muy bonita; está hecha un _____.
3. Estoy hasta la madre con mi jefe; mañana si me dice media cosita, lo voy a mandar a freír _____.
4. Hola, Enrique, ¿qué tal? ¿Cómo está la media _____?
5. ¡Qué lugar más simpático! De veras, es una _____.

E. En el restaurante. You're at a restaurant. Do the following:

1. Say "Evening" to the hostess.   _____

2. Call the waiter.   _____

3. Order a drink.   _____

4. Say you want your steak well done.   _____

5. Tell your friends "Enjoy the meal."   _____

6. When your friends leave, tell them you hope all goes well with them.   _____

REPASO 3

Review of Chapters 11–15

(50 points)

A. Crucigrama. Solve the following crossword puzzle. (1-16)

Horizontal:
   2. un tipo ya no joven, un señor
   5. antes de tomar, se dice "____"
   7. mandar por fax
   8. no simpático
   11. mandar por correo electrónico
   13. antes de comer, se dice "Buen ____"
   14. insultar, ofender con palabrotas
   15. de ninguna manera; ni a la ____

Vertical:
   1. maravilloso: pura ____ (Costa Rica)
   3. no funciona; no ____
   4. historias: déjate de ____
   6. rostro; al mal tiempo buena ____
   8. náusea; me da ____
   9. límite: esto es el ____
   10. esposo(a): media ____
   12. café (Costa Rica); fantástico: una ____ (Colombia)

B. ¿Qué podemos decir de ti? What can we say about you, my friend? Many things. Match each Spanish description to the correct English meaning. (Two English meanings will not be used.)

17. __Tienes careto hoy.
18. __Duermes a lo chancho chingo.
19. __Estás hecho(-a) un mango.
20. __No se puede contigo.
21. __Eres mono(-a).
22. __Cambias mucho de tema.
23. __Estás hasta la madre.
24. __No fumas pitillos.

a. You're cute.
b. You don't smoke cigarettes.
c. You are impossible to deal with.
d. You're as gullible as they come.
e. You change topics a lot.
f. You look all washed out today.
g. You are fed up.
h. You kick up your heels.
i. You've become very attractive.
j. You sleep like a log.

C. La terminación perfecta. Find the right word from the list to end each sentence. (Two words will not be used.)

ocupado	platos	jamones	guayaba	amamos
cabeza	pizca	madre	pasta	Dios
fuerza	tonterías	ratito	barril	

25. Vamos a brindar. ¡Para las que _____!
26. No comprendo la situación. No tiene pies ni _____.
27. Aquí vive mi familia. Te voy a presentar a mis _____.
28. El director no está contento. Tiene cara de teléfono _____.
29. Esas ideas son ridículas. ¡Qué _____!
30. No tengo interés en esa historia. Me importa _____.
31. ¿Cuándo va a volver mi amigo? Sabe _____.
32. Esta vez yo no voy a pagar la cuenta. ¡Ni a la _____!
33. Gabriela viene pronto. Va a estar aquí en un _____.
34. ¡Qué mentira! No voy a tragarme esa _____.
35. Esa niña no me trata con cortesía. No tiene ni _____ de educación.
36. Dos cervezas de _____, por favor.

D. Palabras revueltas. Unscramble the words and write the Spanish expressions from the list that are hidden in the mixed-up letters. Two expressions from the list will not be used.

estar hasta la coronilla	sueña con pájaros preñados
no juegues	me sacaste de onda
se me hace la boca agua	todo el santo día
ni chicha ni limonada	sin ton ni son

37. You see something but can't make out what it is. It's neither fish nor fowl. **[in chachi in landoima]** _____.

38. A friend did the unexpected. You tell him that he surprised the heck out of you. **[em ascesat ed anod]** ¡ _____!

39. Those people work *all day long:* **[doot le otsna ída]** _____.

40. Aurora is always dreaming up hairbrained schemes. **[eñasu noc josaprá sopderañ]** _____.

41. It's time to be serious. You tell your companion to stop fooling around. **[¡on seuguje!]** ¡ _____!

42. The situation is without rhyme nor reason! **[¡nis not in nos!]**
    ¡ _____!

E. Pero, ¿qué querrán decirme? Choose the correct meaning for the following Spanish words or expressions.

43. Your Mexican friends tell you they are leaving for **gringolandia.** Where are they going? To . . .
    a. a shopping center
    b. a video arcade
    c. the U.S.A.

44. A Costa Rican says to you: **¡Momentico!** which means . . .
    a. Wait a minute!
    b. Get moving!
    c. Tell me the time!

45. A Venezuelan reacts to your suggestions with the comment, **¡Puras vainas!** What's she saying?
    a. Great ideas!
    b. Total nonsense!
    c. That's confusing!

46. One way of saying *no* in many parts of Latin America is
    a. ¡**naranjas!**
    b. ¡**bananas!**
    c. ¡**mangos!**

47. If a Latin American sends you **a freír papas,** it means that he
    wants you to . . .
    a. buy food
    b. get lost
    c. have a good time

48. Isabel says to you, **Me topé con Manolo.** She means she . . .
    a. bumped into Manolo
    b. fell in love with Manolo
    c. danced with Manolo

49. Your pal says to you: ¡**Basta ya!** What is he saying?
    a. Hurry up!
    b. Cut it out!
    c. Speak louder!

50. A lot of your friends from Central America refer to this one guy as
    a **pendejo,** so you figure that he probably is . . .
    a. pretty brilliant
    b. a crazy character
    c. a real jerk

Answers to Exercises (¡A usted le toca! and Repasos)

Chapter 1
A. Responda, por favor. 1. b 2. a 3. c 4. b 5. b 6. c

B. Sinónimos. 1. h 2. d 3. b 4. g 5. c 6. a 7. f 8. e

C. Y tú, ¿qué tal? Possible answers: 1. Estoy encantado(-a) de la vida (feliz como una lombriz). 2. Estoy en la gloria. 3. Más o menos. 4. Por aquí (Aquí nomás), trabajando. 5. Estoy crudo(-a). Estoy enguayabado(-a). Estoy de goma. Tengo resaca (guayabo, la mona). 6. Estoy rendido(-a). Estoy hecho(-a) pinole. 7. Estoy agüitado(-a).

D. ¿Cómo se dice . . . ? Possible answers (**tú** form): 1. ¿Cómo te va? 2. ¿Cómo te ha ido? 3. ¿Qué tal? 4. ¿Qué me cuentas? 5. ¿Qué onda?

Chapter 2
A. ¿Qué dicen realmente? 1. b 2. b 3. a 4. c 5. c

B. Chilenismos. 1. despelote 2. siútico 3. pololear 4. gallos 5. El poto 6. copuchar 7. cuñas

C. Palabras revueltas. 1. palo de escoba 2. hacen la vista gorda 3. ¡no es justo! 4. meter la cuchara 5. ¡se dio un ataque de caspa! 6. está todo derretido con ella

D. ¿Qué falta? 1. nada / d 2. cual / e 3. bola / b 4. flauta / f 5. moscas / a 6. gorda / c

E. Responda, por favor. 1. Esta cola no avanza porque los funcionarios están copuchando. Nos hacen la vista gorda. No nos dan bola. Ese gallo está todo derretido con la fulana allí. Es un despelote. Tenemos que reclamar. 2. No te hagas mala sangre. Los trámites siempre redemoran. La pura verdad. Tenemos que comernos el buey. 3. ¡Un poco de respeto, por favor! ¡Qué descaro! Ud. es un rajado. No puede entrar aquí primero como si nada. Eso no es justo. Tenga la bondad de esperar su turno como todos.

263

Chapter 3
A. Sinónimos. 1. i 2. d 3. e 4. a 5. h 6. b 7. c 8. f 9. g
B. ¿Qué es? 1. vacilón 2. pana 3. cero a la izquierda 4. fresa
5. aguafiestas 6. gorila
C. ¿Qué falta? 1. hechos / b 2. está / f 3. Dichosos / a 4. vagando / g
5. nunca / c 6. quedamos / d 7. de / e
D. ¿Qué dice usted . . . ? Possible answers: 1. Este . . . , Bueno . . . ,
Pues . . . 2. ¡Sí, vamos a vacilar! 3. Gracias, pero tengo mucho que hacer.
E. Invitaciones. Possible answers (**tú** form): 1. ¿Qué te parece si vamos a
una fiesta? ¿Te gustaría ir a una fiesta? 2. Asómate a las ocho.
3. No me dejes plantado(-a). No tires bomba. No me dejes con los
churquitos (colochos) hechos. 4. No veo la hora de salir.

Chapter 4
A. Sinónimos. 1. d 2. e 3. a 4. f 5. c 6. b
B. Antónimos. 1. d 2. e 3. a 4. b 5. f 6. c
C. ¿Qué falta? 1. Podría Ud. decirme 2. derecho 3. cachondeando
4. brazo partido 5. los huesos 6. un apuro
D. La palabra exacta. 1. b 2. a 3. c 4. b 5. c 6. a
E. ¿Qué dice usted? 1. ¡Oiga, señor! ¿Podría usted decirme cómo llegar
al Hotel Colonial? 2. Mucho gusto. Me llamo _____. 3. Para llegar al
Café La Perla, camina derecho cinco cuadras (manzanas *in Spain*) y
luego dobla a la izquierda en la Calle Flores, y allí mismo lo vas a ver a
la derecha. 4. ¡Oiga, señor! (*or* ¡Camarero!) ¿Podría usted decirme
dónde están los baños (servicios, cuartos de baño, el excusado, el cuarto
para señoras, el cuarto para caballeros)?

Chapter 5
A. La palabra completa. 1. c 2. d 3. g 4. e 5. a 6. f 7. b
B. En otras palabras. 1. paro 2. De pronto 3. Estoy de mal genio 4. Me
tronaron 5. mina 6. fatal 7. frita 8. requete 9. cuate 10. camellar 11. la
divina garza 12. buena onda
C. ¿Qué falta? 1. mi hija 2. nada 3. universidad 4. Muchas gracias.
5. estoy 6. Nada más 7. va a hacer
D. Una conversación por teléfono. 1. Por lo pronto 2. de paseo
3. Okey 4. Ojalá 5. una nueva chamba 6. volveré a llamar

E. Favores. Possible answers (**tú** form): 1. ¿Me haces un paro? 2. No seas pesado(-a). 3. No puedo, porque tengo que camellar (chambear). 4. Okei, sale y vale.

Chapter 6
A. ¡Misterio, misterio! 1. paracaidista 2. pisco 3. tocayos
B. Sinónimos. 1. e 2. f 3. a 4. c 5. g 6. b 7. d
C. Completar la frase. 1. olla 2. caballero 3. antigua 4. alma 5. bien 6. piola
D. Situaciones. 1. (to my hostess:) Ud. está muy guapa (in Argentina, muy paquete) esta noche. Está como una reina. La casa se ve muy bonita y bien arreglada. La comida (in Perú: el papeo) estuvo rica (rico). ¡Qué delicia! (to my host:) Ud. está muy guapo (caballero) esta noche. 2. ¡Qué ocurrencia! (or: ¡nada de eso!) ¿Cómo cree? No debe decir eso. (or: Usted es muy amable. Favor que Ud. me hace.) 3. María (or: Juan) es una buena persona. Me cae muy bien. 4. María (or: Juan) no me cae bien. Se cree la divina pomada. No es muy amable.

Chapter 7
A. En otras palabras. 1. plena 2. se ponen 3. platicar 4. Sales hasta en la sopa. 5. Nítida. 6. notas 7. imagínate 8. rompimos 9. esfumado 10. ¡No puede ser! 11. extrañado 12. Total 13. qué bárbaro
B. ¿Qué falta? 1. trapos / g 2. baraja / e 3. cotorreo / a 4. torta / c 5. sopa / f 6. que / h 7. hacer / b 8. metiche / d
C. Amigos falsos. 1. pregnant 2. gross thing, word, expression; vulgarity 3. aroused, excited (usually sexually) 4. success 5. soup 6. well brought up 7. to bring about, make real
D. Sinónimos. 1. f 2. e 3. a 4. c 5. d 6. b
E. En una situación informal, ¿qué dice usted . . . ? Possible answers (**tú** form): 1. Chócala. 2. ¿Cachas? ¿Cachaste? ¿Viste? 3. Está que arde. 4. ¡Chanfle! ¡Cielo verde! ¡Diantre! ¡Dianche! ¡Híjole! ¡Huy! ¡Rayos!

Chapter 8
A. ¿Qué falta? 1. cuernos 2. medias 3. besos 4. ojitos 5. copas 6. cobrar
B. Palabras revueltas. 1. un buen partido 2. tengo que cortar 3. juega para el otro equipo 4. dígame 5. bueno 6. mi amor

C. Dos modos de hablar. 1. e 2. a 3. d 4. c 5. b

D. ¿Qué se dice? 1. Bueno, operadora, quisiera (quiero) llamar por cobrar al siguiente número . . . 2. Amorcito, corazón, querido(-a), mi amor, mi cielo, mi corazoncito, mi negro(-a), mi vida, tesoro, te quiero y te amo mucho. 3. Besos y abrazos.

Chapter 9

A. ¿Qué es? 1. supercoco 2. pelado 3. chaparro 4. zanahoria 5. estrafalario 6. cursi 7. chicle 8. plástico

B. Características. 1. height 2. nose 3. ears 4. stomach 5. beard 6. hands 7. feet 8. gluttonous 9. a whiner 10. bossy 11. angry 12. sleepyhead 13. irresponsible 14. "fraidy-cat"

C. Sinónimos. 1. e 2. g 3. a 4. h 5. d 6. b 7. c 8. f

D. ¿Qué falta? 1. gente / g 2. pilas / d 3. pierde / f 4. menear / b 5. Epa / c 6. oreja / e 7. basta / a

E. Mi hermano. Possible answers: Mi hermano es chaparro y rubio. Es muy mandón. Nunca cumple con sus promesas porque es muy faltón. Es comilón y panzón. Es muy abusivo. ¡Qué hermano más pasmado!

Chapter 10

A. ¿Qué quiere decir? 1. c 2. g 3. f 4. h 5. d 6. b 7. e 8. a

B. ¿Dónde estamos—en Argentina o en México? 1. A (niños, *kids*) 2. M (soborno, *bribe*) 3. M (amigo, *pal*), (groseros, *crude*) 4. A (amigo, *pal*), (autobús escolar, *school bus*) 5. A (se divierten, *have a good time*) 6. M (me confundo, *I get confused*) 7. M (comida servida antes de la cena, *appetizers*) 8. A (comida servida antes de la cena, *appetizers*) 9. M (¿Cómo? *Excuse me, what did you say?*) 10. A (sobornos, *bribes*)

C. Completar la frase. 1. bien puestos 2. de menos 3. mayúsculo 4. por el suelo 5. que sí 6. escándalo 7. como una lechuga 8. increíbles 9. por debajo de la mesa

D. ¡Insultos y palabrotas! 1. b 2. c 3. b 4. d 5. a

E. Reacciones. 1. ¡Qué cochinadas hacen! Son corruptos. Todo lo hacen por debajo de la mesa. La situación está por el suelo. 2. Nos llama a todos una bola de pendejos. Se nos encabrona. Se pone fúrico (furioso). Nos grita "¡Me están chingando!" Nos mienta la madre. Y agarra a todos por parejo. 3. ¡Hola, cabrón [pinche cabrón *in Mexico*), boludo *in Argentina,* huevón *in Chile*]! ¿Cómo estás?

Chapter 11
A. Al contrario. Possible answers: 1. antipático 2. de ninguna manera
3. ton ni son 4. a palos (a la fuerza, loco[-a]) 5. en serio 6. ratito
7. sirve
B. En otras palabras. 1. no tiene pies ni cabeza 2. Puras vainas. 3. se me
van a cruzar los cables 4. ¡Naranjas! 5. Ni hablar. 6. Sabe Dios.
7. maestro
C. Cognados. 1. surfear 2. cliquear 3. faxear 4. emailear 5. hacer un
download 6. hacer un backup
D. ¡Falta algo! 1. pájaros / e 2. topo / f 3. tragar / b 4. Basta / c
5. onda / a 6. jugar / d
E. Responda, por favor. Possible answers (**tú** form): 1. ¡Qué va! ¡No
hablas en serio! 2. Déjate de cuentos. Ya está bien de cuentos. 3. No
voy a tragarme esa guayaba. ¡No juegues! 4. ¡Qué invente! ¡Qué tontería! ¡Qué ridículo!

Chapter 12
A. Completar las frases. 1. d 2. a 3. g 4. e 5. h 6. f 7. c 8. i 9. b
B. Tiquismos. 1. pequeñito, auto 2. de nada 3. ¿qué se puede hacer?
4. ¡fantástico!, costarricenses 5. plato de arroz y otras cosas, el café
6. ¡qué lástima!
C. Palabras revueltas. 1. un desahogo 2. se dio cuenta. 3. se armó la
gorda. 4. ¡Achará! 5. está destrozado. 6. ¡qué dicha!
D. ¡Faltan los animales! 1. cabra, c 2. chancho, e 3. perra, d 4. pajarita,
a 5. burro, f 6. rana, b
E. ¿Qué diría usted? 1. Lo siento muchísimo. La (te) acompaño en su (tu)
dolor. Estoy con usted (contigo) y con su (tu) familia. Quiero darles el
pésame. ¡Achará! (Costa Rica) ¿Diay? (Costa Rica) Cuente Ud. (cuenta)
conmigo. 2. Ánimo, amigo. Se le (te) fue la pajarita, ¿y qué? Al mal
tiempo, buena cara. Ud. vale (tú vales) mucho. Ya va (vas) a conocer a
otra chica simpática. No es para tanto. Cuente Ud. (cuenta) conmigo.
Answers to "Los animales en los refranes ticos." 1. C 2. F 3. H 4. B
5. I 6. A 7. E 8. G 9. D

Chapter 13
A. Responda, por favor. 1. a 2. b 3. b 4. c
B. 1. b 2. a 3. a 4. b 5. b 6. b

C. ¡Falta algo! 1. santo / c 2. ocupado / f 3. chocolate / d 4. cosita / a 5. madre / e 6. raya / b

D. En otras palabras. 1. hasta la madre 2. bravo 3. tranquilízate 4. fregada 5. naco 6. pizca

E. ¿Cómo se dice . . . ? Possible answers (**tú** form): 1. Tranquilízate. Cálmate. 2. No se puede contigo. 3. Estoy hasta la madre (las cejas, la coronilla). 4. ¡Esto es el colmo! 5. Ya te pasaste. Te pasaste de la raya.

Chapter 14

A. Antónimos. 1. d 2. c 3. f 4. e 5. a 6. b

B. En España, ¿cómo se dice? 1. os apetece 2. boquerón 3. vosotros 4. patatas 5. pelmazo 6. ¡Mozo!, tapas 7. una perra

C. Selecciones. 1. b 2. d 3. c 4. d 5. a

D. Palabras revueltas. 1. a rajatablas 2. hasta el gorro 3. la boca agua 4. cambiando de tema . . . 5. me dan asco

E. Situaciones. 1. Buenos días. (Buenas tardes.) Dos finos (sherries), por favor. (or: Dos cervezas, etc.) ¿Hay tapas? 2. No me gusta la comida picante. Prefiero la comida suave. (Or: the reverse.) Soy vegetariano(-a) a rajatablas. Se me antoja mucho la comida china (mexicana, francesa, cubana, etc.). Me encantan (in Spain, me apetecen) los mariscos (or: las patatas). Ahora, cambiando de tema . . . 3. Buenas tardes, ¿qué piensa usted de la música que tocan (de la comida que sirven) aquí?

Answers to "Expresiones con alimentos." 1. D 2. A 3. F 4. J 5. B 6. H 7. E 8. I 9. C 10. G

Chapter 15

A. Antónimos. 1. d 2. f 3. a 4. c 5. e 6. b

B. En otras palabras. 1. jefes 2. media naranja 3. chiquitines 4. pongo 5. fría 6. momentico 7. tata 8. mona 9. ¡Fondo blanco! 10. rapidingo

C. ¡Brindemos! Possible answers: 1. ¡(Arriba, abajo) Al centro y p'adentro! ¡Fondo blanco! 2. ¡Salud! ¡Chin chin!

D. ¡Falta algo! 1. limonada 2. mango 3. papas (espárragos) 4. naranja 5. soda

E. En el restaurante. Possible answers: 1. Buenas. 2. ¡Oiga, señor (joven, amigo)! 3. Un jugo (una cerveza, etcétera), por favor. Quisiera . . . 4. Que esté bien cocido el bistec. 5. ¡Buen provecho! 6. ¡Que les vaya bien!

Repaso 1 (Review of Chapters 1–5)

A.

1	2	3	4	5	6	7	8	9	10	11	12	13
		[1]F					[2]C	E	R	O		
[3]G	O	R	D	A			H					
				[4]V	A	C	I	L	O	N		
		S					S					
	[5]F	A	T	[6]A	L		P			[7]B		
		S		S		[8]D	A			R		
	[9]A	G	U	A	F	I	E	S	T	A	S	
	P			D		V				Z		
	U			O		I				O		
	R			S		N			[10]L			
	O				[11]M	A	N	Z	A	N	A	
									N			
				[12]C	H	A	M	B	A			

B. ¿Qué podemos decir de los hermanos Sánchez? 15. l 16. j 17. g 18. a 19. k 20. h 21. b 22. c 23. d 24. e

C. La terminación perfecta. 25. canoa 26. huesos 27. corte 28. madre 29. escoba 30. cuchara 31. relajo 32. paro 33. leche 34. churquitos 35. moscas 36. amolado

D. Palabras revueltas. 37. ¡es lo máximo! 38. me tronaron 39. está en la gloria 40. feliz como una lombriz. 41. está en la olla 42. está toda derretida

E. Pero, ¿que querrán decirme? 43. c 44. b 45. b 46. a 47. a 48. b 49. c 50. b

Repaso 2 (Review of Chapters 6–10)

A.

		¹T				²T				³M	
		A		⁴G		I		⁵P	I	B	E	S
		P		U		C				N	
⁶G	U	A	N	A	C	O			⁷C	H	E
		S		G				⁸C	O		A
				U				U	C		R
		⁹C	H	A	P	A	R	R	O	
		H						S		
		A		¹⁰C	O	M	I	L	O	N
		P								
		I								
¹¹Z	A	N	A	H	O	R	I	A		

B. ¿Qué podemos decir de mis amigos y yo? 14. f 15. e 16. k 17. b 18. l 19. a 20. m 21. c 22. i 23. g 24. d

C. La terminación perfecta. 25. olla 26. oreja 27. piola 28. medias 29. cuernos 30. baraja 31. partido 32. lechuga 33. revueltos 34. asustón 35. alma 36. menos

D. Palabras revueltas. 37. ¡Es un comelibros! 38. ¡Tiene los pantalones bien puestos! 39. chapada a la antigua 40. juega para el otro equipo 41. se comió la torta antes de la fiesta 42. ponte las pilas

E. Pero, ¿que querrán decirme? 43. b 44. b 45. a 46. c 47. a 48. b 49. b 50. b

Repaso 3 (Review of Chapters 11–15)

A.

1	2	3	4	5	6	7	8	9	10	11	12
[1]V			[2]M	A	E	[3]S	T	R	O		
I						I					
D		[4]C				R					
[5]S	A	L	U	D		[6]C		V			
		E		[7]F	A	X	E	A	R		
		N		R							
[8]A	N	T	I	P	A	T	I	[9]C	O		[10]N
S		O						O			A
C		S	[11]E	M	A	I	L	E	A	R	
O		[12]S				M					A
	[13]P	R	O	V	E	C	H	O			N
		D					N				J
[14]P	U	T	E	A	R		[15]F	U	E	R	Z	A

B. **¿Qué podemos decir de ti?** 17. f 18. j 19. i 20. c 21. a 22. e 23. g 24. b

C. **La terminación perfecta.** 25. amamos 26. cabeza 27. jamones 28. ocupado 29. tonterías 30. madre 31. Dios 32. fuerza 33. ratito 34. guayaba 35. pizca 36. barril

D. **Palabras revueltas.** 37. ni chicha ni limonada 38. ¡Me sacaste de onda! 39. todo el santo día 40. Sueña con pájaros preñados. 41. ¡No juegues! 42. sin ton ni son

E. **Pero, ¿qué querrán decirme?** 43. c 44. a 45. b 46. a 47. b 48. a 49. b 50. c

Spanish–English Glossary

The following vocabulary list includes both active and passive expressions from the chapters, as well as vocabulary from the **¡A usted le toca!** sections and **Repasos** that is essential in order to do the exercises. Literal meanings are given in parentheses in English. For verbs with stem-changes, the change in stem (e.g., **ie, ue**) is given in parentheses. The numbers in brackets refer to the chapter in which the word or expression was introduced; [R] refers to the **Repasos.**

a brazo partido   (to a broken arm) to the limit (describing how hard someone is working) [4]

a lo chancho chingo   (long-tailed pig) like a rock (describing how well someone sleeps) [12]

a la derecha   to the right [4]

a la izquierda   to the left [4]

¿A qué te dedicas?   (**tú** form) What do you do for a living? [14]

a rajatabla   (to board breaking) at any cost, fanatical [14]

A saber.   (To be known.) Who knows? [11]

a la suerte de la olla   (to the luck of the pot) potluck [6]

a toda madre   (at full mother) great, fantastic (Mexico, Central America) [1]

abajo   down [4]

el abrazo   hug, embrace [8]

abusadísimo   very sharp, very clever (Mexico) [10]

abusado(-a)   sharp, clever (Mexico) [10]

abusivo(-a)   someone who takes advantage of others, sponge (Mexico: **abusón, abusona**) [9]

¡Achará!   What a shame! (Costa Rica) [12]

acompañar: Lo (La) acompaño en su dolor.   (I accompany you [**usted**] in your pain.) Please accept my condolences. [12]

aguantarse   to control oneself [8]

el, la aguafiestas   party-pooper [3]

agüitado(-a)   "down," tired, low (Mexico, Central America) [1]

ahí   there (close to the person spoken to) [4]

ahorita   (diminutive of **ahora**) right now, sooner than now (not used in Spain or Southern Cone; in Cuba, it means "in a little while") [6]

Ajá.   Uh-huh. I see. [9]

el ajo   garlic [8]

Al mal tiempo, buena cara.   (To bad weather, a good face.) When the going gets tough, the tough get going. [12]

al contrario   on the contrary [11]

al tiro   (at the throw) right now (Chile) [6]

allí   there (far from the person spoken to) [4]

Aló.   Hello. (Common way of answering the telephone in some Latin American countries) [8]

los amigos del alma   (friends of the soul) buddies, pals [6]

la amiguita   dear friend, little friend (female) [12]

amolado(-a): Te dejaron bien amolado(-a).   (They left you [**tú**] ruined, a wreck.) They wore you to a frazzle. [1]

el amorcito, la amorcita   (little love) sweetheart [8]

antipático(-a)   disagreeable, unpleasant [11]

antojarse   to provoke a craving (in someone); **Se me antoja una manzana.** I have a taste for an apple. [14]

los antojos   cravings [14]

el antro   dive, seedy bar or club (Spain) [14]

el apellido de soltera   maiden name of a married woman [6]

el apellido   last name [6]

apetecer   (to awaken one's appetite) to provoke a desire or yearning in someone; **Me apetece una sopa.** I have a taste for soup. (Spain) [14]

el apodo   nickname [8]

el aprovechado, la aprovechada   someone who takes advantage of others, opportunist [9]

el apuro: Usted me saca de un apuro.   You are getting me out of a difficulty. [4]

aquel, aquella   that (referring to a thing or person far from the person spoken to) [4]

aquellos, aquellas   those (referring to things or people far from the person spoken to) [4]

aquí here [4]

aquí nomás ([I'm] Just here) nothing is new. (Mexico, Central America) [1]

la arepa corn bread (Venezuela) [2]

armar escándalo to raise a fuss [10]

arrepentirse (ie) to regret, have second thoughts [5]

arriba up [4]

¡Arriba, abajo, al centro y p'adentro! (Up, down, to the center, and inside!) Down the hatch! Sometimes this is just said as, **¡Al centro y p'adentro!** [15]

el asco nausea or stomach upset [14]

Así quedamos. (That's how we'll remain.) That's how we'll leave it, agreed. [3]

así que . . . so . . . [7]

asomarse to show up [3]

asustón, asustona easily frightened, "fraidy-cat" [9]

el ataque de caspa (dandruff attack) fit, tantrum [2]

el auto car [12]

la aventura adventure; love affair [8]

¡Ay, bendito! (Blessed one!) Bless my soul!, used to express sympathy, common in Puerto Rico [7]

¡Bacán! ¡Bac! Great! Fantastic! (Ecuador, Puerto Rico, Colombia [also: **bacano**]) [9]

la bachata party (Dominican Republic) [3]

el bailorio party, dance (Ecuador) [3]

bajar to go down; to get off [4]

bajo(-a) short, low [9]

el baño bathroom [4]

el bar place to drink; food is also served [15]

barbudo bearded, with a heavy beard [9]

¡Basta ya! Enough already! That's enough! [11]

el bayú party (Caribbean) [3]

el bembé party (Caribbean) [3]

bendito(-a) blessed; sometimes used ironically for the opposite, e.g., **¡Ese bendito coche!** That damn (blessed) car! [14]

el beso kiss [8]; **besos y abrazos** (kisses and hugs) hugs and kisses (common ending for a letter to a friend) [8]

el besuqueo smooching [8]

la bici (short for **bicicleta**) bicycle [5]

bien educado(-a) well brought up [7]

blanco y negro black and white [8]

bobo(-a) foolish [13]

las bolas balls; testicles; **tener bolas** to be brave (vulgar) (Argentina, Chile, Uruguay) [10]

el boli (short for **bolígrafo**) pen [5]

bolo(-a) drunk (Central America) [1]

el boludo lazy dope (vulgar) (Argentina) [10]

la bomba: Lo pasamos bomba. We have a good time (spend it bomb). (Argentina) [10]

el bondi school bus (Argentina) [10]

la botana appetizers (Mexico) [10]

bravo(-a) brave; angry [13]

el briago, la briaga drunkard (Mexico, Central America) [9]

la bronca fight, argument [13]

la bruja witch [6]

¡Buen provecho! ([Take] Good advantage!) Enjoy your meal! [15]

buena gente (good people) nice, kind person or people [9]

buena onda (good sound wave) good deal or thing [5]

buena moza lovely [6]

Buenas. (Good) Afternoon/Evening. [15]

Bueno. (Good) normal way of answering the telephone in Mexico [8]

Bueno . . . a hesitation word, like "uh, well . . ." [3]

el burro donkey [12]

la cabra female goat [4]

el cabrón son of a bitch (vulgar) [10]

la cabronada dirty trick [13]

los cabros, las cabras (goats) kids, children (Chile, Peru) [2]

¿Cachas? (present tense) Do you catch the drift? Get it?; **¿Cachaste?** (past tense) Did you catch the drift? Got it? (**tú** forms) [7]

el cachón horn of an animal; **tener cachones** to have horns, meaning that a person's spouse or sweetheart is cheating on him or her (Costa Rica) [4]

cachondearse (de alguien) to make fun of or tease (someone) [4]

caerse por acá   to drop in here [6]

el cafiche   pimp (Argentina) [2]

cagar   to shit; to make a mistake (vulgar) [10]

Caigo.   (I fall.) I understand. [8]

la cajetilla   pack (of cigarettes) [14]

caliente   hot (temperature) [14]

calle abajo   down the street [4]

calle arriba   up the street [4]

el callejón: en un callejón sin salida   in a hopeless situation (blind alley) [12]

el camarero, la camarera   waiter, waitress [14]

cambiando de tema   changing the subject (theme) [14]

camellar   (to camel) to work [5]

el camello   (camel) work, job [5]

el camión   truck; bus (Mexico); **camión de carga** truck (Mexico) [2]; **camión escolar** school bus (Mexico) [10]

cansado(-a)   tired [R]

¡Carajo!   (reference to male organ) expletive used to express disgust or annoyance (vulgar, especially in Latin America) [13]; **¿Qué carajo hacías?** What the hell were you doing? [13]

¡Caramba!   Jeeze! Darn it! (euphemism of **¡Carajo!,** vulgar) [13]

¡Caray!   Jeeze! Darn it! (euphemism of **¡Carajo!,** vulgar) [3]

el careto   (white-faced mask) face that suggests fatigue or worry [14]

el carro   car (Mexico, Central America) [12]

casado   (married man) Costa Rican dish of rice, beans, meat or fish, and salad [12]

el castellano   the Spanish language [10]

el CD-ROM   CD-ROM [11]

un cero a la izquierda   (a zero to the left) worthless, no good [3]

cerquita   very near (diminutive of **cerca**) [4]

la chacra   country cottage (Peru) [6]

la chamba   work or job [5]

chambear   (also, **chambiar**) to work [5]

¡Chanfle!   Good grief! (used to express surprise or when there is a problem) [7]

chapado(-a) a la antigua   old-fashioned [6]

chaparro(-a)   short (Mexico, Central America) [9]

los chapines   slang term for Guatemalans [6]

chasgracias (short for **muchas gracias**) [5]

chato(-a) (pug-nosed) affectionate nickname [8]

chau, chau bye-bye (used mainly in Argentina, Chile, and Uruguay) [8]

el chavo, la chava guy, girl [1]

che friend, pal (Argentina, Uruguay) [8]

chévere great, fantastic (most of Latin America except the Southern Cone; most common in Caribbean areas, Venezuela, Colombia) [3]

los chiches a woman's breasts, "tits" (Mexico); knicknacks, trinkets (Chile) [8]

el chicle (chewing gum) someone hard to get rid of [9]

chico(-a) (used in direct address) friend, pal [3]

¡Chin chin! (imitating the sound of glass clinking) Cheers! [15]

chingado(-a) (chinga'o[-a]) ripped, torn; screwed (vulgar f-word in Mexico and Central America); to break; **chingarse** to get upset (Spain) [10]

chingar to rip, tear; to screw (vulgar f-word in Mexico and Central America); to break; **chingarse** to get upset (Spain) [10]

chiquitico(-a) very, very tiny (Costa Rica and parts of the Caribbean) [12]

el chiquitín, la chiquitina kid, small child [15]

los chismorreos gossip [7]

chiviar to gamble, play dice (Mexico, Central America) [11]

Chócala. (Hit it.) Put it here. (**tú** form, said with a handshake) [7]

chogusto (short for **mucho gusto**) [5]

chulo(-a) cute, good-looking [3]

chupar to drink alcohol (Peru, Chile) [6]

un(a) churro(-a) bárbaro(-a) (savage fritter) good-looking man or woman [8]

el ciberamigo, la ciberamiga cyberfriend, friend over the Net [11]

¡Cielo verde! (Green sky!) Holy smoke!, used to express that something is surprising or unusual [7]

cincuentón, cincuentona fiftyish (the **-ón** is an augmentative, emphasizing age) [7]

¡Claro que sí! ¡Claro que no! Of course it is! Of course not! [10]

¡Claro! Sure! Clearly! Of course! [7]

Claro, y los chanchos vuelan. Right, and that's likely (pigs fly). (sarcastic) [2]

cliquear to click (e.g., on a computer mouse) [11]

cobrar to charge [8]

el coche car [12]

la cochinada (pig act) dirty trick [10]

el cochino pig [10]

coco   (coconut; masculine and feminine) smart, intelligent

coger   to take, catch, grab; to screw (vulgar) (Argentina, Uruguay, Mexico, and some parts of Central America) [4]

la coima   bribe (Argentina, Uruguay) [10]

los cojones   testicles; **¡Cojones!** common expletive in Spain [10]

cojonudo(-a)   (having large testicles) term of condemnation roughly equivalent to *god-damn* or *son of a bitch;* also used for praising something very good, e.g., **¡Esta comida está cojonuda!** This meal is god-damn tasty! (vulgar) (Spain) [14]

la cola   (tail of an animal) line or queue of people waiting [2]

el, la cole   (short for **colega**) colleague, friend, pal [5]

la comay   (**comadre**) ("co-mother" of one's child) close female friend [7]

el comelibros   (bookeater) bookworm [9]

comer el sanduche antes del recreo   (to eat the sandwich before recess) to enjoy something before it should be enjoyed [7]

comer la torta antes de la fiesta   (to eat the cake before the party) to enjoy something before it should be enjoyed [7]

comerse el buey   (to eat up the ox) to put up with something you don't like [2]

comilón, comilona   gluttonous [9]

Como quiera.   As you like. [15]

como agua para chocolate   (like water for chocolate) at the boiling point, because of either anger or passion (Mexico) [13]

como cocodrilo en fábrica de carteras   (like a crocodile in a wallet factory) nervous [1]

como perro en canoa   (like a dog in a canoe) nervous [1]

como si nada   (as if nothing) just like that, like you don't have a care in the world [4]

¿Cómo cree(s)?   How can you think that? (disclaimer after a compliment) [6]

¿Cómo diré?   How shall I put it (say this)? [7]

¿Cómo está la movida?   How's the action? [7]

¿Cómo que . . . ?   What do you mean . . . ?; **¿Cómo que perdiste el dinero?** What do you mean you (**tú**) lost the money? [9]

¿Cómo te ha ido?   (How has it gone for you?) How have you (**tú**) been? [1]

¿Cómo te sientes hoy?   How are you (**tú**) feeling today? [4]

¿Cómo te va?   (How's it going for you?) How are you (**tú**)? [1]

¿Cómo?   Excuse me? What (did you say)? [2]

el compa   close male friend (from **compadre**) [1]

común average, ordinary; **el hombre común** the common man [14]

con mucho gusto (with great pleasure) you're welcome (Costa Rica) [12]

¡Coño! (reference to the female organ) expletive roughly equivalent to *Goddamn!* (vulgar, especially in Latin America) [14]

el contrapiropo amusing comment a woman says to a man who has made a street compliment (**piropo**) [6]

la copa wine glass; (alcoholic) drink; **tomar una copa** to have a drink [10]

copuchar to gossip (Chile) [2]

el coraje courage; anger (Mexico); **tener coraje** to be brave; to be angry (Mexico) [2]

el corazón (heart) darling [8]

cortar (to cut) to hang up (the phone) [8]

el correo mail [5]

la cosa: una media cosita (half a little thing) every little thing; **una gran cosota** a big deal [13]; **cosas para picar** (things to pick at) appetizers (Chile) [10]

creerse la divina garza to think one is hot stuff (the divine heron) [5]

creerse la divina pomada to think one is hot stuff (the divine cream) [6]

creerse el (la) muy muy to think one is hot stuff (the very very) [1]

el cretino, la cretina idiot [13]

la criada maid (Spain) [6]

la criatura (creature) baby [9]

la cruda (rawness) hangover (Mexico, Central America) [1]

crudo(-a) hung over (Mexico, Central America) [1]

cruzar: ¿Se te cruzaron los cables? (Did your cables get crossed?) Are you crazy? [11]

el cuadernícolas very serious student who studies a lot, from **cuaderno**, *notebook* [9]

la cuadra block of a street (Latin America); stable (Spain) [4]

cuando la rana eche pelos (when the frog sprouts hair) the twelfth of never, when hell freezes over [12]

el cuarto room; **cuarto de baño** bathroom [4]; **cuarto de discusión** chatroom [11]; **cuarto para caballeros** men's room [4]; **cuarto para señoras (damas)** ladies' room [4]

el cuate, la cuata pal, good friend (Central America, Mexico) [5]

Cuente conmigo. (**usted** form) Count on (with) me. [12]

el cuerno horn [8]

cuico(-a) ostentatious snob (Chile) [2]

¡Cuidado! (Care!) Watch out! Be careful! [14]

el culo ass [vulgar] [2]

las cuñas (props, wedges) connections (social, political, etc.) (Chile) [2]

cursi corny, too cute or sentimental [9]

el danzón dance [3]

dar a luz to give birth (to give to the light) [8]

dar asco (to give nausea) to make (someone) sick to his or her stomach [14]

dar bola a alguien (to give someone the ball) to pay attention to someone [2]

dar calabazas (to give pumpkins) to reject someone or stand him or her up [3]

dar una patada to (give a) kick [15]

dar el pésame (to give the "it weighs on me") to express one's sympathy in case of a death or misfortune [12]

dar plantón to stand (someone) up (Spain) [3]

dar la vuelta to make a turn (to the right or left) (Latin America) [4]

darle en la madre to hurt someone where they are vulnerable (emotionally or physically) [15]

darse cuenta to realize (give oneself account) [12]

de barril (from the barrel) draft (beer) [15]

de los pies a la cabeza from head to toe [8]

de mal humor in a bad mood [4]

de mal talante in a bad mood (Spain) [4]

de nada you're welcome [12]

de ninguna manera no way, in no manner [11]

de nuevo again [3]

de película like a movie, great [1]

de remate (terminally) hopelessly, completely [6]

dejar to leave [R]; **dejar con los churquitos (colochos) hechos** to leave (someone) waiting (with their curls done) (Caribbean, Central America) [3]; **dejar con los ruleros puestos** (to leave someone with their rollers in) to stand (someone) up (Chile) [3]; **dejar plantado(-a)** (to leave [someone] planted) to stand (someone) up [3]

Déjate de cuentos. Enough of your stories. [11]

demorar to take a long time [2]

depender de to depend on [12]

la depre (short for **depresión**) depression [5]

Derecho al infierno contigo. Straight to hell with you. [13]

derecho straight ahead [4]

desahogarse (to undrown oneself) to get rid of worry by talking with a friend about a problem [12]

el desahogo (undrowning) outpouring of feeling with a friend [12]

desde luego of course [4]

la despedida de soltera send-off party for the bride before her wedding [6]

Destápate. (**tú** form) (Uncork yourself). Open up. [7]

destrozado(-a) broken up, upset [12]

el día feriado day off [9]

el diablo vendiendo cruces (the devil selling crosses) hypocrite [14]

¡Diablos! (Devils!) expletive equivalent to *Damn it!* [14]

¡Diantre(s)! or **¡Dianche!** (Devil!) Holy smoke!, used to express surprise or dismay [7]

¿Diay? But what can one do? (Costa Rica) [12]

Dichosos los ojos que te están viendo. (Fortunate the eyes that are looking at you.) Great to see you. Also **Dichosos los ojos.** [3]

Diga. (Tell.), **Dígame.** (Tell me.) normal way of answering the telephone in Spain [8]

¡Dios mío! (My God!) My goodness! [7]

¡Dios santo! (Holy God!) My goodness! [7]

la dirección address [4]

la dirección (casilla) electrónica e-mail address [11]

doblar to turn, make a turn (to the right or left) (Latin America) [4]

doler (ue): Me duelen hasta los huesos. (Even my bones ache.) I'm aching all over. [4]

el don Juan Don Juan, womanizer [3]

donde te dicen *hijito* sin conocerte (where they call you *my son* without knowing you) bordello, house of prostitution [11]

dormilón, dormilona describing someone who sleeps a lot, sleepyhead [9]

dormir (ue) a lo chancho chingo to sleep like a rock (long-tailed pig) [12]

echar chispas (to throw off sparks) to fume, be angry [5]

echar de menos to miss (throw for less) someone or something far away [10]

echar flores (to throw flowers) to compliment [6]

echar putadas to insult with offensive names (vulgar) [13]

echar relajo (to throw off or make a rumpus) to have a blast (Mexico) [1]

éjele hey (interjection like **oye**, listen) [7]

el elefante elephant [12]

elogiar to praise [6]

el email e-mail (pronounced with the sound of e-mail in English) [11]

emailear to e-mail (pronounced with the sound of e-mail in English) [11]

emocionado(-a) excited [7]

la empleada maid, employee (Chile) [6]

en serio seriously [8]

en un callejón sin salida in a hopeless situation (blind alley) [12]

encabronado(-a) angry (Mexico, Central America, Puerto Rico, many South American countries) [13]

encabronar to make (someone) angry (wild, like a goat) [13]; **encabronarse** to become angry (wild, like a goat) [10]

Encantado(-a). (Enchanted.) Pleased to meet you. [4]

encantado(-a) de la vida charmed or enchanted with life, very happy [1]

encantar: Me encanta(n). (It enchants me./ They enchant me.) I love it (them). [14]

enguayabado(-a) hung over (Colombia) [1]

enojado(-a) angry [2]

enojón, enojona hostile or angry [9]

¡Epa! Hey! Could I have your attention, please! (Caribbean) [4]; **¡Epa, epa!** interjection expressing surprise or shock [9]

Eres como arroz blanco: te veo hasta en la sopa. (You're like white rice: I see you even in the soup.) I see you (**tú** form) everywhere. [7]

¡Es lo máximo! It's (He's, She's) fantastic (the maximum)! [3]

Es un buen partido. He (She) is a good match (for marriage). [8]

Es un problema mayúsculo. It's a major (capital letter) problem. [10]

el escuintle twerp, insignificant boy (Mexico) [2]

ese, esa that (referring to a thing or person close to the person spoken to) [4]

esfumarse to disappear into thin air [7]

Eso no es justo. That is not fair (just). [2]

esos, esas those (referring to things or people close to the person spoken to) [4]

el espantapájaros scarecrow [9]

la esquina corner of two streets (The corner of two walls is **el rincón.**) [4]

Está (usted) como una reina. You look like (as beautiful as) a queen. [6]

Está cabrón. It's unbearable. (vulgar) [13]

Está hecha un mango. (She's become a mango.) She's very beautiful. [15]

Está por el suelo. It's in the pits, in a bad way (down on the floor). [10]

Está que arde. (It's burning.) It's at fever pitch. [7]

estar bolo(-a) to be drunk (Central America) [9]

estar crudo(-a) to be hung over (to be raw) (Mexico, Central America) [1]

estar de goma (to be made of gum, rubber) to be hung over (Central America) [1]

estar en la gloria (to be in one's glory) to be in seventh heaven, on cloud nine [1]

estar en la olla (to be in the pot) to be in hot water, in trouble [5]

estar frito(-a) (to be fried) to be sunk, in trouble [5]

estar geto(-a) to be drunk (Colombia) [9]

estar hasta la madre, hasta las cejas (eyebrows), **hasta la coronilla** (crown of the head) to be up to here, fed up; to have "had it" [13]

estar más serio que un burro en lancha (to be more serious than a donkey in a rowboat) to look worried [12]

estar pedo(-a) to be drunk (vulgar) [9]

estar seco(-a) (to be dry) to be broke, without money (Argentina) [9]

estar todo(-a) derretido(-a) to be completely under the spell (melted) [2]

Estás como nunca. (You [**tú**] are like never.) You look better than ever. [3]

Este . . . Uh . . . , Well . . . (hesitation word) [3]

¡Esto es el colmo! This is the last straw (the brim, limit, culmination)! [13]

estos, estas these [4]

Estoy a sus órdenes. I am at your service. [4]

Estoy con ustedes. I am with you. (expressing sympathy for misfortune) [12]

Estoy hasta el gorro con . . . I'm fed up (up to the cap) with . . . (Spain) [14]

Estoy hecho(-a) polvo. (I'm made into dust.) I'm exhausted. [4]

Estoy satisfecho(-a). I'm full (satisfied, in the sense of not wanting to eat any more). [14]

Estoy sin blanca. I'm flat broke (without a white one). (Spain) [14]

estrafalario(-a) strange, weird (usually referring mainly to dress) [9]

el excusado (the excused place) bathroom (euphemism) [4]

exitado(-a) aroused, excited (usually sexually) [7]

extrañado(-a) surprised, perplexed [7]

Ey. Yes. [15]

facilingo very easy [15]

faltón, faltona irresponsible, describing someone who doesn't do what they are supposed to do [9]

la fanfarria party (Puerto Rico) [3]

la farra   party (Colombia) [3]

fatal   (fatal) terrible, the pits [5]

Favor que usted me hace.   (Favor that you do me.) How nice of you to say so. [6]

el fax   fax [11]

faxear   to fax [11]

feliz como una lombriz   happy as a lark (worm) [1]

fenomenal   (phenomenal) great, super (Spain) [14]

feote(-a)   very ugly or very run down (**-ote** augmentative) [12]

la feria   (fair or day off) money (Mexico, Central America) [9]

Fíjese (usted). Fíjate (tú).   Just imagine. [7]

el fino   sweet sherry wine [14]

finolis   exaggeratedly refined, uppity (Spain) [14]

¡Fondo blanco!   (White bottom [of glass]!) Bottoms up! [15]

flaco(-a)   (skinny) affectionate nickname [8]

fregado(-a)   useless, messed up, ruined [13]

fregar (ie)   (to scour, rub [the wrong way]) to mess up, ruin, jerk around [13]

freír   to fry [R]; **mandar a freír papas (espárragos)** (to send to fry potatoes [asparagus]) to tell (someone) to get lost [15]

la fresa   (strawberry) a young woman who is innocent but also a bit disdainful or spoiled, usually living with her parents [3]

la fría   (cold one) a beer [15]

frito(-a)   (fried) in trouble [5]

fufurufo(-a)   stuck up [1]

el fulano, la fulana   so and so (to refer to someone you don't know) [2]; **fulano(-a) de tal** John (Jane) Doe [2]

fúrico(-a)   furious (Mexico) [10]

el gallo   (rooster) guy (Chile, Peru, some parts of Central America) [2]

los garabatos   scribblings, grafitti; swear words, bad words (Chile) [10]

la garza   heron; **creerse la divina garza** to think you're (one is) hot stuff (the divine heron) [5]

la gauchada   an immense favor (Argentina) [2]

el gaucho   Argentine cowboy [2]

el genio: no saber qué hacerse del mal genio   to be in such a bad mood one doesn't know what to do [5]

el gilipollas   jerk, dope (vulgar) (Spain) [14]

el golpe de teléfono   (hit with the telephone) phone call (Uruguay, Argentina) [8]

la gorda (fat one) ten-cent coin (Spain) [14]

gordo(-a) (fat) fat plum; darling; **gordito(-a)** (chubby) honey, dear [8]

gracias a Dios thank God [12]

Gringolandia (Gringoland) the United States [15]

la grosería ("gross" thing, expression, etc.) vulgar or obscene word, swear word [7]

la guachafita party (Venezuela) [3]

la guagua baby (Ecuador, Chile); bus (Caribbean) [9]

guapo(-a) attractive, gorgeous; brave (Caribbean) [6]

la guarra hussy, loose woman [4]

la guayaba: No voy a tragarme esa guayaba. I'm not going to swallow that nonsense (guava). [11]

güero(-a) blond(e), fair (Mexico) [2]

hacer un catorce (to make a fourteen) to do (someone) a favor (Colombia) [5]

hacer cola (to make a tail) to wait in line [2]

hacer un download (un backup) to download (back up) (computer file) [11]

hacer ojitos (to make little eyes) to flirt [8]

hacer un paro (to make a stop) to do (someone) a favor (Central America, Mexico) [5]

hacer la vista gorda (to do the fat look) to ignore [2]

hacerse + adj. to become + adj. [7]

hacerse bolas (to make balls of yourself) to get balled up, to get confused [10]

harto(-a) fed up [13]

hasta las cejas (up to the eyebrows) fed up [13]

hasta la coronilla (up to the crown of the head) fed up [13]

hasta el gorro (up to the cap) fed up [14]

hasta la madre (up to the mother) fed up [13]

hecho(-a) pinole ground down, exhausted (Mexico) [1]

la hermana sister [R]

el hermano brother [R]

el hijo de su (puta madre), also **el hijueputa** son of a gun (of a bitch) (vulgar) [13]

el hijo (la hija) natural illegitimate child [8]

¡Híjole! Wow! (expression of surprise), Darn! [7]

el hogar home, home life, hearth [12]

¡Hombre!   (Man!) term of address for either a man or a woman [3]

la home   home (from the English influence) [9]

¡Hostias!   (Hosts!) a strong expletive implying religious sacrilege and roughly equivalent to *God damn it!* (vulgar) [14]

hostigar   to annoy, badger, bug; **Que hostigas.** How you bug a person. [5]

el huaso   Chilean cowboy [2]

la huevada   stupid action typical of a **huevón** or **huevona** (vulgar) [10]

las huevas   testicles (vulgar, variant of **huevos** in Chile) [10]

el huevón, la huevona   lazy dope (vulgar) (Chile, Mexico, Central America) [10]

los huevos   eggs; testicles; **tener huevos** to be brave (vulgar) (Mexico, Central America, Chile) [10]

¡Huy!   Wow! (expression of surprise), Ouch! (expression of pain) [7]

la iglesia   church [14]

Imagínese (usted). Imagínate (tú).   Just imagine. [7]

las ínfulas   airs [6]

las intenciones honradas   honorable intentions [4]

ir de juerga   to go out on the town, party [3]

ir de parranda   to go out on the town, party [3]

ir subiendo   (to go ascending) to keep on going up [4]

ir y venir   coming and going [8]

–ísimo(-a)   superlative ending that makes adjectives more intense, e.g., **buenísimo** (very, very good), **hermosísima** (very, very beautiful) [12]

–ito(-a), –cito(-a), –illo(-a), –ico(-a)   diminutive endings added to words to indicate small size or sentiment, such as affection [14]

los jamones   (hams) parents (Andean countries) [15]

la jarana   party (Mexico, Spain, Peru) [3]

el jefe (la jefa)   (boss) husband (wife) [10, 11]

los jefes   (bosses, chiefs) parents [15]

el jerez   sherry wine [14]

¡Jesús!   (after a sneeze); **¡Jesús, María y José!** (after three sneezes) Gesundheit! [7]

joder   to screw, bother, trick, or "bug" someone; to break (something), commonly used but vulgar [7]

jodido(-a)   (past participle of **joder**) screwed, messed up, commonly used but vulgar [7]

joer from **joder**; interjection used in Spain, something like *Damn!* [9]

Juega para el otro equipo. He/She is homosexual (plays for the other team). [8]

jugar (ue) to bet; **jugarse la pasta** to bet one's money (paste) (Spain) [11]

juntos pero no revueltos together but not romantically involved (mixed) [8]

¡La pucha! softened form of **¡La puta!**, equivalent to *Darn it!* [8]

la lana (wool) money [1]

lanzado(-a) referring to someone who takes advantage of others (Colombia, Spain) or who is simply aggressive [9]

lejos far [R]

la ley law [8]

los limeños people from Lima, Peru [6]

la lisura smoothness, sincerity; obscene word, swear word (Peru) [10]

la llamada (telefónica) (phone) call [8]

llamar a larga distancia to call long distance [8]

llamar a portes revertidos (or **a portes pagados**) to call collect (Spain) [8]

llamar en otra línea to call on another line [8]

llamar por cobrar to call collect [8]

el llanero Venezuelan or Colombian cowboy [2]

llevar: llevarse bien to get along well [R]; **Llévame (tú) de paseo.** Take me on an outing. [5]

llorón, llorona describing a crybaby, whiner [9]

Lo (La) acompaño en su dolor. (I accompany you [**usted**] in your pain.) Please accept my condolences. [12]

Lo pasamos bomba. We have a good time (spend it bomb). (Argentina) [10]

Lo siento muchísimo. (I feel it very, very much.) I am very, very sorry. [12]

lo mismo de siempre the same as always [8]

el loco, la loca guy, girl (Ecuador, Colombia, Venezuela) [9]

m'ijo, m'ija (short for **mi hijo, mi hija**) my son, my daughter [5]

la madre: ¡La madre que te parió! (The mother who bore you!) insult similar to *son of a bitch* [14]; **Me importa madre.** I don't give a darn. [13]; **¡Ni madre!** No way! [13]; **puras madres** things of little value [13]

el maestro (teacher, master) middle-aged or older man, guy [11]

maje buddy, pal (used only among males) (Costa Rica) [10]

mala leche (bad milk) conflictive or difficult person [2]

mala nota   (bad note) unpleasant thing or person, bad news [7]

maldecir   to swear [14]

maldito(-a)   damn [14]

malhablado(-a)   crude in speaking habits [14]

el malnacido, la malnacida   (badly-born person) bastard [13]

mamacita   (little mama) term of address derived from **mamá**, used with affection to a girl or woman; also, **mamita, mami** [3]

mamasota   (big mama) term of address a bit vulgar, meaning *cheesecake,* good-looking woman [3]

'mana ('manita)   forms of **hermana,** sister (used to address a female friend) [1]

mandar a freír papas (espárragos)   (to send to fry potatoes [asparagus]) to tell (someone) to get lost [15]

mandarse un discurso   to deliver a sermon (speech) [2]

¿Mande?   Excuse me? What (did you say)? (Mexico) [2]

mandón, mandona   describing someone who likes to give orders, bossy [9]

un manguito   a good-looking person [15]

'mano ('manito)   forms of **hermano,** brother (used to address a male friend) [1]

manudo(-a)   (9) having large hands

manyar   to eat [6]

la manzana   (apple) block of a street (Spain) [4]

la máquina   machine; car (Cuba) [12]

el maricón, la maricona   somewhat derogatory way of saying homosexual (lesbian) [8]

la marimacha   girl with masculine manners, tomboy; used in some places for lesbian [8]

martes 13, jueves 13   Tuesday the 13th, Thursday the 13th (considered unlucky days in Spanish-speaking countries) [6]

Más o menos.   (More or less.) Okay. [1]

Más sabe el diablo por viejo que por diablo.   (The devil knows more because he's old than because he's the devil.) saying suggesting that old people have a lot of wisdom [14]

Más vale solo(-a) que mal acompañado(-a).   Better alone than in bad company (badly accompanied). [12]

más feo(-a) que mandado a hacer   uglier than a toad (than if designed for it) (Costa Rica) [12]

más loco(-a) que una cabra   crazier than a she-goat [12]

las mate   (short for **matemáticas**) math [5]

máximo: ¡Es lo máximo! It's (He's, She's) fantastic (the maximum)! [3]

mayúsculo(-a) capital (letter); **problema mayúsculo** major problem [10]

Me cae bien. He (She, It) pleases (suits) me. [6]

¡Me cago en Dios! (I shit on God!) strong expletive implying sacrilege and roughly equivalent to *I don't give a damn!* (vulgar) [14]

Me catearon. (They searched me.) I flunked, failed. (Spain) [5]

Me cortaste la nota. (You cut off my note.) You threw me off, messed me up. [11]

Me da asco. It makes me sick to my stomach (gives me nausea). [14]

Me duelen hasta los huesos. (Even my bones ache.) I'm aching all over. [4]

Me encanta(n). (It enchants me./ They enchant me.) I love it (them). [14]

Me hago bolas. I get confused, balled up (make balls to myself). (Mexico) [10]

Me rasparon. (They grated me.) I flunked, failed. (Venezuela) [5]

Me sacaste de onda. You knocked me out of kilter, threw me off. [11]

Me tiré. (I threw myself.) I flunked, failed. (Colombia) [5]

Me tronaron. (They blasted me.) I failed. (Central America, Mexico) [5]

la media naranja (half orange) spouse, sweetheart (male or female) [15]

las medias stockings [8]

menear el bote (to rock or move the boat) to dance [9]

mentar (ie) la madre (to mention the mother) to insult someone by suggesting the moral impurity of his or her mother [10]

la mesa: Todo lo hacen por debajo de la mesa. They do everything in a corrupt manner (under the table). [10]

el mesero, la mesera waiter, waitress (Mexico, Central America) [14]

meter la cuchara (to put in the soup spoon) to butt into someone else's business [2]

meterse en el sobre (to put oneself in one's envelope) to go to bed (Ecuador) [9]

metiche nosy [7]

mi amor my love [8]

mi bomboncito (my little piece of candy) darling, love [8]

mi cielo (my heaven) sweetheart, darling [8]

mi negro(-a) (my black one) sweetheart, darling [8]

mi reina (my queen) sweetheart [8]

mi santa (my saint) sweetheart [8]

mi vida (my life) sweetheart, darling [8]

¡Miércoles! (Wednesday!) Heck! euphemism for **¡Mierda!** [10]

¡Mierda!   Shit! (common expletive) (vulgar) [10]

la mina   girl (South America), woman (in the Argentine Lunfardo dialect used in tangos) [2]

¡Mirad!   Look! (familiar plural **vosotros[-as]** command form of the verb **mirar)** (Spain) [14]

molestar   to bother (false cognate that does not mean *molest* in the sexual sense) [14]

Un momentico.   Just a moment. (Colombia, Venezuela, Costa Rica) [15]

mono(-a)   cute; (Colombia) blond [15]

montar un cotorreo   to start a gab session [7]

la mordida   (bite) bribe (Mexico, Central America) [10]

mosquearse   (to have flies) to smell a rat (be suspicious) (Spain) [4]

mostrar (ue) los dientes   (to show teeth) to smile [2]

el mouse   mouse (computer) [11]

mover (ue) el esqueleto   (to move one's skeleton) to dance (Spain) [9]

la movida   the action, the scene; **en la movida** "with it," where the action is [7]

el mozo   (boy, lad, youngster) waiter [14]

la mucama   maid (Argentina) [6]

la muchacha   girl; maid (Mexico) [6]

Mucho gusto.   (Much pleasure.) Pleased to meet you. [4]

el mujeriego (mujerero)   womanizer [3]

el Mundial   world soccer championship [10]

muy especial   very special (sometimes used ironically to mean *difficult*) [10]

na'a (nada)   nothing [5]

Nacho   nickname for **Ignacio** [8]

el naco, la naca   jerk (Mexico) [13]

Nada de eso.   (None of that.) Not at all. [6]

¡Naranjas!   (Oranges!) No! [11]; **¡Naranjas de la China!** (Oranges from China!) No! (Spain) [11]

narizón, narizona   having a big nose [9]

negro(-a)   black, black one; sweetheart, darling [6]

el nerdo   nerd [9]

el ñero, la ñera   companion, friend (short for **compañero** or **compañera**) [5]

Ni a la fuerza.   (Not even by force.) Not on your life. No way. [11]

Ni a palos.   (Not even with blows of a stick.) No way. [11]

Ni de vaina. (Not even as a husk.) No way. (Venezuela) [11]

Ni hablar. Don't even think (talk) about it. [11]

Ni loco(-a). (Not even crazy.) No way. [11]

ni chicha ni limonada (neither chicha, an alcoholic beverage usually made from corn, nor lemonade) neither fish nor fowl [15]

ni pizca de educación not a pinch of good manners (upbringing) [13]

el niño (la niña) bien well-brought-up (upper-class) boy (girl) [4]

nítido(-a) (clear, bright) great, perfect, correct, very acceptable [7]

No debe(s) decir eso. You shouldn't say that. [6]

No es lo mismo. It's not the same. [10]

No es para tanto. It's not as bad as all that (for so much). [12]

No está en na'a (nada). He or she is out of it (not in anything). [3]

¡No habla(s) en serio! You're not serious (talking seriously)! [11]

No juegue (usted). No juegues (tú). Don't play around. [11]

No me cabrées. (**tú** form) (Don't be a goat.) Don't make me mad. (Spain) [4]

No me dejes con los churquitos (colochos) hechos. (**tú** form) Don't leave me waiting (with my curls done). (Caribbean, Central America) [3]

No me dejes con los ruleros puestos. (**tú** form) (Don't leave me with my rollers in.) Don't stand me up. (Chile) [3]

No me dés plantón. (**tú** form) Don't stand me up. (Spain) [3]

No me jodas. (**tú** form) Don't bug (bother, screw) me. (vulgar in some regions and inoffensive in others) [10]

No me mosquées. (**tú** form) Don't bug me. Don't make me suspicious. (Spain) [4]

No puede ser. It can't be. [7]

No se puede contigo. Things are impossible with you (**tú**). [13]

No seas pelma. (**tú** form) Don't be a bore. (Spain) [14]

No seas pelmazo(-a). (**tú** form) Don't be a pain (mass of undigested food). (Spain) [5]

No seas pesado(-a). (**tú** form) Don't be a pain (heavy, weighty). (Latin America) [14]

No seas tímido(-a). (**tú** form) Don't be shy. [4]

No sirve. It's no good. It doesn't work (serve). [11]

No te agüites. (**tú** form) Don't let yourself get down, upset. (Mexico, Central America) [1]

No te hagas mala sangre. (**tú** form) Don't get upset (make bad blood for yourself). [2]

No te sulfures. (**tú** form) Don't get so steamed up. [13]

No tengas pena. (**tú** form) Don't be shy (have sorrow). (Latin America) [4]

No tengo ni una perra (ni una gorda). I don't have even a cent (dog coin, fat one). [14]

No tiene pies ni cabeza. (It has neither feet nor head.) It makes no sense. [11]

No veo la hora de salir. I can't wait (see the hour) to go out. [13]

No voy a tragarme esa guayaba. I'm not going to swallow that nonsense (guava). [11]

no pegar los ojos en toda la noche to not sleep a wink (glue the eyes) the whole night [12]

no saber qué hacerse del mal genio to be in such a bad mood one doesn't know what to do [5]

Nos lukeamos. (We'll see each other.) See you. (from the English *to look)* [3]

Nos watchamos. (We'll see each other.) See you. (from the English *to watch)* [3]

la(s) nota(s) news [7]

nuevamente again [3]

o sea that is; that is to say [5]

¡Oiga! (**usted** form of **oír**) (Listen!) Excuse me, may I speak with you? (used to get attention of passerby, waiter, etc.) [4]

¡Oiga, señor(ita)! (Listen, sir/miss!) Waiter! Waitress! [15]

Oigo. (I'm hearing.) normal way of answering the phone among Cubans [8]

los ojitos little eyes (diminutive of **ojos**) [8]

Okei. OK. (from the English expression) [5]

la olla: estar en la olla to be in trouble, hot water (in the pot) [5]

-on(-a), -ote(-a), -acho(-a) augmentative endings added to words to indicate large size or other qualities, often negative, such as ugliness, poor condition, etc. [12]

onda: ser buena onda to be a good thing, a good deal, a good person [5]

ordinario(-a) common, low-class, tacky [14]

orejón, orejona having big ears [9]

os to you (all); object pronoun for **vosotros(-as)** forms; **¿Os gusta el vino?** Do you (both, all) like the wine? (Spain) [14]

Oye. (**tú** form of **oír**) Listen. Hey. [1]

pa' (para) que sepas just so you (**tú**) know [13]

la pachanga, el pachangón party [3]

padrísimo(-a)   fantastic, super (Mexico) [1]

la pajarita   (female bird) little dove, sweetheart [12]

la palabrota   swearword, vulgar word (**-ota** is an augmentative form added to **palabra**, *word*) [7]

palancón, palancona   very tall (from **palanca**, a lever or stick) [9]

el palo de escoba   (broomstick) person who is too skinny [2]

el, la pana   (male or female) friend, buddy, pal (from **panal**, honeycomb) (Venezuela, Ecuador, Colombia) [3]

panzón, panzona   having a large stomach, pot-bellied [9]

la papa   potato (Latin America) [6]

papear   (to potato) to eat (Peru, Central America) [6]

el papeo   (potato feast) dinner (Peru) [6]

paquete   (package) chic, well-turned out [6]

¡Para las que amamos!   For those whom we love! (a toast) [15]

¿Para qué?   (For what?) You're welcome. [4]

el paracaidista   (parachutist) freeloader [6]

parece Volkswagen con las puertas abiertas   (he or she looks like a Volkswagen with the doors open) i.e., having very large ears [9]

los pasa palos   (things to go along with **palos** [sticks]) appetizers, slang for *drinks* (Venezuela) [10]

pasar las noches en vela   (to spend the nights on watch) to spend sleepless nights [12]

pasarla bien (pasarlo bien)   to have a good time [3]

pasarlo en grande   (to pass or spend it big) to have a great time (Spain) [3]

pasarlo piola   to be in a bad way economically (Peru) [6]

pasarse de la raya   to be out of line (go over the line) [13]

el paseo   walk; stroll traditionally taken by Spanish and Latin Americans in the late afternoon [14]

pasmado(-a)   foolish, stupid [9]

la pasta   (dough) money (Spain) [14]

la pataleta   (kicking fit) fit, tantrum [2]

la patata   potato (Spain) [14]

las patatas bravas   spicy potato dish (Spain) [14]

patos: Se caen los patos asados.   (Roasted ducks are falling.) It's too hot. (Chile) [2]

patudo(-a)   ([ugly] bigfoot) pushy or brazen person (Argentina, Chile, Uruguay) [2]

pegajoso(-a)   sticky, referring to someone who is hard to get rid of or shake off [9]

pelado(-a)   penniless, broke (from **pelar**, to peel); bald, smooth [9]; shameless (Mexico) [13]; **chistes pelados** off-color jokes (Mexico) [10]

el pelma   idiot, boring person (Spain) [14]

la pelota   ball [10]

la pendejada   silly or stupid thing to do; trick (vulgar) (Mexico, Central America) [10)

pendejear   to behave in a foolish or stupid way (vulgar) [13]

el pendejo, la pendeja   kid, child (Argentina); stupid jerk (vulgar) (Mexico, Central America) [10]

el pepepato   vain rich man (Chile) [2]

la pera: ¡Las tías sois la pera!   You women are the limit (the pear)! (Spain) [4]

la perra   (female dog) ten-cent coin [14]

el perro   dog [R]; **como perro en canoa** (like a dog in a canoe) nervous [1]

pesado(-a)   heavy, boring, a drag [5]

pésame: dar el pésame   (to give the "it weighs on me") to express sympathy [12]

el pibe, la piba   kid, young person (Argentina) [10]

las picadas   appetizers (Argentina) [10]

picado(-a) de la curiosidad   burning (itching) with curiosity [14]

picante   (stinging) spicy hot [14]

picudo(-a)   well-connected and clever (Mexico) [10]

pinche   blasted, damn (**pinche viejo, pinche máquina**, etc.) (Mexico, Central America) [9]; **pinche cabrón** insult similar to *rotten bastard* (vulgar) (Mexico) [10]; **el pinche** kitchen worker (Spain) [10]

el piola   sponge, someone who wants a free ride (Argentina) [9]

el piropo   street compliment [6]

el pisco   grape brandy (Chile, Peru) [6]

el pitillo   cigarette (Spain) [14]

pituco(-a)   affected snob (Chile) [2]

planchar la oreja   (to iron one's ear) to go to bed (Ecuador, Venezuela, Colombia) [9]

plantado(-a): dejar plantado(-a)   (to leave [someone] planted) to stand (someone) up [3]

un plantón   (a planting) a standing up (of someone); also, someone who stands someone else up [3]

plástico(-a)   (plastic) artificial, hypocritical [9]

la plata   (silver) money (Latin America) [8]

platicar   to talk, chat [7]

el plato   plate, dish [12]

pleno(-a)   whole, complete; **en plena calle** in the middle of the street; **en pleno invierno** in the middle of winter [7]

Pobre pero caballero.   Poor but dignified (a gentleman). [6]

¡Pobrecito!   Poor (little) thing! [12]

¿Podría usted decirme . . . ?   Could you tell me . . . ? [4]

la polilla de biblioteca   (library moth) bookworm [9]

el pollo   chicken, chick [12]

pololear   (to buzz around like a bee) to go steady with someone (Chile) [2]

el pololo, la polola   (bumblebee) sweetheart, steady boyfriend or girlfriend (Chile) [2]

los pompis   (bubbles) buttocks, rear end (Mexico) [2]

ponerle los cuernos   (to put the horns on him or her) to cheat on one's spouse or lover [8]

ponerse   + adj. to become + adj. [9]

ponerse a   + inf. (to set or put oneself to doing something) to begin to (do something) [7]

ponerse las pilas   (to put in one's batteries) to get with it, get going [9]

poquitín   a little bit [6]

Por aquí (trabajando, estudiando).   (I'm) Just here (working, studying), nothing is new. [1]

Por aquí, vagando.   (I'm) Just here, goofing (wandering) around. [3]

¿Por qué andas tan bravo(-a)?   Why are you (**tú**) so angry? [13]

¡Por supuesto!   Of course! [10]

por acá   around here [4]

por allá, por ahí   around there [4]

por la flauta   (by the flute) by heaven [2]

por parejo   equally [10]

por si las moscas   (because if the flies) just in case (Chile, Peru, Central America) [2]

por supuesto   of course [10]

porfa   (short for **por favor**) please [5]

el porro   marihuana joint [14]

los porteños   people from Buenos Aires [6]

el poto   rear end, butt, bottom (Chile) [2]

preguntar cómo llegar a . . . (to ask how to arrive at . . .) to ask for directions to . . . [4]

Primero Dios. (First God.) God willing. (often heard when an action is proposed or some statement of optimism is made) (Central America) [5]

probar (ue) (to prove) to try for the first time (food, clothing, a sport, etc.) [14]

el, la profe (short for **profesor** or **profesora**) prof, professor [5]

pronto soon [4]

pronto: de pronto suddenly; **por lo pronto** for now [5]

Pues . . . a hesitation word, like "uh, well . . ." [3]

¡Pura chepa! Nonsense! (Colombia) [11]

¡Pura leche! Nonsense! (Colombia) [11]

¡Pura paja! (Pure straw!) Complete nonsense! [11]

pura verdad (pure truth) right you are [2]

¡Pura vida! (Pure life!) fantastic, wonderful (Costa Rica) [12]

¡Puras vainas! (Pure husks!) Complete nonsense! [11]

¡Puros disparates! Complete nonsense! [11]

la puta whore [7]

putear, echar putadas to insult with offensive names (vulgar) [13]

el puto male whore; pimp [10]

puto(-a) (pimp or whore) blasted, damn (vulgar); **la puta máquina** the blasted machine; **no hacer ni puto caso** not to pay any damn attention [7]

¡Qué barbaridad! (What barbarity!) Good grief! [7]

¡Qué bárbaro! (How barbarous!) Good grief! [7]

¡Qué buitre! (What a vulture!) What a wolf! [3]

¡Qué burdel! (What a bordello!) What a mess! (Argentina, Uruguay) [2]

¡Qué cocodrilo! (What a crocodile!) What a wolf! [3]

¿Qué crees? (What do you [**tú**] think?) Guess what? [1]

¡Qué delicia! (What a delight!) How delicious! [6]

¡Qué descarado(-a)! What a scoundrel, rascal! [3]

¡Qué descaro! What nerve (brazenness)! [2]

¡Qué despelote! (What an unravelling ball!) What a mess! (Chile, Uruguay, Argentina) [2]

¡Qué dicha! What luck (bliss)! (Costa Rica) [12]

¡Qué don Juan! What a Don Juan! [3]

¡Qué follón! What a mess! (vulgar) (Spain) [2]

¡Qué gorila!   (What a gorilla!) What a wolf! [3]

¡Qué habré hecho yo para merecer tal preciosura!   What could I have done to deserve such beauty (such preciousness)! [3]

¡Qué laberinto!   (What a labyrinth!) What a mess! (Peru) [2]

¡Qué lástima!   What a shame! [12]

¿Qué le pongo al señor?   What shall I serve (put before) the gentleman? (Spain) [15]

¡Qué lío!   (What a bundle!) What a mess! [2]

¿Qué me cuentas?   (What do you [**tú**] tell me?) What's happening? [1]

¡Qué mujeriego (mujerero)!   (What a womanizer!) What a wolf! [3]

Que no.   No. [5]

¿Qué notas me cuentas?   (What notes are you telling me?) What news can you tell me? [7]

¡Qué ocurrencia!   The very idea! [6]

¿Qué onda(s)?   (What sound wave[s]?) What's happening? [1]

¡Qué padre!   (What a father!) Great! How fantastic! [1]

¡Qué perra vida!   What a horrible (dog's) life! [12]

¡Qué quilombo!   (What a bordello!) What a mess! (Argentina, Uruguay) [2]

¿Qué rayos pasa?   What the dickens (lightning rays) is happening? [7]

¡Qué ridículo!   How ridiculous! [11]

¿Qué tal?   How are things? [1]

¿Qué tal anda(s)?   How are you? (Spain) [1]

¿Qué te parece (si . . .)?   How does it seem to you (**tú**) (if . . .)? How about (if . . .)? [3]

Que te (le, les) vaya bien.   May all go well with you. [15]

¡Qué tontería(s)!   What nonsense! [11]

¡Qué va!   Oh, come on! [11]

¡Qué zambrote!   (What a Moorish party!) What a mess! (Costa Rica) [2]

querido(-a)   dear [4]

¡Qui úbole!   a greeting, like **¡Hola!** [1]

Quieres que te reciba como si fueras el rey.   You (**tú**) want me to welcome you as if you were the king. [13]

la rabieta   fit, tantrum; **darse (agarrarse) una rabieta** to have a fit [8]

la rana   frog; **cuando la rana eche pelos** (when the frog sprouts hair) the twelfth of never, when hell freezes over [12]

rapidingo   very quick [15]

ratito: en un ratito   in a little while [11]

el ratón de biblioteca   (library rat) bookworm [9]

¡Rayos!   (Lightning rays!) Good grief!, Blast! (a bit old-fashioned, used to express surprise or when there is a problem) [7]

realizar   to make real or concrete, as a plan [7]

recopado(-a)   super, fantastic (filled with many trophies) [10]

redemorar   to take a really long time [2]

la regañada   scolding, bawling out [10]

regio(-a)   great, beautiful (Colombia, Ecuador) [15]

el remo   (oar) sponge, leech (Ecuador) [9]

rendido(-a)   (rendered) exhausted [1]

requete   intensifier used with adjectives or adverbs, meaning *very* + adjective or adverb [5]; **requete interesante** very, very interesting [12]

resimpático(-a)   very nice and empathetic [12]

respeto: un poco de respeto   a little respect [2]

el reventón de primera   (blowout of first) first-class bash (Mexico, Central America) [1]

rico(-a)   delicious [14]

romper   to break [12]; **romper con alguien** to break up with someone [7]; **romperle la madre**   to hurt someone where they are vulnerable (emotionally or physically) [13]

roto(-a)   broken; low-class bum with bad manners (Chile) [2]; **roto(-a) con plata** low-class person with money, *nouveau riche* (Chile) [2]

la ruca   girl, woman (Latin America excl. Southern Cone) [1]

el rumbón   (from **rumba**) dance [3]

Sabe Dios.   God knows. [11]

sabroso(-a)   tasty [14]

sacar los trapos al sol   (to take the rags or clothes out into the sun) to give someone the low-down, air the dirty laundry [7]

sacarse la polilla   (to get the moths off) to dance (Mexico) [9]

Sale y vale.   (It goes/turns out and it's worth it.) It's a deal. [5]

Sales hasta en la sopa.   (You [**tú**] turn up even in the soup.) I see you everywhere. [7]

salir embarazada   to be (turn out) pregnant [7]

¡Salud!   (also, Mexico: **¡Salucitas!**) (Health!) To your health! [15]

Santo que no me quiere, basta con no rezarle. (Saint that doesn't like me, it's enough not to pray to him.) There's no need to bother with someone who doesn't care about me. [9]

santos en la corte (saints at court) connections [2]

Se armó la gorda. (The fat one got armed.) There was a big blowup. [12]

sea: o sea . . . that is . . . (hesitation phrase) [5]

Se caen los patos asados. (Roasted ducks are falling.) It's too hot. (Chile) [2]

Se comió el sanduche antes del recreo. (The sandwich was eaten before recess.) Something was enjoyed before it should have been. [7]

Se comió la torta antes de la fiesta. (The cake was eaten before the party.) Something was enjoyed before it should have been. [7]

Se cree el (la) muy muy. He (She) thinks he's (she's) hot stuff (the very very). [1]

Se cree la divina pomada. She thinks she's hot stuff (the divine cream). [6]

Se le (te) fue la pajarita. (The little bird went away from you.) Your lover flew the coop. [12]

Se me antoja(n) . . . I have a taste for . . . [14]

Se me caen las medias (los calzones). (My stockings [pants] are falling down.) I'm excited by that good-looking guy. [8]

Se me hace agua la boca. My mouth is watering (becoming water). [14]

¿Se te cruzaron los cables? (Did your cables get crossed?) Are you crazy? [11]

se (te) lo juro I swear to you [5]

ser aguafiestas (to be a water-party) to be a party-pooper [3]

ser buena gente (to be good people) to be nice, kind [9]

ser como arroz blanco (to be like white rice) to be seen everywhere [7]

ser el as de la baraja (to be the ace of the deck) to make oneself scarce [7]

la serpiente snake [12]

los servicios públicos public washrooms [4]

la servilleta napkin; maid (Peru) [6]

si Dios quiere (if God wants) God willing (often heard when an action is proposed or some statement of optimism is made) [5]

Si se quema la casa, no pierde nada. If the house burns down, he or she won't lose anything. [9]

si te apetece if you like (Spain) [14]

siempre always [R]

simón yeah (variant of **sí**) [3]

la simpatía   openness and interest in others [12]

sin blanca   (without a white one) broke, without money (Spain) [14]

sin una gorda   (without a fat one) broke, without a cent (Spain) [14]

sin ton ni son   (without tone or sound) without rhyme or reason [11]

la sirvienta   maid [6]

siútico(-a)   affected and pretentious snob (Chile) [2]

el soborno   bribe [10]

la sobremesa   after-dinner conversation at the table [6]

la soda   (soda) café that sells reasonably priced food (Costa Rica) [12]; **ser una soda** to be terrific (Colombia) [15]

sólo un pelito   just a tiny bit (little hair) [6]

soñar con pájaros preñados   (to dream of pregnant birds) to be crazy, thinking of the impossible [11]

suave   bland, non-spicy (food); smooth, soft [14]

sucio(-a)   dirty, soiled [8]

sudar la gota gorda   (to sweat the fat drop) to sweat bullets, sweat it out [2]

el sueño   dream; sleep; **tener sueño** to be sleepy [R]

sulfurarse   to get steamed up [13]

surfear la Red (Internet)   to surf the Net [11]

tal por cual   (such for which) out-and-out, dyed-in-the-wool [2]

tan fresco(-a) como una lechuga   as fresh as a daisy (lettuce) [10]

tanto   so much [12]

las tapas   appetizers [14]

el tata   father; **los tatas** parents, father and mother; also, grandparents [15]

los tartarabuelos   great-grandparents [15]

Te amo.   I love you (often in a spiritual way). [8]

Te dejaron bien amolado(-a).   (They left you [**tú**] ruined, a wreck.) They wore you to a frazzle. [1]

Te estás cachondeando de mí.   (**tú** form) You are making fun of (batting horns with) me. (somewhat vulgar) (Spain) [4]

Te quiero.   I love (want) you (often in a physical way); also used for simple affection [8]

la tele   (short for **televisión**) television [5]

Tenemos que reclamar.   We have to demand our rights (clamor). [2]

tener una cara de teléfono ocupado   (to have a face like a busy telephone) to be angry [13]

tener un careto   (to have a white-faced mask) to look really bad because of worry or lack of sleep (Spain) [14]

tener coraje   to have courage; to be angry (Mexico) [2]

tener éxito   (to have success) to be successful [7]

tener ganas de . . .   to feel like . . . [4]

tener guayabo   (to have a guava tree) to be hung over (Colombia) [1]

tener mala leche   (to have bad milk) to be in a grouchy mood [2]

tener la mona   (to have the monkey) to be hung over (Chile) [1]

tener mucha suerte   (to have a lot of luck) to be very lucky [8]

tener mucho culo   (to have a lot of ass) to be very lucky (vulgar) (Uruguay) [8]

tener pinta de   to look like [14]

tener resaca   (to have undertow) to be hung over (Argentina, Uruguay, Spain) [1]

tener un ratón   (to have a mouse) to be hung over (Venezuela) [1]

tener unas tablas increíbles   to have good preparation (boards) (Argentina) [10]

Tenga la bondad de . . .   (**usted** form) (Have the goodness of . . .) Be so good as to . . . [2]

Tengo que cortar.   I have to hang up (cut) (the phone). [8]

el tenorio   womanizer, don Juan [6]

el tesoro   (treasure) sweetheart, darling [8]

los ticos   Costa Ricans [4]

tinto   red (wine); **el tinto** (Colombia) coffee; **¿Te provoca un tinto?** Would you like some coffee? (Colombia) [2]

el tío, la tía   (uncle, aunt) guy or fellow, gal or woman [4]

el tipo   (type) guy, fellow [8]

tirar arroz   (to throw rice) to criticize [6]

tirar bomba   (to throw a bomb) to stand (someone) up (Caribbean) [13]

el tocayo, la tocaya   person with the same first name as yours or someone else's [6]

todo el santo día   the whole live-long day [13]

Todo lo hacen por debajo de la mesa.   They do everything in a corrupt manner (under the table). [10]

todo lo contrario   (all the contrary) just the opposite [8]

To'el tiempo pa'lante.   (All the time forward.) Onward and upward. [7]

tomado(-a)   drunk (Latin America) [8]

tomar una copa   to have a drink (wine glass) [8]

tontear   to behave in a foolish or stupid way [13]

toparse con   to bump into, run across [11]

torcer (ue) (to twist, turn) to make a turn (to the right or left) (Spain) [4]

total que (total that) so, in short [7]

los trámites bureaucratic procedures [2]

Tranquilícese (usted). Tranquilízate (tú). Calm down. [13]

el trasero rear end, butt (bum in Canada and England) [2]

el traste pot, dish, pan (Mexico); rear end, backside (in many other countries) [2, 10]

el trome expert, wizard (Perú) [6]

¡Tu madre! (Your mother!) strong insult that suggests the moral impurity of someone's mother [10]

tú you (intimate singular) [4]

la u (short for **universidad**) university [5]

¡Un momentico, por favor! Just a little moment, please! (Colombia, Venezuela, Costa Rica) [12]

usted you (formal singular); abbreviated **Ud.** or **Vd.** [4]

Usted es muy amable. (You are very kind.) [6]

Usted me saca de un apuro. You are getting me out of a difficulty. [4]

ustedes you (formal plural); abbreviated **Uds.** or **Vds.** [4]

vacilar to party, have a good time; to kid or joke; **¡Vamos a vacilar!** Let's party! [3]

el vacilón good time, party; comic, entertaining person; **Allá se formaba un vacilón.** A party was taking shape (getting going) there. [3]

Vaya uno a saber. Who knows? [11]

¡Váyase (usted) a la porra! ¡Vete (tú) . . . ! Go to the devil! [13]

¡Váyase (usted) al diablo (al infierno)! ¡Vete (tú) . . . ! Go to the devil (to hell)! [13]

¡Váyase (usted) a la mierda! ¡Vete (tú) . . . ! (vulgar) Go to hell (to shit)! [10]

el vejete old man [7]

verde green; natural, referring to sex; **chistes (historias) verdes** jokes (stories) about sex; **estar muy verde** (to be very green) to be innocent, not socially active (Spain) [9]; **viejo verde** old man still interested in sex, "dirty" old man [8]

los veteranos (veterans) parents (Argentina, Uruguay) [8]

la vida: ¡La vida me sonríe! (Life is smiling on me!) What a stroke of luck! [12]

el viejo, la vieja (old man, old woman) husband, boyfriend (wife, girlfriend) [11]

¿Viste? (Did you [tú] see?) See? [7]

volver (ue) a + inf. (to return to + inf.) to do (something) again [5]

vos colloquial form of *you* (intimate singular) (Argentina, Uruguay, Chile, Colombia, Central America) [4]

vos sos you (familiar) are (instead of **tú eres**) in Argentina, Uruguay, Chile, Colombia, Central America [8]

vosotros, vosotras you (all) (plural of intimate *you* for friends or family in many parts of Spain) [4]

el water (from water closet, pronounced "vater") bathroom [4]

Y de la vida, ¿qué más? (And of life, what more?) What else is happening in your life? [7]

¿Y eso? (And that?) What does that mean? [1]

Ya está bien de cuentos. Enough of your stories. [11]

¡Ya me encabronaste (tú)! Now you've really got me furious! (vulgar) [13]

¡Ya te pasaste (tú)! You've gone too far (passed yourself)! [13]

ya tú sabe' you know (already) [7]

la zanahoria (carrot) young person who is innocent, not socially active or "with it" (Ecuador, Venezuela, Colombia) [9]

los zapallos people from Lima [6]